T0140300

Essential Spectrum-based Fault Localization

Xiaoyuan Xie • Baowen Xu

Essential Spectrum-based
Fault Localization

Xiaoyuan Xie
School of Computer Science
Wuhan University
Wuhan, Hubei, China

Baowen Xu
Department of Computer Science
and Technology
Nanjing University
Nanjing, Jiangsu, China

ISBN 978-981-33-6181-2   ISBN 978-981-33-6179-9   (eBook)
https://doi.org/10.1007/978-981-33-6179-9

This Springer imprint is published by the registered company Springer Nature Singapore Pte Ltd.
The registered company address is: 152 Beach Road, #21-01/04 Gateway East, Singapore 189721,
Singapore

Foreword

I never forget the day when I first realized the importance of software quality. It was in 1979 when I was doing my undergraduate study and introduced to programming language. One day, I learned the story about Mariner 1, the first spacecraft in the American Mariner program, which was launched on July 22, 1962, but had to be destroyed after veering off course due to equipment failure and an error in coded computer instructions. The post-flight review found that a missing hyphen in coded computer instructions allowed transmission of incorrect guidance signals. Even though this mission was later achieved by Mariner 2, the loss of Mariner 1 was as high as 18.5 million US dollars. Significantly, this epic software bug impressed me and influenced my following academic career.

After I started my master's degree program supervised by Prof. Zhenyu Wang, I gained a deeper understanding of programming languages (such as Ada, AED, ALGOL60, ALGOL68, ALGOL W, APL, BASIC, BCPL, BLISS, C, CLU, COBOL, Concurrent Pascal, CORAL66, Edison, Eiffel, Euclid, Euler, FORTH, FORTRAN IV, FORTRAN 77, GPSS, JOVIAL, LIS, LISP, Modula, Modula-2, Modula-3, NPL, Oberon, Pascal, PL/I, PL/M, PLZ/SYS, PROLOG, SETL, SIMULA, SmallTalk, SNOBOL, SPL/I). In that age, though programs were not in large scale or with complex structures, testing and debugging were actually very challenging due to the lack of supporting mechanisms and facilities. Initiated by my study on programming language principles, design, and implementation, a belief that I should also do studies on software quality assurance becomes stronger and stronger.

I was one of the first researchers who systematically studied software quality in China. In 1986, I published the first paper in China, enumerating various issues in C programming languages that can introduce risks in software. I also compared several popular programming languages in that age, such as Ada and Pascal, discussing principles and metrics for good programming languages. Right around the same time, I worked on program analysis and slicing. I proposed a method for backward dependence analysis. Under my supervision, my students also developed a series of methods for static and dynamic program analysis, dependence analysis in concurrent programs, monadic slicing for programs with pointers, etc.

Since 1995, we have started to realize the importance of software measurements in producing high-quality software systems. We proposed approaches to measuring class cohesion based on dependence analysis, package cohesion based on client usage, and methods to further improve software architecture design. Around 2000, we initiated our first project on software testing. After that, my research group kept putting many efforts in this area, and have harvested abundant achievements over the past two decades, which cover combinatorial testing, regression testing, evolutionary testing, metamorphic testing, web testing, and test case prioritization and reduction. We also cared about software reliability and security. Based on the accumulations in testing and analysis, our group was able to develop a series of theories and methodologies in software fault localization and defect prediction, which have exerted profound influences in these areas. Recently, we expanded our directions to testing and debugging for artificial intelligent systems, crowdsourcing software engineering, empirical software engineering, and knowledge graph.

Over the past 30 years, our group has obtained many important research results, which are highly praised by international peers and exert great impact in relevant fields. We have undertaken over 70 research projects from the National Natural Science Foundation of China, the Ministry of Education, the Ministry of Science and Technology, Jiangsu Province, institutions, and famous enterprises. The group has published more than 500 papers, including top venues such as *ACM Transactions on Software Engineering and Methodology*, *IEEE Transactions on Software Engineering*, the International Conference on Software Engineering, The ACM Joint European Software Engineering Conference and Symposium on the Foundations of Software Engineering, and the International Joint Conference on Artificial Intelligence. We have also built close connections and collaboration with many prestigious universities and institutes, including Purdue University, Nanyang Technological University, University of California Irvine, University College London, and Columbia University.

We have developed multiple systems including CRL/Ada language and its generation system, Ada program analysis and understanding system (APAUS), software maintenance and support system for Ada reverse engineering (ARMS), embedded software testing support system (ETS), software quality assurance system (SQAS), and testing platform for large and complex systems (Testeres). Through participation in various projects, we also built up large-scale benchmarks of real-life data. From these data, we conducted empirical studies and have provided useful and convincing insights.

Such a long period of research gives us good accumulation in both theory and practice. And hence we are planning a series of books on relevant areas of program analysis, testing, and evolution. We hope they will appear in the near future.

Nanjing University, China   Baowen Xu

Preface

Program debugging has always been a difficult and time-consuming task in software development. Back in the 1970s, when researchers proposed the concept of program slicing, automatic program fault localization became an ambition for efficiently debugging the program. Since then, various trials were performed to get closer to this goal, among which spectrum-based fault localization (SBFL) is one of the most widely studied families of techniques.

SBFL was first proposed around 2000. Different from traditional slicing-based methods, SBFL became popular because of its lightweight and practicability. Since 2000, this area has seen thousands of techniques derived from various perspectives. As a consequence, it becomes very important and urgent to compare the actual performance among different SBFL techniques. In fact, before 2013, many empirical studies were conducted to investigate this question. However, they were strongly dependent on the experimental setup, and hence can hardly be considered as sufficiently comprehensive due to the huge number of possible combinations of various factors in SBFL. In other words, these empirical studies did not reveal the essence of SBFL performance.

Therefore, we propose to draft this book, whose orientation is not to introduce various SBFL techniques, or to compare their empirical performance. Instead, this book aims to provide a deep understanding on the essence of this area, talking about its essential theories. Specifically, this book introduces a series of set-based theoretical frameworks, which reveal the intrinsic performance hierarchy among different SBFL techniques. In addition, this book also discusses two emerging challenges of "oracle problem" and "multiple faults" and introduces promising solutions.

The target audience of this book are mainly graduate students and researchers who work in the areas of software analysis, testing, debugging, and repairing, and are seeking deep comprehension of SBFL.

Wuhan University, China
Nanjing University, China

Xiaoyuan Xie
Baowen Xu

Acknowledgments

Our research is partially supported by the National Natural Science Foundation of China under Grant numbers 61832009, 61972289, 61772263, 61572375, 61472178, 91418202, 61170071.

We want to express our gratitude to our long-term collaborators (alphabetic order on the surnames):

- Prof. Tsong Yueh Chen (Swinburne University, Australia)
- Prof. Yang Liu (Nanyang Technological University, Singapore)
- Prof. T. H. Tse (Hong Kong University)
- Prof. W. Eric Wong (University of Texas at Dallas, USA)
- Prof. Shin Yoo (Korea Advanced Institute of Science and Technology, South Korea)
- Prof. Xiangyu Zhang (Purdue University, USA)

We sincerely thank the graduate student Yi Song in our group for his contributions in editing. We also sincerely appreciate the constructive suggestions from the reviewers, as well as the efforts of Springer Editor Jane Li and Project Coordinator Priya Shankar.

Contents

Chapter 1
Introduction

Abstract It is commonly recognized that debugging and fault localization are important but expensive activities in software engineering. Currently, many techniques have been proposed towards the automatic fault localization, among which spectrum-based fault localization (referred to as SBFL in this book) has received a lot of attention due to its simplicity and effectiveness. As the first chapter of this book, Chap. 1 will first introduce the history of automatic debugging, then briefly introduce the basis of SBFL, and finally give a literature review by covering three research directions in SBFL, namely, "risk evaluation formulas," "parallel debugging," and "combining deep learning with SBFL."

1.1 Assurance of Software Quality

It is commonly recognized that testing and debugging are important but expensive activities in software engineering. Attempts to reduce the number of faults in software are estimated to consume 50% to 80% of the total development and maintenance effort [14].

Software testing utilizes concrete test cases to dynamically reveal the problems in the program system. Over the past few decades, this area has seen a massive amount of studies, in test case generation, prioritization, oracle problem alleviation, etc. For example, popular automatic test case generation methods include evolutionary testing, combinatorial testing, new coverage-based testing, etc. [11, 12, 35, 46, 54, 55, 58, 63]. And for regression testing and prioritization, people derived methods based on various criteria [17, 18, 57]. About 20 years ago, metamorphic testing was proposed [6, 7] and now has become one or the most promising solutions to oracle problem [16, 47, 50].

Finding failure test cases can be a starting point of debugging. Debugging is a complex activity, which may involve program analysis, fault prediction, fault localization, fault repairing, etc. Program analysis generally includes dependency extraction [8–10, 24, 52], slicing [53, 56, 61], and type inference [51, 60]. With the information obtained from analysis, people derived a variety of methods for automatic fault prediction, localization, repairing, etc. [13, 28, 39, 45, 48, 49, 59, 62, 64, 69, 71].

In this book, we will mainly focus on an automatic fault localization technique, namely, spectrum-based fault localization.

1.2   Automatic Fault Localization

Fault localization aims to pinpoint the possible positions of the faults based on various information and hence gives debuggers hints for fault fixing. However, this activity always involves a great amount of manual jobs. For example, a typical debugging process usually begins when the failures of a program are observed. Then, a debugger will focus on a particular failed execution and manually set a series of breakpoints in the program. By inspecting and altering the internal states at these breakpoints and iteratively re-executing the program with this test case, the debugger will locate the fault for this failure.

Obviously, such a great amount of manual involvement makes the fault localization very resource consuming and not effective. Therefore, automation of this task becomes very important, which can significantly increase its effectiveness and decrease its cost.

Currently, many techniques have been proposed towards the automatic fault localization. Some of them use various information to isolate a set of program entities that are likely to be faulty, based on different heuristics [4, 15, 20, 36, 40, 67]. For example, Zhang et al. [67] have utilized different types of dynamic slices associated with failed test cases, as the set of suspicious statements of being faulty. However, these techniques always have difficulties in compromising between the effectiveness and precision. Generally speaking, a large suspicious set of program entities usually has better precision since it has more chance to contain the faults; however, it has to sacrifice the effectiveness since more program entities need to be examined. Moreover, these techniques usually involve complicated program analysis and hence are not efficient enough to be adopted in practice.

Therefore, people have proposed another promising automatic fault localization technique, spectrum-based fault localization (referred to as SBFL in this book). Instead of isolating the suspicious program entities, SBFL ranks program entities according to their risks of being faulty. Generally speaking, SBFL first collects the information from software testing, including various program spectra and the associated testing result, in terms of *failed* or *passed*, of each individual test case. The program spectrum can be any granularity of program entities (e.g., statements, branches, blocks, etc.) and any type of run-time information (e.g., the binary coverage status, the execution frequency, etc.) [22, 37]. With this information, SBFL then uses different formulas to evaluate the risk of containing a fault for each program entity and gives a risk ranking list. SBFL intends to highlight program entities which strongly correlate with program failures, and these entities are regarded as the likely faulty locations [2].

Compared with the other debugging techniques, SBFL is much easier to be implemented and adopted in practice. Actually, it has received a lot of attention due to its simplicity and effectiveness. Some recent studies in SBFL were focused on proposing new approaches that are distinguished from each other in the selection of program spectrum, the choice of formula used for evaluating risk values for each program entity, etc., in order to improve the accuracy of the diagnosis. Some typical risk evaluation formulas include Pinpoint [5], Tarantula [26], Ochiai [1], etc. On the other hand, some studies have aimed to compare the performance of different SBFL techniques or to investigate how can different factors (e.g., number of failed test cases, size of test suite, selection of coverage criterion, tie-breaking scheme for statements with the same risk values, etc.) affect the performance of a particular SBFL technique and how to adjust them to obtain a better performance [1, 3, 23, 25, 38].

As a family of fault localization methods with over two-decade history, spectrum-based fault localization has been extensively studied. This book will mainly focus on those studies beyond the basic SBFL process.

1.3   Basis in Spectrum-Based Fault Localization

As a dynamic approach, SBFL basically utilizes two types of information collected during software testing, namely, testing results and program spectrum. The testing result associated with each test case records whether a test case is *failed* or *passed*, while a program spectrum is a collection of data that provides a specific view on the dynamic behavior of software [21, 37]. Generally speaking, it records the run-time profiles about various program entities for a specific test suite. The program entities could be statements, branches, paths, basic blocks, etc., while the run-time information could be the binary coverage status, the execution frequency, the program state before and after executing the program entity, etc. In practice, there are many kinds of combinations [21, 22]. The most widely adopted combination involves statement and its binary coverage status in a test execution [4, 40, 41]. In this book, we will follow the common practice to use this combination as a representative of the program spectrum.

Let us consider a program $PG=<s_1, s_2, \ldots, s_n>$ with n statements and executed by a test suite of m test cases $TS=\{t_1, t_2, \ldots, t_m\}$. Figure 1.1 shows the essential information required by SBFL.

RE records all the testing results associated with the test cases, in which p indicates *passed* and f indicates *failed*. And matrix *MS* represents the program spectrum, where the element in the ith column and jth row represents the coverage information of statement s_i, by test case t_j, with 1 indicating s_i is executed and 0 otherwise. In other words, the jth row represents the *execution slice* of t_j.

For each statement s_i, these data can be represented as a vector of four elements, denoted as $A_i=<a_{ef}^i, a_{ep}^i, a_{nf}^i, a_{np}^i>$, where a_{ef}^i and a_{ep}^i represent the number of test cases in *TS* that execute statement s_i and return the testing result of *failure*

$$PG : (s_1 \quad s_2 \quad \cdot \quad \cdot \quad \cdot \quad s_n)$$

$$TS : \begin{pmatrix} t_1 \\ t_2 \\ \vdots \\ t_m \end{pmatrix} \quad MS : \begin{pmatrix} 1/0 & 1/0 & & & 1/0 \\ 1/0 & 1/0 & & & 1/0 \\ \vdots & \vdots & \cdot & \cdot & \vdots \\ 1/0 & 1/0 & & & 1/0 \end{pmatrix} \quad RE : \begin{pmatrix} p/f \\ p/f \\ \vdots \\ p/f \end{pmatrix}$$

Fig. 1.1 Essential information for SBFL

or *pass*, respectively, and a^i_{nf} and a^i_{np} denote the number of test cases that do not execute s_i and return the testing result of *failure* or *pass*, respectively. Obviously, the sum of these four parameters for each statement should always be equal to the size of the test suite. An example is shown in Fig. 1.2.

In Fig. 1.2, program PG has four statements $\{s_1, s_2, s_3, s_4\}$, and test suite TS has six test cases $\{t_1, t_2, t_3, t_4, t_5, t_6\}$. As indicated in RE, t_1 and t_5 give rise to *passed* runs, and the remaining four test cases give rise to *failed* runs. Matrix MS records the binary coverage information for each statement with respect to every test case. Matrix MA is such defined that its ith column represents the corresponding A_i for s_i. For instance, in this figure, $a^1_{np}=0$ for s_1 means that no test case in the current test suite gives a testing result of *pass* without executing s_1; $a^4_{ef}=4$ for s_4 represents that s_4 is executed by four test cases which can detect failure.

A risk evaluation formula R is then applied on each statement s_i to assign a real value that indicates its risk of being faulty. All formulas follow the same intuition

$$PG : (s_1 \quad s_2 \quad s_3 \quad s_4)$$

$$TS : \begin{pmatrix} t_1 \\ t_2 \\ t_3 \\ t_4 \\ t_5 \\ t_6 \end{pmatrix} \quad MS : \begin{pmatrix} 1 & 1 & 0 & 0 \\ 0 & 0 & 0 & 1 \\ 0 & 0 & 1 & 1 \\ 1 & 0 & 0 & 1 \\ 1 & 0 & 0 & 0 \\ 1 & 0 & 1 & 1 \end{pmatrix} \quad RE : \begin{pmatrix} p \\ f \\ f \\ f \\ p \\ f \end{pmatrix}$$

$$MA : \begin{array}{l} a^i_{ef} \\ a^i_{ep} \\ a^i_{nf} \\ a^i_{np} \end{array} \begin{pmatrix} 2 & 0 & 2 & 4 \\ 2 & 1 & 0 & 0 \\ 2 & 4 & 2 & 0 \\ 0 & 1 & 2 & 2 \end{pmatrix}$$

Fig. 1.2 An example

that statements associated with more *failed* and less *passed* testing results should have higher risks. For example, formula Tarantula is defined as follows [26].

$$R_T(s_i) = \frac{a_{ef}^i}{a_{ef}^i + a_{nf}^i} \bigg/ \left(\frac{a_{ef}^i}{a_{ef}^i + a_{nf}^i} + \frac{a_{ep}^i}{a_{ep}^i + a_{np}^i} \right)$$

A statement with a higher risk value is interpreted to have a higher possibility to be faulty, which therefore should be examined with higher priority. Hence, after being assigned with the risk values, all statements are sorted descendingly according to their risk values. An effective formula should be able to make the faulty statements as the top in the list as possible.

For the performance measurement of the risk evaluation formulas, the majority of the SBFL community used the same metric or its equivalent, which is the percentage of the code that **needs** (or **needs not**) to be examined before the faulty statement is identified. Such a metric is used with the assumption of *perfect bug detection* that the fault can always be identified once it is examined [42]. In [42], the percentage of code that **needs** to be examined before the faults are identified is referred to as the *EXAM* score, which will be adopted in this book. Obviously, a lower *EXAM* score indicates a better performance.

1.4 Some Research Directions in SBFL

1.4.1 Risk Evaluation Formulas

Risk evaluation formula is a core component in SBFL. Hence one of the most popular research directions in SBFL is the design of effective formulas, aiming at ranking the faulty statements as high in the risk list as possible.

Apart from the above Tarantula, there are many other risk evaluation formulas. Early ones include Jaccard [5], AMPLE [66], CBI Inc. [30, 31], Ochiai [1], SOBER [32], Wong [42], etc., which are based on different similarity measurements. Recently, a series of innovative risk evaluation formulas, such as Crosstab [43] and DStar (D*) [44], were proposed. Crosstab is a crosstab-based statistical technique which constructs a crosstab for each executable statement. A statistic can be computed to determine the risk value of the individual statement based on the corresponding crosstab subsequently. DStar (D*) is a technique that can suggest suspicious locations for fault localization automatically. No prior knowledge is required on program structure or semantics in this approach. The authors stated that DStar (D*) was more effective in locating faults than all the other techniques compared to it.

Generally speaking, different formulas were developed from different intuitions or designed to serve different purposes. But no matter from what intuitions the formulas were derived, they should all comply with the expectation that statements associated with more failed and less passed testing results should have higher faulty risks.

With more and more formulas proposed, some people started to compare their performance via empirical studies. Risk evaluation formulas, including Pinpoint, Ample, Tarantula, Jaccard, and Ochiai, were investigated by Abreu et al. [1, 2]. Their experiments employed Siemens Suite, which is composed of seven programs as a benchmark. An important conclusion of this study is that Ochiai performs better than the other formulas. More specifically, Ochiai has been observed to improve 5% on average over the next best technique in terms of the amount of code that needs to be examined. In 2009, Abreu et al. revisited Jaccard, Tarantula, and Ochiai using Siemens Suite and Space [3], pointing out that all the three formulas can provide a useful diagnosis, but Ochiai led to a better diagnosis than the others. Besides, Jones et al. have compared Tarantula with four non-SBFL approaches, namely, Set union, Set intersection, Nearest Neighbor, and Cause Transitions [25]. Their study showed that Tarantula outperforms the other four approaches in both the effectiveness and the efficiency.

Later, some researchers have investigated the performance of risk evaluation formulas from a semi-theoretical perspective. As the first attempt, Lee et al. have proved that formula Tarantula always produces identical ranking list as formula q_e, and hence they are equivalent [29]. This pilot study was followed by a more comprehensive investigation by Naish et al. [34], where over 30 formulas were studied and more equivalence relations were identified, using the same definition of equivalence as [29]. Naish et al. [34] also investigated the non-equivalence relations, using a hybrid approach, with a model program and a group of multisets of execution paths. The multiset of execution paths is the abstraction of the path coverage information and the testing results of each concrete test suite, with respect to the model program.

In this study, for a risk evaluation formula, the performance score with respect to a multiset of execution paths is 0 if the risk of the faulty statement is less than any other statement. Otherwise, the score is $1/k$, where k denotes the number of statements (including the faulty statement) having equal risk values as the faulty statement. The overall performance of a formula is measured by the total score, which is the sum (or average) of the scores over all possible distinct multisets of t execution paths that contain at least one failed test case. When the number of possible multisets is not too large, all the possible multisets were used to evaluate the performance; while for large numbers of multisets, a random sample of them is used, which is selected according to a uniform distribution of the combinations of path coverage and testing results. This study proposes two optimal formulas which are equivalent with respect to their model program and the total score. A comprehensive empirical study on 30 formulas is conducted, to compare the performance among non-equivalent formulas, as well as to investigate the impacts of various factors, including test suite size, error detection accuracy, the number of failed test cases, and the execution frequency of the buggy code.

1.4.2 Parallel Debugging

Recently, SBFL on the multi-fault scenario has drawn attentions of the community. The main difficulty for the multi-fault scenario is to establish associations between failed executions and the corresponding faults. Currently, there are two commonly adopted approaches. One is OBA (One-Bug-at-A-time), that is, faults are one by one localized sequentially (which is also known as sequential debugging). The other one is parallel debugging, where several developers localize faults simultaneously.

Many researchers have argued that parallel debugging can be more helpful than sequential debugging, in terms of its efficiency and relatively satisfactory effectiveness. There are four key components in designing good parallel debugging methods, namely, clustering algorithm, fingerprinting function, distance metric, and evaluation metric.

- As an effective method for mining the similarity between data, the clustering process can make data with similar characteristics form a cluster spontaneously, so it is widely used by researchers to discover the "Fault → Failure" relationship. Jones et al. used agglomerative hierarchical clustering to cluster failed cases [27] and developed a technique that computes the stopping criterion based on fault localization information. Three clustering algorithms, DBSCAN, K-means, and K-medoids, were mentioned by Gao et al. in [19]. They argued that DBSCAN is not appropriate for fault localization because failed cases for some faults might be excluded during clustering, since they may fall in low-density regions. They also pointed out that K-medoids has shown to be very robust in comparison to the K-means clustering algorithm for the presence of noise or outliers, thus generally producing high-quality clusters.
- Failed test cases are too abstract to be measured in distance calculation. They must be represented in a mathematical form until they can be used for clustering. A fingerprinting function that extracts signatures from failures achieves this request in general. Liu et al. discussed six representative failure proximities in [33], namely, FP (Failure Point)-Based Proximity, ST (Stack Trace)-Based Proximity, CC (Code Coverage)-Based Proximity, PE (Predicate Evaluation)-Based Proximity, DS (Dynamic Slicing)-Based Proximity, and SD (Statistical Debugging)-Based Proximity. Inspired by this study, many researchers proposed to use rank proximity, that is, to employ the suspiciousness ranking of all statements based on a given fault localization technique, to represent an individual failed test case.
- In addition to the clustering algorithm, distance metric also plays an important role in parallel debugging. Zakari et al. have argued that clustering algorithms with Euclidean distance, Jaccard distance, or Hamming distance are indeed problematic and inappropriate in parallel debugging [65]. Kendall tau distance counts the number of pairwise disagreements between two rankings of the same size, which can ideally match the intuition that rankings with more pairwise disagreements should be given greater distance. A revised Kendall tau distance was proposed in [19].

- In SBFL, *EXAM* score and *CNSE* (Cumulative Number of Statements Examined) are the two most widely used evaluation metrics. However, in parallel debugging, the evaluation metrics need to be redesigned because faults are localized and fixed simultaneously. Jones et al. proposed D (the total developer expense) and FF (the critical expense to a failure-free program), to evaluate the effectiveness of the parallel debugging technique.

1.4.3 Combining Deep Learning with SBFL

Recently, we have seen deep learning techniques applied in various software engineering activities, including SBFL. Deep learning techniques can capture the potential features of given data and then generate a data-based model with limited human interaction. In SBFL, the developer obtains the risk value of each statement based on the coverage information gathered by executing PG against TS and then generates rankings to help debuggers localize the fault(s) in PG. The core of SBFL is to find the mapping relationship between coverage information and risk values, while the advantage of deep learning is to mine data features and generate models to predict such relationships. In recent years, we have seen achievements in this direction. Two representative methods are DNN-FL and CNN-FL.

1. To find the complex nonlinear relationship between the coverage of each test case in the test suite TS and its execution result, Zheng et al. proposed DNN-FL for determining the correlation between each statement in the program PG and the failed execution [70]. This method first constructs and trains a deep neural network and then generates a set of virtual test cases with the same number of executable statements in PG (each virtual case covers only one statement) followed by inputting these virtual cases into the trained DNN; thus, the risk value of each statement could be output within DNN. The detailed steps are as follows:

   - Step 1: Construct a deep neural network containing an input layer, an output layer, and an appropriate number of hidden layers;
   - Step 2: The coverage data c_{t_i} and execution result r_{t_i} of TS were input as training samples into the DNN model, allowing DNN to learn the complex nonlinear relationship between coverage data and execution results;
   - Step 3: Input the coverage data of m virtual test cases $c_{v_1}, c_{v_2}, \ldots, c_{v_m}$ into the trained DNN; the generated m outputs $r_{v_1}, r_{v_2}, \ldots, r_{v_m}$ will reflect the risk values of the m executable statements in PG, respectively;
   - Step 4: Conduct descending ranking for $r_{v_1}, r_{v_2}, \ldots, r_{v_m}$, i.e., rank all executable statements in PG according to their corresponding risk values to form a ranking.
   - Step 5: Check the statement in PG one by one based on the ranking until the fault(s) are localized.

2. As the scale of PG increases, Zhang et al. have argued that the number of statements included in PG will increase substantially, and the traditional deep neural network needs to set more hidden layers and parameters to satisfy the needs of data mining, which is bound to result in higher costs [68]. This deficiency of DNN can be eliminated by three merits of the convolutional neural network (CNN), that is, local connections, parameter sharing, and down-sampling in pooling. Firstly, the local connections can be accomplished by making a convolutional kernel much smaller than input data; thus the learning efficiency of CNN can be improved by reducing the number of parameters. Secondly, with the benefit of parameter sharing, CNN can scan input data with fewer parameters, which significantly reduces the cost of network training, particularly when the input data is large. Thirdly, the pooling layer in CNN simplifies the processed data through down-sampling, further reducing the number of output parameters and enhancing the generation ability of the model. Based on these considerations, Zhang et al. combined CNN with SBFL and proposed CNN-FL, which contains four steps.

- Step 1: Construct a convolutional neural network with an input layer (the size is determined by the number of executable statements in PG), two convolutional layers, two pooling layers, two rectified linear units ($ReLU$), several fully connected layers (the number of nodes in each layer is related to the size of PG), and an output layer (the number of nodes is 1);
- Step 2: The coverage data and execution results of test cases in TS are split into multiple batches and then fed to CNN in turn for training the network;
- Step 3: Construct virtual test cases equal to the number of executable statements in PG, and each virtual test case covers only one statement in PG, that is, the statement i corresponding to x_i is only covered by the virtual test case t_i. Input the virtual case t_i ($i = 1, 2, \ldots, N$) into the trained CNN to obtain the corresponding output, the output of t_i represents the likelihood that x_i contains a bug, indicating the suspiciousness of statement i of being defective. Since t_i only covers one entity, statement i, the output is actually the risk value of statement i;
- Step 4: All executable statements in PG are ranked to form a ranking in descending order of risk values, and the debugger localizes the fault(s) in PG accordingly.

1.5 Structure of This Book

In this book, we will cover two parts in SBFL. The first part is about the essential theories of SBFL. Chapter 2 introduces the theoretical framework that reveals the intrinsic relations among different risk evaluation formulas. In Chap. 3, we show how to use the framework to compare various risk evaluation formulas and demonstrate a performance hierarchy among these formulas. Chapter 4 further explains the sufficient and necessary condition to a general maximal formula. In Chap. 5, we introduce an extended framework, which can be used to analyze hybrid SBFL methods. And Chap. 6 will discuss the practicality of the introduced frameworks.

The second part is about some emerging challenges in SBFL. Chapter 7 focuses on the widely existed "oracle problem" and introduces a solution with "metamorphic slice." And Chap. 8 targets at another widely studied challenge, namely, "multiple-fault localization," where two approaches are elaborated.

Finally, we conclude this book in Chap. 9.

References

1. Abreu R, Zoeteweij P, Gemund AJV (2006) An evaluation of similarity coefficients for software fault localization. In: Proceedings of the 12th Pacific Rim International Symposium on Dependable Computing, pp 39–46. https://doi.org/10.1109/PRDC.2006.18
2. Abreu R, Zoeteweij P, Gemund AJV (2007) On the accuracy of spectrum-based fault localization. In: Proceedings of Testing: Academic and Industrial Conference Practice and Research Techniques-MUTATION, pp 89–98. https://doi.org/10.1109/TAIC.PART.2007.13
3. Abreu R, Zoeteweij P, Golsteijn R, Gemund AJV (2009) A practical evaluation of spectrum-based fault localization. J Syst Softw 82(11):1780–1792. https://doi.org/10.1016/j.jss.2009.06.035
4. Agrawal H, Horgan JR, London S, Wong WE (1995) Fault localization using execution slices and dataflow tests. In: Proceedings of the 6th International Symposium on Software Reliability Engineering, pp 143–151. https://doi.org/10.1109/ISSRE.1995.497652
5. Chen MY, Kiciman E, Fratkin E, Fox A, Brewer E (2002) Pinpoint: problem determination in large, dynamic internet services. In: Proceedings of the 32th IEEE/IFIP International Conference on Dependable Systems and Networks, pp 595–604. https://doi.org/10.1109/DSN.2002.1029005
6. Chen TY, Cheung SC, Yiu SM (1998) Metamorphic testing: a new approach for generating next test cases. Technical Report HKUST-CS98-01, Department of Computer Science, Hong Kong University
7. Chen TY, Kuo FC, Tse TH, Zhou Z (2003) Metamorphic testing and beyond. In: Proceedings of the 11th Annual International Workshop on Software Technology and Engineering Practice, pp 94–100. https://doi.org/10.1109/STEP.2003.18
8. Chen Z, Xu B, Yang H (2001) Detecting dead statements for concurrent programs. In: Proceedings of the 1st IEEE International Workshop on Source Code Analysis and Manipulation, pp 67–74. https://doi.org/10.1109/SCAM.2001.972667
9. Chen Z, Xu B, Yang H, Zhao J (2002) Concurrent ada dead statements detection. Inf Softw Technol 44(13):733–741. https://doi.org/10.1016/S0950-5849(02)00106-4
10. Chen Z, Zhou Y, Xu B, Zhao J, Yang H (2002) A novel approach to measuring class cohesion based on dependence analysis. In: Proceedings of the 18th International Conference on Software Maintenance, pp 377–384. https://doi.org/10.1109/ICSM.2002.1167794
11. Chen Z, Xu B, Yang H (2003) Test coverage analysis based on program slicing. In: Proceedings of the 2003 IEEE International Conference on Information Reuse and Integration, pp 559–565. https://doi.org/10.1109/IRI.2003.1251465
12. Chen Z, Xu B, Nie C (2007) Comparing fault-based testing strategies of general boolean specifications. In: Proceedings of the 31st Annual International Computer Software and Applications Conference, pp 621–622. https://doi.org/10.1109/COMPSAC.2007.91

13. Chen Z, Chen TY, Xu B (2011) A revisit of fault class hierarchies in general boolean specifications. ACM Trans Softw Eng Methodol 20(3):13:1–13:11. https://doi.org/10.1145/2000791.2000797

14. Collofello JS, Woodfield SN (1989) Evaluating the effectiveness of reliability-assurance techniques. J Syst Softw 9(3):191–195. https://doi.org/10.1016/0164-1212(89)90039-3

15. DeMillo RA, Pan H, Spafford EH (1996) Critical slicing for software fault localization. In: Proceedings of ACM SIGSOFT International Symposium on Software Testing and Analysis, pp 121–134. https://doi.org/10.1145/226295.226310

16. Dong G, Nie C, Xu B, Wang L (2007) An effective iterative metamorphic testing algorithm based on program path analysis. In: Proceedings of the 7th International Conference on Quality Software, pp 292–297. https://doi.org/10.1109/QSIC.2007.15

17. Fang C, Chen Z, Xu B (2012) Comparing logic coverage criteria on test case prioritization. Sci China Inf Sci 55(12):2826–2840. https://doi.org/10.1007/s11432-012-4746-9

18. Feng Y, Chen Z, Jones JA, Fang C, Xu B (2015) Test report prioritization to assist crowdsourced testing. In: Nitto ED, Harman M, Heymans P (eds) Proceedings of the 10th Joint Meeting on Foundations of Software Engineering, pp 225–236. https://doi.org/10.1145/2786805.2786862

19. Gao R, Wong WE (2019) Mseer-an advanced technique for locating multiple bugs in parallel. IEEE Trans Softw Eng 45(3):301–318. https://doi.org/10.1109/TSE.2017.2776912

20. Gupta N, He H, Zhang X, Gupta R (2005) Locating faulty code using failure-inducing chops. In: Proceedings of the 20th IEEE/ACM International Conference on Automated Software Engineering, pp 263–272. https://doi.org/10.1145/1101908.1101948

21. Harrold MJ, Rothermel G, Wu R, Yi L (1998) An empirical investigation of program spectra. In: Proceedings of the 1st ACM SIGPLAN-SIGSOFT Workshop on Program Analysis for Software Tools and Engineering, pp 83–90. https://doi.org/10.1145/277631.277647

22. Harrold MJ, Rothermel G, Sayre K, Wu R, Yi L (2000) An empirical investigation of the relationship between spectra differences and regression faults. Softw Test Verification Reliab 10(3):171–194. https://doi.org/10.1002/1099-1689(200009)10:3<171::AID-STVR209>3.0.CO;2-J

23. Jiang B, Chan WK (2010) On the integration of test adequacy, test case prioritization, and statistical fault localization. In: Proceedings of the 10th International Conference on Quality Software, pp 377–384. https://doi.org/10.1109/QSIC.2010.64

24. Jiang S, Xu B, Shi L (2006) An approach to analyzing recursive programs with exception handling constructs. SIGPLAN Not 41(4):30–35. https://doi.org/10.1145/1147214.1147220

25. Jones JA, Harrold MJ (2005) Empirical evaluation of the tarantula automatic fault-localization technique. In: Proceedings of the 20th IEEE/ACM International Conference on Automated Software Engineering, pp 273–282. https://doi.org/10.1145/1101908.1101949

26. Jones JA, Harrold MJ, Stasko J (2002) Visualization of test information to assist fault localization. In: Proceedings of the 24th International Conference on Software Engineering, pp 467–477. https://doi.org/10.1145/581396.581397

27. Jones JA, Bowring JF, Harrold MJ (2007) Debugging in parallel. In: Proceedings of ACM SIGSOFT International Symposium on Software Testing and Analysis, pp 16–26. https://doi.org/10.1145/1273463.1273468

28. Ju X, Chen X, Yang Y, Jiang S, Qian J, Xu B (2017) An in-depth study of the efficiency of risk evaluation formulas for multi-fault localization. In: Proceedings of the 2017 IEEE International Conference on Software Quality, Reliability and Security Companion, pp 304–310. https://doi.org/10.1109/QRS-C.2017.58

29. Lee HJ, Naish L, Ramamohanarao K (2009) Study of the relationship of bug consistency with respect to performance of spectra metrics. In: Proceedings of the 2nd IEEE International Conference on Computer Science and Information Technology, pp 501–508. https://doi.org/10.1109/ICCSIT.2009.5234512

30. Liblit B (2004) Cooperative bug isolation. PhD thesis, University of California

31. Liblit B, Naik M, Zheng AX, Aiken A, Jordan MI (2005) Scalable statistical bug isolation. In: Proceedings of ACM SIGPLAN Conference on Programming Language Design and Implementation, pp 15–26. https://doi.org/10.1145/1064978.1065014

32. Liu C, Fei L, Yan X, Han J, Midkiff SP (2006) Statistical debugging: a hypothesis testing-based approach. IEEE Trans Softw Eng 32(10):831–848

33. Liu C, Zhang X, Han J (2008) A systematic study of failure proximity. IEEE Trans Softw Eng 34(6):826–843. https://doi.org/10.1109/TSE.2008.66

34. Naish L, Lee HJ, Ramamohanarao K (2011) A model for spectra-based software diagnosis. ACM Trans Softw Eng Methodol 20(3):101–132. https://doi.org/10.1145/2000791.2000795

35. Nie C, Xu B, Shi L, Wang Z (2006) A new heuristic for test suite generation for pair-wise testing. In: Proceedings of the 18th International Conference on Software Engineering & Knowledge Engineering, pp 517–521

36. Renieris M, Reiss S (2003) Fault localization with nearest neighbor queries. In: Proceedings of the 18th IEEE International Conference on Automated Software Engineering, pp 30–39. https://doi.org/10.1109/ASE.2003.1240292

37. Reps T, Ball T, Das M, Larus J (1997) The use of program profiling for software maintenance with applications to the year 2000 problem. In: Proceedings of the 6th European Software Engineering Conference held jointly with the 5th ACM SIGSOFT International Symposium on Foundations of Software Engineering, vol 6, pp 432–449. https://doi.org/10.1007/3-540-63531-9_29

38. Santelices R, Jones JA, Yu Y, Harrold MJ (2009) Lightweight fault-localization using multiple coverage types. In: Proceedings of the 31st International Conference on Software Engineering, pp 56–66. https://doi.org/10.1109/ICSE.2009.5070508

39. Shi Q, Huang J, Chen Z, Xu B (2016) Verifying synchronization for atomicity violation fixing. IEEE Trans Softw Eng 42(3):285–301. https://doi.org/10.1109/TSE.2015.2477820

40. Wong WE, Qi Y (2006) Effective program debugging based on execution slices and inter-block data dependency. J Syst Softw 79(7):891–903. https://doi.org/10.1016/j.jss.2005.06.045

41. Wong WE, Sugeta T, Qi Y, Maldonado JC (2005) Smart debugging software architectural design in SDL. J Syst Softw 76(1):15–28. https://doi.org/10.1016/j.jss.2004.06.026

42. Wong WE, Debroy V, Choi B (2010) A family of code coverage-based heuristics for effective fault localization. J Syst Softw 83(2):188–208. https://doi.org/10.1016/j.jss.2009.09.037

43. Wong WE, Debroy V, Xu D (2012) Towards better fault localization: a crosstab-based statistical approach. IEEE Trans Syst Man Cybern 42(3):378–396. https://doi.org/10.1109/TSMCC.2011.2118751

44. Wong WE, Debroy V, Gao R, Li Y (2014) The DStar Method for Effective Software Fault Localization. IEEE Trans Reliab 63(1):290–308. https://doi.org/10.1109/TR.2013.2285319

45. Wu D, Chen L, Zhou Y, Xu B (2015) How do developers use C++ libraries? An empirical study. In: Xu H (ed) Proceedings of the 27th International Conference on Software Engineering and Knowledge Engineering, pp 260–265. https://doi.org/10.18293/SEKE2015-9

46. Xie X, Shi L, Nie C, He Y, Xu B (2005) A dynamic optimization strategy for evolutionary testing. In: Proceedings of the 12th Asia-Pacific Software Engineering Conference, pp 568–575. https://doi.org/10.1109/APSEC.2005.6

47. Xie X, Ho JWK, Murphy C, Kaiser G, Xu B, Chen TY (2011) Testing and validating machine learning classifiers by metamorphic testing. J Syst Softw 84(4):544–558

48. Xie X, Chen TY, Kuo FC, Xu B (2013) A theoretical analysis of the risk evaluation formulas for spectrum-based fault localization. ACM Trans Softw Eng Methodol 22(4):31:1–31:40. https://doi.org/10.1145/2522920.2522924

49. Xie X, Wong WE, Chen TY, Xu B (2013) Metamorphic slice: an application in spectrum-based fault localization. Inf Softw Technol 55(5):866–879. https://doi.org/10.1016/j.infsof.2012.08.008

50. Xie X, Zhang Z, Chen TY, Liu Y, Poon PL, Xu B (2020) Mettle: a metamorphic testing approach to assessing and validating unsupervised machine learning systems. IEEE Trans Reliab. https://doi.org/10.1109/TR.2020.2972266

51. Xu B (1993) On subprograms with A variable number of parameters of varying types. SIGPLAN Not 28(2):14–20. https://doi.org/10.1145/157352.157353
52. Xu B, Chen Z (2001) Dependence analysis for recursive java programs. SIGPLAN Not 36(12):70–76. https://doi.org/10.1145/583960.583969
53. Xu B, Chen Z, Yang H (2002) Dynamic slicing object-oriented programs for debugging. In: Proceedings of the 2nd IEEE International Workshop on Source Code Analysis and Manipulation, pp 115–122. https://doi.org/10.1109/SCAM.2002.1134111
54. Xu B, Nie C, Shi L, Chu WCC, Yang H, Chen H (2003) Test plan design for software configuration testing. In: Proceedings of the International Conference on Software Engineering Research and Practice, pp 686–692
55. Xu B, Xu L, Nie C, Chu WCC, Chang C (2003) Applying combinatorial method to test browser compatibility. In: Proceedings of the 5th International Symposium on Multimedia Software Engineering, pp 156–162. https://doi.org/10.1109/MMSE.2003.1254437
56. Xu B, Qian J, Zhang X, Wu Z, Chen L (2005) A brief survey of program slicing. ACM SIGSOFT Softw Eng Notes 30(2):1–36. https://doi.org/10.1145/1050849.1050865
57. Xu L, Xu B, Chen Z, Jiang J, Chen H (2003) Regression testing for web applications based on slicing. In: Proceedings of the 27th International Computer Software and Applications Conference, pp 652–656. https://doi.org/10.1109/CMPSAC.2003.1245411
58. Xu L, Xu B, Nie C, Chen H, Yang H (2003) A browser compatibility testing method based on combinatorial testing. In: Proceedings of the 3rd International Conference on Web Engineering. Lecture Notes in Computer Science, vol 2722, pp 310–313. https://doi.org/10.1007/3-540-45068-8_60
59. Xu Z, Liu P, Zhang X, Xu B (2016) Python predictive analysis for bug detection. In: Zimmermann T, Cleland-Huang J, Su Z (eds) Proceedings of the 24th ACM SIGSOFT International Symposium on Foundations of Software Engineering, pp 121–132. https://doi.org/10.1145/2950290.2950357
60. Xu Z, Zhang X, Chen L, Pei K, Xu B (2016) Python probabilistic type inference with natural language support. In: Zimmermann T, Cleland-Huang J, Su Z (eds) Proceedings of the 24th ACM SIGSOFT International Symposium on Foundations of Software Engineering, pp 607–618. https://doi.org/10.1145/2950290.2950343
61. Yang Y, Zhou Y, Lu H, Chen L, Chen Z, Xu B, Leung HKN, Zhang Z (2015) Are slice-based cohesion metrics actually useful in effort-aware post-release fault-proneness prediction? An empirical study. IEEE Trans Softw Eng 41(4):331–357. https://doi.org/10.1109/TSE.2014.2370048
62. Yang Y, Harman M, Krinke J, Islam SS, Binkley DW, Zhou Y, Xu B (2016) An empirical study on dependence clusters for effort-aware fault-proneness prediction. In: Lo D, Apel S, Khurshid S (eds) Proceedings of the 31st IEEE/ACM International Conference on Automated Software Engineering, pp 296–307. https://doi.org/10.1145/2970276.2970353
63. Yang Y, Jiang Y, Zuo Z, Wang Y, Sun H, Lu H, Zhou Y, Xu B (2019) Automatic self-validation for code coverage profilers. In: Proceedings of the 34th IEEE/ACM International Conference on Automated Software Engineering, pp 79–90. https://doi.org/10.1109/ASE.2019.00018
64. Yoo S, Xie X, Kuo FC, Chen TY, Harman M (2017) Human competitiveness of genetic programming in spectrum-based fault localisation: theoretical and empirical analysis. ACM Trans Softw Eng Methodol 26(1):4:1–4:30. https://doi.org/10.1145/3078840
65. Zakari A, Lee SP (2019) Parallel debugging: an investigative study. J Softw Evol Process 31(11):e2178. https://doi.org/10.1002/smr.2178
66. Zeller A (2002) Isolating cause-effect chains from computer programs. In: Proceedings of the 10th ACM SIGSOFT Symposium on Foundations of Software Engineering, pp 1–10. https://doi.org/10.1145/605466.605468
67. Zhang X, He H, Gupta N, Gupta R (2005) Experimental evaluation of using dynamic slices for fault location. In: Proceedings of the 6th International Symposium on Automated Analysis-Driven Debugging, pp 33–42. https://doi.org/10.1145/1085130.1085135
68. Zhang Z, Lei Y, Mao X, Li P (2019) Cnn-fl: an effective approach for localizing faults using convolutional neural networks. In: Proceedings of the 26th International Conference

on Software Analysis, Evolution and Reengineering, pp 445–455. https://doi.org/10.1109/SANER.2019.8668002

69. Zhao Y, Yang Y, Lu H, Zhou Y, Song Q, Xu B (2015) An empirical analysis of package-modularization metrics: implications for software fault-proneness. Inf Softw Technol 57:186–203. https://doi.org/10.1016/j.infsof.2014.09.006

70. Zheng W, Hu D, Wang J (2016) Fault localization analysis based on deep neural network. Math Problems Eng 2016:1–11. https://doi.org/10.1155/2016/1820454

71. Zhou Y, Yang Y, Lu H, Chen L, Li Y, Zhao Y, Qian J, Xu B (2018) How far we have progressed in the journey? An examination of cross-project defect prediction. ACM Trans Softw Eng Methodol 27(1):1:1–1:51. https://doi.org/10.1145/3183339

Chapter 2
A Theoretical Framework for Spectrum-Based Fault Localization

Abstract An important research direction of spectrum-based fault localization (SBFL) is the effectiveness of risk evaluation formulas. In the past two decades, many relevant studies have adopted an empirical approach, which can hardly be considered as sufficiently comprehensive because of the huge number of combinations of various factors in SBFL. Though some studies aimed at overcoming the limitations of the empirical approach, none of them has provided a completely satisfactory solution. Therefore, in this chapter, we introduce a theoretical framework proposed by us (Xie et al (2013) ACM Trans Softw Eng Methodol 22(4):31:1–31:40), which can compare and analyze the effectiveness of any given risk evaluation formulas, without conducting any experiments. This framework is built on a concept of set division of all program statements, and this division is defined by the given formula. In Sect. 2.3 we show the proof of the set division for 30 commonly adopted formulas, which will be used in the following chapters.

2.1 Comparison Among Risk Formulas

As introduced in Sect. 1.4.1, one of the most essential tasks in SBFL is the **risk evaluation**. An effective risk evaluation formula is very crucial to provide a good fault localization performance for SBFL. With more and more formulas proposed, some people started to compare their performance, in order to identify the formulas with the "best" performance [1–4]. In all these studies, empirical approaches were conducted to investigate and measure the effectiveness of the risk evaluation formulas. In order to make the experimental results more reliable, people have used various approaches to control the threats to validity. For example, they adopted the same performance metric or its equivalents, the standardized experimental setup,

Part of this chapter ©2013 ACM. Reprinted, with permission from ACM Transactions on Software Engineering and Methodology; October 2013. Vol. 22, No. 4, Article 31, 1–40. https://doi.org/10.1145/2522920.2522924 (Ref. [8]).

and the unified benchmarks. In addition, both the mutation analysis and real-life case studies were conducted.

However, the limitations of these empirical approaches shall not be ignored. In an experimental analysis, the performance of a risk evaluation formula strongly depends on the experimental setup. Different combinations of various test suites, testing objects, fault types, etc. may affect the experimental results. Even though people have adopted the unified setup and benchmarks, these empirical studies can hardly be considered as sufficiently comprehensive due to the huge number of combinations of all the possible variations. In other words, the experimental results are still the sampled observations and cannot conclusively identify the most effective formulas.

2.2 A Set-Based Framework

Therefore, in this chapter, we will introduce a set-based framework, to theoretically analyze and compare risk evaluation formulas [8]. Different from empirical studies, a theoretical analysis can reveal the most essential principles and properties of SBFL.

As discussed in Chap. 1, in SBFL, given a program and a test suite, the matrix MA can be constructed accordingly. A risk evaluation formula R uses MA to assess the risk of being faulty for all statements, according to which, all statements will be sorted descendingly. Such a ranking list is then used to assist debugging. Therefore, the relative risk values rather than the absolute risk values of all statements are the key factor determining the $EXAM$ score for a formula R.

Given a ranking list in descending order of the risk values evaluated by a formula R, we can divide all statements into three disjoint sets, S_B^R, S_F^R, and S_A^R, with respect to an arbitrary s_f, as follows.

Definition 2.2.1 (Set division) Given a program with n statements $PG=<s_1, s_2, \ldots, s_n>$, a test suite of m test cases $TS=\{t_1, t_2, \ldots, t_m\}$, and a risk evaluation formula R, vector $A_i=<a_{ef}^i, a_{ep}^i, a_{nf}^i, a_{np}^i>$ can be constructed for each statement s_i, and $R(s_i)$ can be computed accordingly. For any faulty statement s_f, the set of program statements $S=\{s_1, s_2, \ldots, s_n\}$ can be decomposed into three mutually exclusive subsets:

(a) S_B^R consists of all statements with risk values higher than the risk value of the faulty statement s_f, that is, $S_B^R = \{s_i \in S | R(s_i) > R(s_f), 1 \le i \le n\}$.
(b) S_F^R consists of all statements with the risk values equal to the risk value of the faulty statement s_f, that is, $S_F^R = \{s_i \in S | R(s_i) = R(s_f), 1 \le i \le n\}$.
(c) S_A^R consists of all statements with the risk values lower than the risk value of the faulty statement s_f, that is, $S_A^R = \{s_i \in S | R(s_i) < R(s_f), 1 \le i \le n\}$.

In the practice of SBFL, a **tie-breaking scheme** is always required to determine the order of the statements with same risk values, and this scheme may affect the performance of SBFL. Different tie-breaking schemes have been developed, including *WORST, BEST, ORIGINAL ORDER*, etc. [5–7]. However, in terms of evaluating the *EXAM* score, there is no need to consider the application or impact of tie-breaking scheme on S_B^R or S_A^R, because by definition, in the final list returned by a risk evaluation formula R, all $s_i \in S_B^R$ are ranked higher than s_f, while all $s_i \in S_A^R$ are ranked lower than s_f. Thus, the ordering of the statements within S_B^R or S_A^R does not affect the ranking of s_f. As a consequence, it is only sensitive on how a tie-breaking scheme distinguishes and ranks $s_i \in S_F^R$.

Actually, a tie-breaking scheme solves the ordering problem that a risk evaluation formula cannot handle. Thus, when focusing on the comparison between different formulas, it is reasonable to expect that the tie-breaking scheme returns consistent results for all formulas. Thus, in the theoretical framework, we require that a tie-breaking scheme preserves the relative order of any pair of statements irrespective of which formula is used. We refer such schemes as consistent tie-breaking schemes, which are defined as follows.

Definition 2.2.2 (Tie-breaking scheme) Given any two statement sets S_1 and S_2, which contain elements with the same risk values, a tie-breaking scheme returns the ordered statement lists O_1 and O_2 for S_1 and S_2, respectively. The tie-breaking scheme is said to be consistent, if all elements common to S_1 and S_2 have the same relative order in O_1 and O_2.

Let us use a simple example to further illustrate the intuition behind this requirement. Given two risk evaluation formulas R_1 and R_2 that return the same S_F^R but different S_B^R, suppose the size of $S_B^{R_1}$ is smaller than the size of $S_B^{R_2}$. Since the order of $s_i \in S_F^R$ in both R_1 and R_2 cannot be decided by these two formulas, that is, it is independent of these formulas, then to make a fair comparison, this order must be identical in R_1 and R_2. Obviously, only by adopting a consistent tie-breaking scheme such identical order can be guaranteed. And in this example, R_1 with smaller S_B^R would have a lower *EXAM* score.

Intuitively speaking, the most straightforward approach towards the theoretical analysis of the performance between two formulas is to compare the sizes of their S_B^R and the numbers of statements that are from S_F^R but ranked before s_f based on the tie-breaking scheme. However, since the sizes of S_B^R and S_F^R depend on the program and test suite, which can be very varying, a size comparison appears to be intractable. The core idea of this theoretical framework is to make use of the subset relationships among S_B^R (or S_F^R) of different formulas, to facilitate the analysis.

Let E_1 and E_2 denote the *EXAM* scores for risk evaluation formulas R_1 and R_2, respectively. There are two types of relations between R_1 and R_2 as follows.

Definition 2.2.3 (Better) R_1 is said to be *better* than R_2 (denoted as $R_1 \rightarrow R_2$) if for any program, faulty statement s_f, test suite, and consistent tie-breaking scheme, we have $E_1 \leq E_2$.

Obviously the relation "$\rightarrow$" is reflexive, that is, we have $R_1 \rightarrow R_1$. Furthermore, this relation is transitive, that is, if $R_1 \rightarrow R_2$ and $R_2 \rightarrow R_3$, we have $R_1 \rightarrow R_3$.

Definition 2.2.4 (Equivalent) R_1 and R_2 are said to be *equivalent* (denoted as $R_1 \leftrightarrow R_2$), if for any program, faulty statement s_f, test suite, and consistent tie-breaking scheme, we have $E_1 = E_2$.

As a reminder, this relation "$\leftrightarrow$" is reflexive, symmetric, and transitive, that is, $R_1 \leftrightarrow R_1$; if $R_1 \leftrightarrow R_2$, then $R_2 \leftrightarrow R_1$; and if $R_1 \leftrightarrow R_2$ and $R_2 \leftrightarrow R_3$, then $R_1 \leftrightarrow R_3$.

With the above definitions, we can have the following theorems and propositions.

Theorem 2.2.1 *For any two risk evaluation formulas R_1 and R_2, $R_1 \leftrightarrow R_2$ if and only if $R_1 \rightarrow R_2$ and $R_2 \rightarrow R_1$.*

Proof Immediately after Definitions 2.2.3 and 2.2.4, this theorem can be proved.

□

Theorem 2.2.2 *Given any two risk evaluation formulas R_1 and R_2, if for any program, faulty statement s_f, and test suite, we have $S_B^{R_1} \subseteq S_B^{R_2}$ and $S_A^{R_2} \subseteq S_A^{R_1}$, then $R_1 \rightarrow R_2$.*

Proof Consider a virtual formula R_3, such that for any program, s_f, and test suite, $S_B^{R_3} = S_B^{R_1}$ and $S_A^{R_3} = S_A^{R_2}$. Let E_3 denote the *EXAM* score of R_3, and let L_1, L_2, and L_3 denote the ranking lists returned by R_1, R_2, and R_3, respectively. Obviously, considering R_1 and R_3, we have $S_B^{R_3} = S_B^{R_1}$, $S_F^{R_1} \subseteq S_F^{R_3}$, and $S_A^{R_3} \subseteq S_A^{R_1}$. If the tie-breaking scheme is consistent, s_f can never have lower ranking in L_1 than in L_3. Therefore, we have $E_1 \leq E_3$. Now, considering R_2 and R_3, we have $S_B^{R_3} \subseteq S_B^{R_2}$, $S_F^{R_2} \subseteq S_F^{R_3}$, and $S_A^{R_3} = S_A^{R_2}$. If the tie-breaking scheme is consistent, s_f always has the same relative order with any element of $S_F^{R_2}$, in both L_2 and L_3. However, all elements in $S_F^{R_3} \setminus S_F^{R_2}$ will definitely be ranked higher than s_f in L_2, but not necessarily be ranked higher than s_f in L_3. As a consequence, $E_3 \leq E_2$.

Therefore, we have $E_1 \leq E_2$. Following immediately from Definition 2.2.3, we have $R_1 \rightarrow R_2$.   □

Theorem 2.2.3 *Given any two risk evaluation formulas R_1 and R_2, if for any program, faulty statement s_f, and test suite, we have $S_B^{R_1} = S_B^{R_2}$, $S_F^{R_1} = S_F^{R_2}$, and $S_A^{R_1} = S_A^{R_2}$, then $R_1 \leftrightarrow R_2$.*

Proof Suppose that for any program, s_f, and test suite, we have $S_B^{R_1} = S_B^{R_2}$ and $S_A^{R_1} = S_A^{R_2}$. In other words, we have $S_B^{R_1} \subseteq S_B^{R_2}$ and $S_A^{R_2} \subseteq S_A^{R_1}$, as well as $S_B^{R_2} \subseteq S_B^{R_1}$ and $S_A^{R_1} \subseteq S_A^{R_2}$. It follows immediately from Theorem 2.2.2 that $R_1 \rightarrow R_2$ and $R_2 \rightarrow R_1$. Therefore, we have $R_1 \leftrightarrow R_2$ after Theorem 2.2.1.   □

2.3   Set Division for Risk Evaluation Formulas

In this section, we will demonstrate the set division for risk evaluation formulas in some commonly adopted SBFL techniques. For the sources of these formulas, please refer to [8]. The definitions for these formulas are listed in Table 2.1.

Next, we will illustrate how to construct S_B^R, S_F^R, and S_A^R for these formulas. First, let us discuss some lemmas. Given a test suite TS, we denote its size as T, the number of *failed* test cases as F, and the number of *passed* cases as P. Obviously, we have $1 \leq F < T$, $1 \leq P < T$, and $P + F = T$. And we have the following lemmas of which the proofs are immediately after the definitions and the above assumptions.

Lemma 2.3.1 *For any $A_i = <a_{ef}^i, a_{ep}^i, a_{nf}^i, a_{np}^i>$, we have $a_{ef}^i + a_{ep}^i > 0$, $a_{ef}^i + a_{nf}^i = F$, $a_{ep}^i + a_{np}^i = P$, $a_{ef}^i \leq F$, and $a_{ep}^i \leq P$.*

Lemma 2.3.2 *For any faulty statement s_f with $A_f = <a_{ef}^f, a_{ep}^f, a_{nf}^f, a_{np}^f>$, if s_f is the only faulty statement in the program, we have $a_{ef}^f = F$ and $a_{nf}^f = 0$.*

With the above lemmas, now we can formally demonstrate the proof for Op1 set division.

Proposition 2.3.1 S_B^{Op1}, S_F^{Op1}, and S_A^{Op1} *for Op1 are equal to the following sets, X^1, Y^1, and Z^1, respectively.*

$$X^1 = \{s_i \mid a_{ef}^f = F \text{ and } a_{ep}^f - a_{ep}^i > 0, 1 \leq i \leq n\} \tag{2.1}$$

$$Y^1 = \{s_i \mid a_{ef}^f = F \text{ and } a_{ep}^f - a_{ep}^i = 0, 1 \leq i \leq n\} \tag{2.2}$$

$$Z^1 = \{s_i \mid (a_{ef}^i < F) \text{ or } (a_{ef}^i = F \text{ and } a_{ep}^f - a_{ep}^i < 0), 1 \leq i \leq n\} \tag{2.3}$$

Proof As stated in Table 2.1, formula Op1 is defined as follows.

$$R_{Op1}(s_i) = \begin{cases} -1 & \text{if } a_{ef}^i < F \\ P - a_{ep}^i & \text{if } a_{ef}^i = F \end{cases}$$

After Definition 2.2.1, we have

$$S_B^{Op1} = \{s_i \mid (a_{ef}^i < F \text{ and } -1 > P - a_{ep}^f)$$
$$\text{or } (a_{ef}^i = F \text{ and } P - a_{ep}^i > P - a_{ep}^f), 1 \leq i \leq n\} \tag{2.4}$$

$$S_F^{Op1} = \{s_i \mid (a_{ef}^i < F \text{ and } -1 = P - a_{ep}^f)$$
$$\text{or } (a_{ef}^i = F \text{ and } P - a_{ep}^i = P - a_{ep}^f), 1 \leq i \leq n\} \tag{2.5}$$

$$S_A^{Op1} = \{s_i \mid (a_{ef}^i < F \text{ and } -1 < P - a_{ep}^f)$$
$$\text{or } (a_{ef}^i = F \text{ and } P - a_{ep}^i < P - a_{ep}^f), 1 \leq i \leq n\} \tag{2.6}$$

Table 2.1 Investigated formulas

Name	Expression
Op1	$\begin{cases} -1 & \text{if } a_{ef} < F \\ P - a_{ep} & \text{if } a_{ef} = F \end{cases}$
Op2	$a_{ef} - \dfrac{a_{ep}}{a_{ep} + a_{np} + 1}$
Jaccard	$\dfrac{a_{ef}}{a_{ef} + a_{nf} + a_{ep}}$
Anderberg	$\dfrac{a_{ef}}{a_{ef} + 2(a_{nf} + a_{ep})}$
Sørensen-Dice	$\dfrac{2a_{ef}}{2a_{ef} + a_{nf} + a_{ep}}$
Dice	$\dfrac{2a_{ef}}{a_{ef} + a_{nf} + a_{ep}}$
Goodman	$\dfrac{2a_{ef} - a_{nf} - a_{ep}}{2a_{ef} + a_{nf} + a_{ep}}$
Tarantula	$\dfrac{a_{ef}}{a_{ef} + a_{nf}} / \left(\dfrac{a_{ef}}{a_{ef} + a_{nf}} + \dfrac{a_{ep}}{a_{ep} + a_{np}} \right)$
qe	$\dfrac{a_{ef}}{a_{ef} + a_{ep}}$
CBI Inc.	$\dfrac{a_{ef}}{a_{ef} + a_{ep}} - \dfrac{a_{ef} + a_{nf}}{a_{ef} + a_{nf} + a_{ep} + a_{np}}$
Wong2	$a_{ef} - a_{ep}$
Hamann	$\dfrac{a_{ef} + a_{np} - a_{nf} - a_{ep}}{a_{ef} + a_{nf} + a_{ep} + a_{np}}$
Simple Matching	$\dfrac{a_{ef} + a_{np}}{a_{ef} + a_{nf} + a_{ep} + a_{np}}$
Sokal	$\dfrac{2(a_{ef} + a_{np})}{2(a_{ef} + a_{np}) + a_{nf} + a_{ep}}$
Rogers&Tanimoto	$\dfrac{a_{ef} + a_{np}}{a_{ef} + a_{np} + 2(a_{nf} + a_{ep})}$
Hamming etc.	$a_{ef} + a_{np}$
Euclid	$\sqrt{a_{ef} + a_{np}}$
Wong1	a_{ef}
Russel & Rao	$\dfrac{a_{ef}}{a_{ef} + a_{nf} + a_{ep} + a_{np}}$
Binary	$\begin{cases} 0 & \text{if } a_{ef} < F \\ 1 & \text{if } a_{ef} = F \end{cases}$
Scott	$\dfrac{4a_{ef}a_{np} - 4a_{nf}a_{ep} - (a_{nf} - a_{ep})^2}{(2a_{ef} + a_{nf} + a_{ep})(2a_{np} + a_{nf} + a_{ep})}$
Rogot1	$\dfrac{1}{2} \left(\dfrac{a_{ef}}{2a_{ef} + a_{nf} + a_{ep}} + \dfrac{a_{np}}{2a_{np} + a_{nf} + a_{ep}} \right)$
Kulczynski2	$\dfrac{1}{2} \left(\dfrac{a_{ef}}{a_{ef} + a_{nf}} + \dfrac{a_{ef}}{a_{ef} + a_{ep}} \right)$
M2	$\dfrac{a_{ef}}{a_{ef} + a_{np} + 2(a_{nf} + a_{ep})}$
Ochiai	$\dfrac{a_{ef}}{\sqrt{(a_{ef} + a_{nf})(a_{ef} + a_{ep})}}$
AMPLE2	$\dfrac{a_{ef}}{a_{ef} + a_{nf}} - \dfrac{a_{ep}}{a_{ep} + a_{np}}$

(continued)

Table 2.1 (continued)

Name	Expression
Wong3	$a_{ef}-h$, where $h=\begin{cases} a_{ep} & \text{if } a_{ep}\leq 2 \\ 2+0.1(a_{ep}-2) & \text{if } 2<a_{ep}\leq 10 \\ 2.8+0.001(a_{ep}-10) & \text{if } a_{ep}>10 \end{cases}$
Arithmetic Mean	$\dfrac{2a_{ef}a_{np}-2a_{nf}a_{ep}}{(a_{ef}+a_{ep})(a_{np}+a_{nf})+(a_{ef}+a_{nf})(a_{ep}+a_{np})}$
Cohen	$\dfrac{2a_{ef}a_{np}-2a_{nf}a_{ep}}{(a_{ef}+a_{ep})(a_{np}+a_{ep})+(a_{ef}+a_{nf})(a_{nf}+a_{np})}$
Fleiss	$\dfrac{4a_{ef}a_{np}-4a_{nf}a_{ep}-(a_{nf}-a_{ep})^2}{(2a_{ef}+a_{nf}+a_{ep})+(2a_{np}+a_{nf}+a_{ep})}$

First, we will prove $S_B^{Op1}=X^1$. S_B^{Op1} defined in (2.4) can be rewritten as:

$$S_B^{Op1}=\{s_i\,|\,a_{ef}^i<F \text{ and } -1>P-a_{ep}^f,\,1\leq i\leq n\}$$

$$\cup\{s_i\,|\,a_{ef}^i=F \text{ and } a_{ep}^f-a_{ep}^i>0,\,1\leq i\leq n\}$$

Since $(-1<P-a_{ep}^f)$ after Lemma 2.3.1, we have

$$\{s_i\,|\,a_{ef}^i<F \text{ and } -1>P-a_{ep}^f,\,1\leq i\leq n\}=\emptyset$$

Therefore, S_B^{Op1} becomes

$$S_B^{Op1}=\{s_i\,|\,a_{ef}^i=F \text{ and } a_{ep}^f-a_{ep}^i>0,\,1\leq i\leq n\}=X^1$$

Similarly, we can prove that $S_F^{Op1}=Y^1$.

Now, consider S_A^{Op1} defined in (2.6). Since $(-1<P-a_{ep}^f)$ after Lemma 2.3.1, $(a_{ef}^i<F \text{ and } -1<P-a_{ep}^f)$ is logically equivalent to $(a_{ef}^i<F)$. Therefore, S_A^{Op1} becomes

$$S_A^{Op1}=\{s_i\,|\,(a_{ef}^i<F) \text{ or } (a_{ef}^i=F \text{ and } a_{ep}^f-a_{ep}^i<0),\,1\leq i\leq n\}=Z^1$$

In conclusion, we have proved that $S_B^{Op1}=X^1$, $S_F^{Op1}=Y^1$ and $S_A^{Op1}=Z^1$. □

Similarly, we can prove the set division for all the remained formulas in Table 2.1. In this section, we present the conclusions in propositions and leave all the detailed proof in Appendix A.

Proposition 2.3.2 S_B^{Op2}, S_F^{Op2}, and S_A^{Op2} for Op2 are equal to the above sets X^1 (2.1), Y^1 (2.2), and Z^1 (2.3), respectively.

Proposition 2.3.3 S_B^R, S_F^R, and S_A^R for Jaccard, Anderberg, Sørensen-Dice, Dice, and Goodman are equal to the following sets, respectively.

$$S_B^R = \{s_i \, | \, a_{ef}^i > 0 \text{ and } 1 + \frac{a_{ep}^f}{F} - \frac{F}{a_{ef}^i} - \frac{a_{ep}^i}{a_{ef}^i} > 0, \, 1 \leq i \leq n\}$$

$$S_F^R = \{s_i \, | \, a_{ef}^i > 0 \text{ and } 1 + \frac{a_{ep}^f}{F} - \frac{F}{a_{ef}^i} - \frac{a_{ep}^i}{a_{ef}^i} = 0, \, 1 \leq i \leq n\}$$

$$S_A^R = \{s_i \, | \, (a_{ef}^i = 0) \text{ or } (a_{ef}^i > 0 \text{ and } 1 + \frac{a_{ep}^f}{F} - \frac{F}{a_{ef}^i} - \frac{a_{ep}^i}{a_{ef}^i} < 0), \, 1 \leq i \leq n\}$$

Proposition 2.3.4 S_B^R, S_F^R, and S_A^R for Tarantula, qe, and CBI Inc. are equal to the following sets, respectively.

$$S_B^R = \{s_i \, | \, a_{ef}^i > 0 \text{ and } \frac{a_{ep}^f}{F} - \frac{a_{ep}^i}{a_{ef}^i} > 0, \, 1 \leq i \leq n\}$$

$$S_F^R = \{s_i \, | \, a_{ef}^i > 0 \text{ and } \frac{a_{ep}^f}{F} - \frac{a_{ep}^i}{a_{ef}^i} = 0, \, 1 \leq i \leq n\}$$

$$S_A^R = \{s_i \, | \, (a_{ef}^i = 0) \text{ or } (a_{ef}^i > 0 \text{ and } \frac{a_{ep}^f}{F} - \frac{a_{ep}^i}{a_{ef}^i} < 0), \, 1 \leq i \leq n\}$$

Proposition 2.3.5 S_B^R, S_F^R, and S_A^R for Wong2, Hamann, Simple Matching, Sokal, Rogers & Tanimoto, Hamming etc., and Euclid are equal to the following sets, respectively.

$$S_B^R = \{s_i \, | \, (a_{ef}^i - F) + (a_{ep}^f - a_{ep}^i) > 0, \, 1 \leq i \leq n\}$$

$$S_F^R = \{s_i \, | \, (a_{ef}^i - F) + (a_{ep}^f - a_{ep}^i) = 0, \, 1 \leq i \leq n\}$$

$$S_A^R = \{s_i \, | \, (a_{ef}^i - F) + (a_{ep}^f - a_{ep}^i) < 0, \, 1 \leq i \leq n\}$$

Proposition 2.3.6 S_B^R, S_F^R, and S_A^R for Wong1, Russell & Rao, and Binary are equal to $\emptyset$, $\{s_i \, | \, a_{ef}^i = F, \, 1 \leq i \leq n\}$, and $\{s_i \, | \, a_{ef}^i < F, \, 1 \leq i \leq n\}$, respectively.

Proposition 2.3.7 S_B^R, S_F^R, and S_A^R for Scott and Rogot1 are equal to the following sets, respectively.

$$S_B^R = \{s_i \, | \, \frac{-F^2 + 4a_{ef}^i P + 2F a_{ef}^i - 2F a_{ep}^i - (a_{ep}^i + a_{ef}^i)^2}{(F + 2P - a_{ep}^i - a_{ef}^i)(F + a_{ef}^i + a_{ep}^i)}$$

$$> \frac{4PF - 4F a_{ep}^f - (a_{ep}^f)^2}{(2F + a_{ep}^f)(2P - a_{ep}^f)}, \, 1 \leq i \leq n\}$$

$$S_F^R = \{s_i \mid \frac{-F^2 + 4a_{ef}^i P + 2Fa_{ef}^i - 2Fa_{ep}^i - (a_{ep}^i + a_{ef}^i)^2}{(F + 2P - a_{ep}^i - a_{ef}^i)(F + a_{ef}^i + a_{ep}^i)}$$

$$= \frac{4PF - 4Fa_{ep}^f - (a_{ep}^f)^2}{(2F + a_{ep}^f)(2P - a_{ep}^f)}, 1 \le i \le n\}$$

$$S_A^R = \{s_i \mid \frac{-F^2 + 4a_{ef}^i P + 2Fa_{ef}^i - 2Fa_{ep}^i - (a_{ep}^i + a_{ef}^i)^2}{(F + 2P - a_{ep}^i - a_{ef}^i)(F + a_{ef}^i + a_{ep}^i)}$$

$$< \frac{4PF - 4Fa_{ep}^f - (a_{ep}^f)^2}{(2F + a_{ep}^f)(2P - a_{ep}^f)}, 1 \le i \le n\}$$

Proposition 2.3.8 S_B^{K2}, S_F^{K2}, and S_A^{K2} for Kulczynski2 are equal to the following sets, respectively.

$$S_B^{K2} = \{s_i \mid a_{ef}^i > 0 \text{ and } \frac{a_{ef}^i F + a_{ef}^i a_{ep}^f - F^2}{F^2 + (F + a_{ep}^f)(F - a_{ef}^i)} - \frac{a_{ep}^i}{a_{ef}^i} > 0, 1 \le i \le n\}$$

$$S_F^{K2} = \{s_i \mid a_{ef}^i > 0 \text{ and } \frac{a_{ef}^i F + a_{ef}^i a_{ep}^f - F^2}{F^2 + (F + a_{ep}^f)(F - a_{ef}^i)} - \frac{a_{ep}^i}{a_{ef}^i} = 0, 1 \le i \le n\}$$

$$S_A^{K2} = \{s_i \mid (a_{ef}^i = 0) \text{ or } (a_{ef}^i > 0 \text{ and } \frac{a_{ef}^i F + a_{ef}^i a_{ep}^f - F^2}{F^2 + (F + a_{ep}^f)(F - a_{ef}^i)} - \frac{a_{ep}^i}{a_{ef}^i} < 0), 1 \le i \le n\}$$

Proposition 2.3.9 S_B^{M2}, S_F^{M2}, and S_A^{M2} for M2 are equal to the following sets, respectively.

$$S_B^{M2} = \{s_i \mid a_{ef}^i > 0 \text{ and } \frac{P + a_{ep}^f}{F} - \frac{2F + P}{a_{ef}^i} + 2 - \frac{a_{ep}^i}{a_{ef}^i} > 0, 1 \le i \le n\}$$

$$S_F^{M2} = \{s_i \mid a_{ef}^i > 0 \text{ and } \frac{P + a_{ep}^f}{F} - \frac{2F + P}{a_{ef}^i} + 2 - \frac{a_{ep}^i}{a_{ef}^i} = 0, 1 \le i \le n\}$$

$$S_A^{M2} = \{s_i \mid (a_{ef}^i = 0) \text{ or } (a_{ef}^i > 0 \text{ and } \frac{P + a_{ep}^f}{F} - \frac{2F + P}{a_{ef}^i} + 2 - \frac{a_{ep}^i}{a_{ef}^i} < 0), 1 \le i \le n\}$$

Proposition 2.3.10 S_B^O, S_F^O, and S_A^O for Ochiai are equal to the following sets, respectively.

$$S_B^O = \{s_i \, | \, a_{ef}^i > 0 \text{ and } (1 + \frac{a_{ep}^f}{F}) \frac{a_{ef}^i}{F} - 1 - \frac{a_{ep}^i}{a_{ef}^i} > 0, 1 \leq i \leq n\}$$

$$S_F^O = \{s_i \, | \, a_{ef}^i > 0 \text{ and } (1 + \frac{a_{ep}^f}{F}) \frac{a_{ef}^i}{F} - 1 - \frac{a_{ep}^i}{a_{ef}^i} = 0, 1 \leq i \leq n\}$$

$$S_A^O = \{s_i \, | \, (a_{ef}^i = 0) \text{ or } (a_{ef}^i > 0 \text{ and } (1 + \frac{a_{ep}^f}{F}) \frac{a_{ef}^i}{F} - 1 - \frac{a_{ep}^i}{a_{ef}^i} < 0), 1 \leq i \leq n\}$$

Proposition 2.3.11 S_B^A, S_F^A, and S_A^A for AMPLE2 are equal to the following sets, respectively.

$$S_B^A = \{s_i \, | \, a_{ef}^i > 0 \text{ and } \frac{P a_{ef}^i - PF + F a_{ep}^f}{F a_{ef}^i} - \frac{a_{ep}^i}{a_{ef}^i} > 0, 1 \leq i \leq n\}$$

$$S_F^A = \{s_i \, | \, a_{ef}^i > 0 \text{ and } \frac{P a_{ef}^i - PF + F a_{ep}^f}{F a_{ef}^i} - \frac{a_{ep}^i}{a_{ef}^i} = 0, 1 \leq i \leq n\}$$

$$S_A^A = \{s_i \, | \, (a_{ef}^i = 0) \text{ or } (a_{ef}^i > 0 \text{ and } \frac{P a_{ef}^i - PF + F a_{ep}^f}{F a_{ef}^i} - \frac{a_{ep}^i}{a_{ef}^i} < 0), 1 \leq i \leq n\}$$

Proposition 2.3.12 S_B^{W3}, S_F^{W3}, and S_A^{W3} for Wong3 have three cases:

(1) If $a_{ep}^f \leq 2$, S_B^{W3}, S_F^{W3}, and S_A^{W3} for Wong3 are equal to the following sets, respectively.

$$S_B^{W3} = \{s_i \, | \, a_{ep}^i \leq 2 \text{ and } (a_{ef}^i - F) + (a_{ep}^f - a_{ep}^i) > 0, 1 \leq i \leq n\}$$

$$S_F^{W3} = \{s_i \, | \, a_{ep}^i \leq 2 \text{ and } (a_{ef}^i - F) + (a_{ep}^f - a_{ep}^i) = 0, 1 \leq i \leq n\}$$

$$S_A^{W3} = \{s_i \, | \, (a_{ep}^i > 2) \text{ or } (a_{ep}^i \leq 2 \text{ and } (a_{ef}^i - F) + (a_{ep}^f - a_{ep}^i) < 0), 1 \leq i \leq n\}$$

(2) If $2 < a_{ep}^f \leq 10$, S_B^{W3}, S_F^{W3}, and S_A^{W3} for Wong3 are equal to the following sets, respectively.

$$S_B^{W3} = \{s_i \, | \, (a_{ep}^i \leq 2 \text{ and } (a_{ef}^i - F) + (0.1 a_{ep}^f - a_{ep}^i) + 1.8 > 0) \text{ or }$$
$$(2 < a_{ep}^i \leq 10 \text{ and } (a_{ef}^i - F) + (0.1 a_{ep}^f - 0.1 a_{ep}^i) > 0), 1 \leq i \leq n\}$$

$$S_F^{W3} = \{s_i \, | \, 2 < a_{ep}^i \leq 10 \text{ and } (a_{ef}^i - F) + (0.1 a_{ep}^f - 0.1 a_{ep}^i) = 0, 1 \leq i \leq n\}$$

$$S_A^{W3}=\{s_i\,|\,(a_{ep}^i\leq2 \text{ and } (a_{ef}^i-F)+(0.1a_{ep}^f-a_{ep}^i)+1.8<0) \text{ or}$$

$$(2<a_{ep}^i\leq10 \text{ and } (a_{ef}^i-F)+(0.1a_{ep}^f-0.1a_{ep}^i)<0) \text{ or}$$

$$(a_{ep}^i>10),\,1\leq i\leq n\}$$

(3) *If $a_{ep}^f>10$, S_B^{W3}, S_F^{W3}, and S_A^{W3} for Wong3 are equal to the following sets, respectively.*

$$S_B^{W3}=\{s_i\,|\,(a_{ep}^i\leq2 \text{ and } (a_{ef}^i-F)+(0.001a_{ep}^f-a_{ep}^i)+2.79>0) \text{ or}$$

$$(2<a_{ep}^i\leq10 \text{ and } (a_{ef}^i-F)+(0.001a_{ep}^f-0.1a_{ep}^i)+0.99>0) \text{ or}$$

$$(a_{ep}^i>10 \text{ and } (a_{ef}^i-F)+(0.001a_{ep}^f-0.001a_{ep}^i)>0),\,1\leq i\leq n\}$$

$$S_F^{W3}=\{s_i\,|\,(a_{ep}^i\leq2 \text{ and } (a_{ef}^i-F)+(0.001a_{ep}^f-a_{ep}^i)+2.79=0) \text{ or}$$

$$(2<a_{ep}^i\leq10 \text{ and } (a_{ef}^i-F)+(0.001a_{ep}^f-0.1a_{ep}^i)+0.99=0) \text{ or}$$

$$(a_{ep}^i>10 \text{ and } (a_{ef}^i-F)+(0.001a_{ep}^f-0.001a_{ep}^i)=0),\,1\leq i\leq n\}$$

$$S_A^{W3}=\{s_i\,|\,(a_{ep}^i\leq2 \text{ and } (a_{ef}^i-F)+(0.001a_{ep}^f-a_{ep}^i)+2.79<0) \text{ or}$$

$$(2<a_{ep}^i\leq10 \text{ and } (a_{ef}^i-F)+(0.001a_{ep}^f-0.1a_{ep}^i)+0.99<0) \text{ or}$$

$$(a_{ep}^i>10 \text{ and } (a_{ef}^i-F)+(0.001a_{ep}^f-0.001a_{ep}^i)<0),\,1\leq i\leq n\}$$

Proposition 2.3.13 S_B^{AM}, S_F^{AM}, and S_A^{AM} *for Arithmetic Mean are equal to the following sets, respectively.*

$$S_B^{AM}=\{s_i\,|\,\frac{a_{ef}^iP-a_{ep}^iF}{(a_{ef}^i+a_{ep}^i)(P+F-a_{ef}^i-a_{ep}^i)+PF}$$

$$>\frac{PF-Fa_{ep}^f}{(F+a_{ep}^f)(P-a_{ep}^f)+PF},\,1\leq i\leq n\}$$

$$S_F^{AM}=\{s_i\,|\,\frac{a_{ef}^iP-a_{ep}^iF}{(a_{ef}^i+a_{ep}^i)(P+F-a_{ef}^i-a_{ep}^i)+PF}$$

$$=\frac{PF-Fa_{ep}^f}{(F+a_{ep}^f)(P-a_{ep}^f)+PF},\,1\leq i\leq n\}$$

$$S_A^{AM} = \{s_i \mid \frac{a_{ef}^i P - a_{ep}^i F}{(a_{ef}^i + a_{ep}^i)(P + F - a_{ef}^i - a_{ep}^i) + PF}$$

$$< \frac{PF - F a_{ep}^f}{(F + a_{ep}^f)(P - a_{ep}^f) + PF}, 1 \le i \le n\}$$

Proposition 2.3.14 S_B^{CO}, S_F^{CO}, and S_A^{CO} for Cohen are equal to the following sets, respectively.

$$S_B^{CO} = \{s_i \mid \frac{a_{ef}^i P - a_{ep}^i F}{P(a_{ef}^i + a_{ep}^i) + F(P + F - a_{ef}^i - a_{ep}^i)}$$

$$> \frac{PF - F a_{ep}^f}{P(F + a_{ep}^f) + F(P - a_{ep}^f)}, 1 \le i \le n\}$$

$$S_F^{CO} = \{s_i \mid \frac{a_{ef}^i P - a_{ep}^i F}{P(a_{ef}^i + a_{ep}^i) + F(P + F - a_{ef}^i - a_{ep}^i)}$$

$$= \frac{PF - F a_{ep}^f}{P(F + a_{ep}^f) + F(P - a_{ep}^f)}, 1 \le i \le n\}$$

$$S_A^{CO} = \{s_i \mid \frac{a_{ef}^i P - a_{ep}^i F}{P(a_{ef}^i + a_{ep}^i) + F(P + F - a_{ef}^i - a_{ep}^i)}$$

$$< \frac{PF - F a_{ep}^f}{P(F + a_{ep}^f) + F(P - a_{ep}^f)}, 1 \le i \le n\}$$

Proposition 2.3.15 S_B^F, S_F^F, and S_A^F for Fleiss are equal to the following sets, respectively.

$$S_B^F = \{s_i \mid -F^2 + 4a_{ef}^i P + 2F a_{ef}^i - 2F a_{ep}^i - (a_{ep}^i + a_{ef}^i)^2$$

$$> 4PF - 4F a_{ep}^f - (a_{ep}^f)^2, 1 \le i \le n\}$$

$$S_F^F = \{s_i \mid -F^2 + 4a_{ef}^i P + 2F a_{ef}^i - 2F a_{ep}^i - (a_{ep}^i + a_{ef}^i)^2$$

$$= 4PF - 4F a_{ep}^f - (a_{ep}^f)^2, 1 \le i \le n\}$$

$$S_A^F = \{s_i \mid -F^2 + 4a_{ef}^i P + 2F a_{ef}^i - 2F a_{ep}^i - (a_{ep}^i + a_{ef}^i)^2$$

$$< 4PF - 4F a_{ep}^f - (a_{ep}^f)^2, 1 \le i \le n\}$$

References

1. Abreu R, Zoeteweij P, Gemund AJV (2006) An evaluation of similarity coefficients for software fault localization. In: Proceedings of the 12th Pacific Rim International Symposium on Dependable Computing, pp 39–46. https://doi.org/10.1109/PRDC.2006.18
2. Abreu R, Zoeteweij P, Gemund AJV (2007) On the accuracy of spectrum-based fault localization. In: Proceedings of Testing: Academic and Industrial Conference Practice and Research Techniques-MUTATION, pp 89–98. https://doi.org/10.1109/TAIC.PART.2007.13
3. Abreu R, Zoeteweij P, Golsteijn R, Gemund AJV (2009) A practical evaluation of spectrum-based fault localization. J Syst Softw 82(11):1780–1792. https://doi.org/10.1016/j.jss.2009.06.035
4. Jones JA, Harrold MJ (2005) Empirical evaluation of the tarantula automatic fault-localization technique. In: Proceedings of the 20th IEEE/ACM International Conference on Automated Software Engineering, pp 273–282. https://doi.org/10.1145/1101908.1101949
5. Wong WE, Wei T, Qi Y, Zhao L (2008) A crosstab-based statistical method for effective fault localization. In: Proceedings of the 1st International Conference on Software Testing, Verification and Validation, pp 42–51. https://doi.org/10.1109/ICST.2008.65
6. Wong WE, Debroy V, Choi B (2010) A family of code coverage-based heuristics for effective fault localization. J Syst Softw 83(2):188–208. https://doi.org/10.1016/j.jss.2009.09.037
7. Xie X, Wong WE, Chen TY, Xu B (2011) Spectrum-based fault localization: testing oracles are no longer mandatory. In: Proceedings of the 11th International Conference on Quality Software, pp 1–10. https://doi.org/10.1109/QSIC.2011.20
8. Xie X, Chen TY, Kuo FC, Xu B (2013) A theoretical analysis of the risk evaluation formulas for spectrum-based fault localization. ACM Trans Softw Eng Methodol 22(4):31:1–31:40. https://doi.org/10.1145/2522920.2522924

Chapter 3
Theoretical Comparison Among Risk Evaluation Formulas

Abstract In this chapter, we will adopt the set-based theoretical framework introduced in Chap. 2 to build a performance hierarchy for the 30 commonly adopted formulas (whose definitions and corresponding set divisions are listed and proved in Sect. 2.3). Overall, we will demonstrate and prove six equivalent formula groups, among which two groups are identified as maximal (including five maximal formulas, namely, Op1, Op2, Wong1, Russell & Rao, and Binary). These theoretical results are no longer suffering from any threats to validity introduced by experiments and hence are definite and reliable.

3.1 Preliminary

With the set-based theoretical framework introduced in Chap. 2, we now can compare any given formulas. Before presenting the detailed analysis, let us first discuss some prerequisite assumptions.

1. The analysis assumes that the SBFL techniques are applied to programs with testing oracle. In other words, for any test case, the testing result of either *fail* or *pass* can be decided. This assumption is adopted in all previous studies, except our work [2].
2. The analysis assumes *"perfect bug detection,"* which is adopted by most of the previous SBFL studies. It assumes that the fault can always be identified once the faulty statement is examined [1].
3. The analysis assumes that the faults are the deterministic faults, that is, a test case will always yield the same testing result of either *failed* or *passed*. This type of faults is not affected by any run-time environment and is also assumed in the majority of previous SBFL studies. Moreover, we will exclude the omission

Part of this chapter ©2013 ACM. Reprinted, with permission from ACM Transactions on Software Engineering and Methodology; October 2013. Vol. 22, No. 4, Article 31, 1–40. https://doi.org/10. 1145/2522920.2522924 (Ref. [3]).

faults, because SBFL is designed to assign risk values to the existent statements. Some previous SBFL experimental studies handled the omission faults by considering the preceding or succeeding statement of the missing statement as the "faulty statement." However, this approach is not completely satisfactory because it could lead to controversy or inconsistency. Furthermore, the "preceding or succeeding" statement may have different interpretations, such as "the line order of source code" or "the order according to the control flow graph." Not all the experimental studies have explicitly clarified their methods of identifying these faults. Thus in order to avoid unnecessary noises, we do not consider the omission faults in this study.

4. The test suite is assumed to have 100% statement coverage, that is, for any s_i, we have $a_{ef}^i + a_{ep}^i > 0$. Also assumed is that the test suite contains at least one passed test case and one failed test case, that is, for any s_i, we have $a_{ep}^i + a_{np}^i > 0$ and $a_{ef}^i + a_{nf}^i > 0$. Intuitively speaking, these assumptions are reasonable because even though we can never justify that a test suite has provided "sufficient" testing information for fault localization, we can at least argue that a test suite with some uncovered statements, or with either solely passed test cases or solely failed test cases, is not sufficient for debugging. More importantly, these assumptions are required to make some formulas (such as Tarantula) totally defined.

3.2 The Performance Hierarchy

In this section, we will show how to apply the framework in Chap. 2 to theoretically compare the 30 formulas (whose definitions and corresponding set divisions are listed and proved in Sect. 2.3). The illustration here will be based on single-fault scenario. This analysis requires inference of the S_B^R, S_F^R, and S_A^R for each formula, which can be found in Appendix A.

3.2.1 Equivalent Cases

First, let us consider the analysis for equivalence relation. From the set division of all the formulas, it is not difficult to find that among the 30 investigated formulas, there are 6 groups of equivalent formulas (which are referred to as "ER1" to "ER6"), as follows.

- ER1 consists of Op1 and Op2.
- ER2 consists of Jaccard, Anderberg, Sørensen-Dice, Dice, and Goodman.
- ER3 consists of Tarantula, q_e, and CBI Inc.

- ER4 consists of Wong2, Hamann, Simple Matching, Sokal, Rogers & Tanimoto, Hamming etc., and Euclid.
- ER5 consists of Wong1, Russell & Rao, and Binary.
- ER6 consists of Scott and Rogot1.

Proposition 3.2.1 *For ER1, we have Op1 ↔ Op2.*

Proof As proved in Proposition 2.3.1 and Appendix A, S_B^R, S_F^R, and S_A^R of both Op1 and Op2 are equal to the sets defined in (2.1), (2.2), and (2.3), respectively, as follows.

$$S_B^R = \{s_i \,|\, a_{ef}^i = F \text{ and } a_{ep}^f - a_{ep}^i > 0, \, 1 \le i \le n\}$$

$$S_F^R = \{s_i \,|\, a_{ef}^i = F \text{ and } a_{ep}^f - a_{ep}^i = 0, \, 1 \le i \le n\}$$

$$S_A^R = \{s_i \,|\, (a_{ef}^i < F) \text{ or } (a_{ef}^i = F \text{ and } a_{ep}^f - a_{ep}^i < 0), \, 1 \le i \le n\}$$

Therefore, we have $S_B^{Op1} = S_B^{Op2}$, $S_F^{Op1} = S_F^{Op2}$, and $S_A^{Op1} = S_A^{Op2}$. Immediately after Theorem 2.2.3, Op1 ↔ Op2. □

Proposition 3.2.2 *For ER2, we have Jaccard ↔ Anderberg ↔ Sørensen-Dice ↔ Dice ↔ Goodman.*

Proof As shown in Proposition 2.3.3 and proved in Appendix A, S_B^R, S_F^R, and S_A^R of each formula R in ER2 are the same as the sets defined in (A.8), (A.9), and (A.10), respectively, as follows.

$$S_B^R = \{s_i \,|\, a_{ef}^i > 0 \text{ and } 1 + \frac{a_{ep}^f}{F} - \frac{F}{a_{ef}^i} - \frac{a_{ep}^i}{a_{ef}^i} > 0, \, 1 \le i \le n\}$$

$$S_F^R = \{s_i \,|\, a_{ef}^i > 0 \text{ and } 1 + \frac{a_{ep}^f}{F} - \frac{F}{a_{ef}^i} - \frac{a_{ep}^i}{a_{ef}^i} = 0, \, 1 \le i \le n\}$$

$$S_A^R = \{s_i \,|\, (a_{ef}^i = 0) \text{ or } (a_{ef}^i > 0 \text{ and } 1 + \frac{a_{ep}^f}{F} - \frac{F}{a_{ef}^i} - \frac{a_{ep}^i}{a_{ef}^i} < 0), \, 1 \le i \le n\}$$

Obviously, for any two formulas R_1 and R_2 of ER2, we have $S_B^{R_1} = S_B^{R_2}$, $S_F^{R_1} = S_F^{R_2}$, and $S_A^{R_1} = S_A^{R_2}$. Immediately after Theorem 2.2.3, $R_1 ↔ R_2$, that is, Jaccard ↔ Anderberg ↔ Sørensen-Dice ↔ Dice ↔ Goodman. □

Proposition 3.2.3 *For ER3, we have Tarantula ↔ q_e ↔ CBI Inc.*

Proof As shown in Proposition 2.3.4 and proved in Appendix A, S_B^R, S_F^R, and S_A^R of each formula R in ER3 are the same as the sets defined in (A.31), (A.32), and (A.33), respectively, as follows.

$$S_B^R = \{s_i \,|\, a_{ef}^i > 0 \text{ and } \frac{a_{ep}^f}{F} - \frac{a_{ep}^i}{a_{ef}^i} > 0,\ 1 \leq i \leq n\}$$

$$S_F^R = \{s_i \,|\, a_{ef}^i > 0 \text{ and } \frac{a_{ep}^f}{F} - \frac{a_{ep}^i}{a_{ef}^i} = 0,\ 1 \leq i \leq n\}$$

$$S_A^R = \{s_i \,|\, (a_{ef}^i = 0) \text{ or } (a_{ef}^i > 0 \text{ and } \frac{a_{ep}^f}{F} - \frac{a_{ep}^i}{a_{ef}^i} < 0),\ 1 \leq i \leq n\}$$

Therefore, for any two formulas R_1 and R_2 of ER3, we have $S_B^{R_1} = S_B^{R_2}$, $S_F^{R_1} = S_F^{R_2}$, and $S_A^{R_1} = S_A^{R_2}$. It follows from Theorem 2.2.3 that Tarantula $\leftrightarrow$ qe $\leftrightarrow$ CBI Inc.   □

Proposition 3.2.4 *For ER4, we have Wong2 $\leftrightarrow$ Hamann $\leftrightarrow$ Simple Matching $\leftrightarrow$ Sokal $\leftrightarrow$ Rogers & Tanimoto $\leftrightarrow$ Hamming etc. $\leftrightarrow$ Euclid.*

Proof As shown in Proposition 2.3.5 and proved in Appendix A, S_B^R, S_F^R, and S_A^R of each formula R in ER4 are equal to the sets defined in (A.42), (A.43), and (A.44), respectively, as follows.

$$S_B^R = \{s_i \,|\, (a_{ef}^i - F) + (a_{ep}^f - a_{ep}^i) > 0,\ 1 \leq i \leq n\}$$

$$S_F^R = \{s_i \,|\, (a_{ef}^i - F) + (a_{ep}^f - a_{ep}^i) = 0,\ 1 \leq i \leq n\}$$

$$S_A^R = \{s_i \,|\, (a_{ef}^i - F) + (a_{ep}^f - a_{ep}^i) < 0,\ 1 \leq i \leq n\}$$

Therefore, for any two formulas R_1 and R_2 of ER4, we have $S_B^{R_1} = S_B^{R_2}$, $S_F^{R_1} = S_F^{R_2}$, and $S_A^{R_1} = S_A^{R_2}$. Immediately after Theorem 2.2.3, we have Wong2 $\leftrightarrow$ Hamann $\leftrightarrow$ Simple Matching $\leftrightarrow$ Sokal $\leftrightarrow$ Rogers & Tanimoto $\leftrightarrow$ Hamming etc. $\leftrightarrow$ Euclid.   □

Proposition 3.2.5 *For ER5, we have Wong1 $\leftrightarrow$ Russell & Rao $\leftrightarrow$ Binary.*

Proof As shown in Proposition 2.3.6 and proved in Appendix A, S_B^R, S_F^R, and S_A^R of each formula R in ER5 are equal to sets $\emptyset$, $\{s_i \,|\, a_{ef}^i = F,\ 1 \leq i \leq n\}$, and $\{s_i \,|\, a_{ef}^i < F,\ 1 \leq i \leq n\}$ defined in (A.63), (A.64), and (A.65), respectively.

Obviously, we have $S_B^{W1} = S_B^{RR} = S_B^B$, $S_F^{W1} = S_F^{RR} = S_F^B$, and $S_A^{W1} = S_A^{RR} = S_A^B$. After Theorem 2.2.3, Wong1 $\leftrightarrow$ Russell & Rao $\leftrightarrow$ Binary.   □

Proposition 3.2.6 *For ER6, we have Scott $\leftrightarrow$ Rogot1.*

Proof As shown in Proposition 2.3.7 and proved in Appendix A, S_B^R, S_F^R, and S_A^R of both Scott and Rogot1 are the same as the sets defined in (A.72), (A.73), and (A.74), respectively, as follows.

$$S_B^R = \{s_i \mid \frac{-F^2 + 4a_{ef}^i P + 2Fa_{ef}^i - 2Fa_{ep}^i - (a_{ep}^i + a_{ef}^i)^2}{(F + 2P - a_{ep}^i - a_{ef}^i)(F + a_{ef}^i + a_{ep}^i)}$$

$$> \frac{4PF - 4Fa_{ep}^f - (a_{ep}^f)^2}{(2F + a_{ep}^f)(2P - a_{ep}^f)}, 1 \le i \le n\}$$

$$S_F^R = \{s_i \mid \frac{-F^2 + 4a_{ef}^i P + 2Fa_{ef}^i - 2Fa_{ep}^i - (a_{ep}^i + a_{ef}^i)^2}{(F + 2P - a_{ep}^i - a_{ef}^i)(F + a_{ef}^i + a_{ep}^i)}$$

$$= \frac{4PF - 4Fa_{ep}^f - (a_{ep}^f)^2}{(2F + a_{ep}^f)(2P - a_{ep}^f)}, 1 \le i \le n\}$$

$$S_A^R = \{s_i \mid \frac{-F^2 + 4a_{ef}^i P + 2Fa_{ef}^i - 2Fa_{ep}^i - (a_{ep}^i + a_{ef}^i)^2}{(F + 2P - a_{ep}^i - a_{ef}^i)(F + a_{ef}^i + a_{ep}^i)}$$

$$< \frac{4PF - 4Fa_{ep}^f - (a_{ep}^f)^2}{(2F + a_{ep}^f)(2P - a_{ep}^f)}, 1 \le i \le n\}$$

Obviously, the sets S_B^R, S_F^R, and S_A^R of Scott are equal to the corresponding sets of Rogot1, respectively. After Theorem 2.2.3, Scott $\leftrightarrow$ Rogot1. □

3.2.2 Non-equivalent Cases

Next, we will show the analysis on non-equivalent relations.

Proposition 3.2.7 *We have ER2 $\to$ ER3, ER2 $\to$ ER4, Ochiai $\to$ ER2, Kulczynski2 $\to$ Ochiai, and M2 $\to$ AMPLE2.*

Proof In this section, we only illustrate the proof for "ER2 $\to$ ER3" and leave the other proof in Appendix B.

In order to prove ER2 $\to$ ER3, it is sufficient to prove Jaccard $\to$ Tarantula. As proved in Appendix A, S_B^J and S_A^J are equal to the sets defined in (A.8) and (A.10), respectively, as follows.

$$S_B^J = \{s_i \mid a_{ef}^i > 0 \text{ and } 1 + \frac{a_{ep}^f}{F} - \frac{F}{a_{ef}^i} - \frac{a_{ep}^i}{a_{ef}^i} > 0, 1 \le i \le n\}$$

$$S_A^J = \{s_i \mid (a_{ef}^i = 0) \text{ or } (a_{ef}^i > 0 \text{ and } 1 + \frac{a_{ep}^f}{F} - \frac{F}{a_{ef}^i} - \frac{a_{ep}^i}{a_{ef}^i} < 0), 1 \le i \le n\}$$

And S_B^T and S_A^T are equal to the sets defined in (A.31) and (A.33), respectively, as follows.

$$S_B^T = \{s_i | a_{ef}^i > 0 \text{ and } \frac{a_{ep}^f}{F} - \frac{a_{ep}^i}{a_{ef}^i} > 0, 1 \leq i \leq n\}$$

$$S_A^T = \{s_i | (a_{ef}^i = 0) \text{ or } (a_{ef}^i > 0 \text{ and } \frac{a_{ep}^f}{F} - \frac{a_{ep}^i}{a_{ef}^i} < 0), 1 \leq i \leq n\}$$

After rearranging the terms in $1 + \frac{a_{ep}^f}{F} - \frac{F}{a_{ef}^i} - \frac{a_{ep}^i}{a_{ef}^i}$ from (A.8) and (A.10), we have

$$1 + \frac{a_{ep}^f}{F} - \frac{F}{a_{ef}^i} \frac{a_{ep}^i}{a_{ef}^i} = \left(\frac{a_{ep}^f}{F} - \frac{a_{ep}^i}{a_{ef}^i} \right) + \left(1 - \frac{F}{a_{ef}^i} \right)$$

Since $1 - \frac{F}{a_{ef}^i} \leq 0$ after Lemma 2.3.1, we have

$$1 + \frac{a_{ep}^f}{F} - \frac{F}{a_{ef}^i} \frac{a_{ep}^i}{a_{ef}^i} \leq \frac{a_{ep}^f}{F} - \frac{a_{ep}^i}{a_{ef}^i} \tag{3.1}$$

Now, we are going to prove $S_B^J \subseteq S_B^T$ and $S_A^T \subseteq S_A^J$.

Firstly, we will prove $S_B^J \subseteq S_B^T$. Assume $s_i \in S_B^J$. Then, we have $(a_{ef}^i > 0$ and $1 + \frac{a_{ep}^f}{F} - \frac{F}{a_{ef}^i} - \frac{a_{ep}^i}{a_{ef}^i} > 0)$ after (A.8). As a consequence, we have $\frac{a_{ep}^f}{F} - \frac{a_{ep}^i}{a_{ef}^i} > 0$ from (3.1). Thus, $s_i \in S_B^T$ after (A.31). Therefore, $S_B^J \subseteq S_B^T$.

Secondly, we will prove $S_A^T \subseteq S_A^J$. Assume $s_i \in S_A^T$. Then, we have either $(a_{ef}^i = 0)$ or $(a_{ef}^i > 0$ and $\frac{a_{ep}^f}{F} - \frac{a_{ep}^i}{a_{ef}^i} < 0)$ after (A.33).

- Consider the case that $(a_{ef}^i = 0)$. Immediately after (A.10), $s_i \in S_A^J$.

- Consider the case that $(a_{ef}^i > 0$ and $\frac{a_{ep}^f}{F} - \frac{a_{ep}^i}{a_{ef}^i} < 0)$. Then, we have $1 + \frac{a_{ep}^f}{F} - \frac{F}{a_{ef}^i} - \frac{a_{ep}^i}{a_{ef}^i} < 0$ after (3.1). Thus, $s_i \in S_A^J$ after (A.10).

In summary, we have proved that $S_A^T \subseteq S_A^J$.

In conclusion, we have $S_B^J \subseteq S_B^T$ and $S_A^T \subseteq S_A^J$. Immediately after Theorem 2.2.2, Jaccard $\rightarrow$ Tarantula. Since Jaccard belongs to ER2 and Tarantula belongs to ER3, we have ER2 $\rightarrow$ ER3.   □

Proposition 3.2.8 *ER1 $\rightarrow$ R (where R stands for Kulczynski2, M2, ER6, Wong3, Arithmetic Mean, Cohen and Fleiss); and R $\rightarrow$ ER1 does not hold.*

Proof In this section, we only illustrate the proof for "ER1 $\rightarrow$ Kulczynski2" and leave the other proof in Appendix B.

In order to prove ER1 $\rightarrow$ Kulczynski2, it is sufficient to prove Op1 $\rightarrow$ Kulczynski2. As proved in Appendix A, S_B^{K2} and S_A^{K2} are equal to the sets defined in (A.81) and (A.83), respectively; and S_B^{Op1} and S_A^{Op1} are equal to the sets defined in (2.1) and (2.3), respectively, as follows.

$$S_B^{Op1}=\{s_i|a_{ef}^i=F \text{ and } a_{ep}^f-a_{ep}^i>0, 1\leq i\leq n\}$$

$$S_A^{Op1}=\{s_i|(a_{ef}^i < F) \text{ or } (a_{ef}^i=F \text{ and } a_{ep}^f-a_{ep}^i<0), 1\leq i\leq n\}$$

We are going to prove $S_B^{Op1}\subseteq S_B^{K2}$ and $S_A^{K2}\subseteq S_A^{Op1}$.

Firstly, we will prove $S_B^{Op1}\subseteq S_B^{K2}$. Assume $s_i\in S_B^{Op1}$. Then, we can have $a_{ef}^i=F>0$ and $(a_{ep}^f-a_{ep}^i)>0$ after (2.1). As a consequence, we have

$$\frac{a_{ef}^i F+a_{ef}^i a_{ep}^f-F^2}{F^2+(F+a_{ep}^f)(F-a_{ef}^i)}-\frac{a_{ep}^i}{a_{ef}^i}=\frac{F^2+Fa_{ep}^f-F^2-Fa_{ep}^i}{F^2}$$

$$=\frac{a_{ep}^f-a_{ep}^i}{F}>0$$

Therefore, $s_i\in S_B^{K2}$ after (A.81). Thus, $S_B^{Op1}\subseteq S_B^{K2}$.

Secondly, we are going to prove $S_A^{K2}\subseteq S_A^{Op1}$. Suppose $s_i\in S_A^{K2}$. Then, after (A.83), we can have either $(a_{ef}^i=0)$ or

$$\left(a_{ef}^i>0 \text{ and } \frac{a_{ef}^i F+a_{ef}^i a_{ep}^f-F^2}{F^2+(F+a_{ep}^f)(F-a_{ef}^i)}-\frac{a_{ep}^i}{a_{ef}^i}<0\right)$$

- Consider the case that $(a_{ef}^i=0)$. Obviously, $a_{ef}^i<F$. Immediately after (2.3), $s_i\in S_A^{Op1}$.

- Consider the case that $(a_{ef}^i>0$ and $\frac{a_{ef}^i F+a_{ef}^i a_{ep}^f-F^2}{F^2+(F+a_{ep}^f)(F-a_{ef}^i)}-\frac{a_{ep}^i}{a_{ef}^i}<0)$. Assume further that $0<a_{ef}^i<F$. After (2.3), we have $s_i\in S_A^{Op1}$. Next, consider the sub-case that $a_{ef}^i=F$. Then we have $\frac{a_{ef}^i F+a_{ef}^i a_{ep}^f-F^2}{F^2+(F+a_{ep}^f)(F-a_{ef}^i)}-\frac{a_{ep}^i}{a_{ef}^i}=\frac{a_{ep}^f-a_{ep}^i}{F}$. Since $\frac{a_{ef}^i F+a_{ef}^i a_{ep}^f-F^2}{F^2+(F+a_{ep}^f)(F-a_{ef}^i)}-\frac{a_{ep}^i}{a_{ef}^i}<0$ and $F>0$, we have $(a_{ep}^f-a_{ep}^i)<0$. Thus, $s_i\in S_A^{Op1}$ after (2.3).

In summary, we have proved that $S_A^{K2}\subseteq S_A^{Op1}$.

In conclusion, we have $S_B^{Op1} \subseteq S_B^{K2}$ and $S_A^{K2} \subseteq S_A^{Op1}$. Immediately after Theorem 2.2.2, Op1 $\rightarrow$ Kulczynski2. And after Proposition 3.2.1, ER1 $\rightarrow$ Kulczynski2.

□

Proposition 3.2.9 *As proved in the above propositions, we have ER1 $\rightarrow$ R (where R stands for Kulczynski2, M2, ER6, Wong3, Arithmetic Mean, Cohen, and Fleiss). Actually, we can also prove that R $\rightarrow$ ER1 **does not** hold.*

Proof Consider a sample program PG_1 in Fig. 3.1, where s_5 is the faulty statement. Table 3.1 lists the A_i for PG_1 with respect to a test suite TS_1. As a reminder, data in Table 3.1 are feasible. Firstly, they comply with Lemmas 2.3.1 and 2.3.2. Secondly, the entry statement s_1 has ($a_{nf}^1=0$) and ($a_{np}^1=0$). Thirdly, for any s_i in Fig. 3.1, the value of element a_{ef}^i or a_{ep}^i is equal to the sum of the corresponding element contributed by all of its directly preceding statements and also equal to the sum of its contribution to all of its directly succeeding statements.

Then, for PG_1 with TS_1, S_B^R, S_F^R, and S_A^R for ER1 are shown as the scenario A in Table 3.3, while the corresponding sets for formulas Kulczynski2, M2, ER6, Wong3, Arithmetic Mean, Cohen, and Fleiss are shown as the scenario B in Table 3.3. Then, using any consistent tie-breaking scheme, the *EXAM* score of ER1 is less than the *EXAM* scores of the other formulas. As a consequence, we have demonstrated that

Fig. 3.1 Sample program PG_1

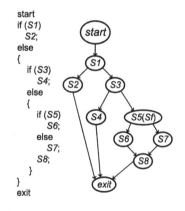

```
start
if (S1)
    S2;
else
{
    if (S3)
        S4;
    else
    {
        if (S5)
            S6;
        else
            S7;
        S8;
    }
}
exit
```

Table 3.1 A_i for PG_1 with TS_1

Statement	$A_i = <a_{ef}^i, a_{ep}^i, a_{nf}^i, a_{np}^i>$
s_1	$<40, 160, 0, 0>$
s_2	$<0, 40, 40, 120>$
s_3	$<40, 120, 0, 40>$
s_4	$<0, 40, 40, 120>$
s_5	$<40, 80, 0, 80>$
s_6	$<39, 1, 1, 159>$
s_7	$<1, 79, 39, 91>$
s_8	$<40, 80, 0, 80>$

$R \to$ ER1 does not hold, where R is Kulczynski2, M2, ER6, Wong3, Arithmetic Mean, Cohen, or Fleiss. Thus, the proposition is proved. $\square$

Apart from the above relations, it can also be found that some formulas do **not** have definite relations between them.

Proposition 3.2.10 *ER1 and ER5 dominate all the other formulas in Table 2.1, but ER1 $\nrightarrow$ ER5 and ER5 $\nrightarrow$ ER1.*

Proof Firstly, we will prove that ER5 $\to$ ER1 does not hold. Consider PG_1 with TS_1 in Table 3.1. It is not difficult to find that the relevant sets for ER1 are as the scenario A in Table 3.3, while for ER5, they are as the scenario C in Table 3.3. If we adopt the *ORIGINAL ORDER* tie-breaking scheme, which is a consistent tie-breaking scheme and ranks all statements in S_F^R according to their original order in program, the *EXAM* score of ER5 is greater than the *EXAM* score of ER1. After Definition 2.2.3, ER5 $\to$ ER1 does not hold.

Secondly, we will prove that ER1 $\to$ ER5 does not hold either. Consider another sample program PG_2 shown in Fig. 3.2, where s_5 is the faulty statement. Table 3.2 gives the A_i for PG_2 with respect to another test suite TS_2. It is not difficult to learn that data in Table 3.2 are feasible. For PG_2 with TS_2, the relevant sets for ER1 are as the scenario D in Table 3.3, while for ER5, they are as the scenario E in Table 3.3. If we adopt the *ORIGINAL ORDER* tie-breaking scheme, the *EXAM* score of ER1 is greater than the *EXAM* score of ER5. After Definition 2.2.3, ER1 $\to$ ER5 does not hold.

The above examples demonstrate that neither ER1 $\to$ ER5 nor ER5 $\to$ ER1 holds. $\square$

With all the above analysis, we found that ER1 actually dominates all the other formulas in Table 2.1, except ER5. In other words, ER1 and ER5 are the 2 maximal

Fig. 3.2 Sample program PG_2

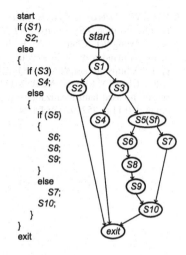

```
start
if (S1)
    S2;
else
{
    if (S3)
        S4;
    else
    {
        if (S5)
        {
            S6;
            S8;
            S9;
        }
        else
            S7;
        S10;
    }
}
exit
```

Table 3.2 A_i for PG_2 with TS_2

Statement	$A_i = <a_{ef}^i, a_{ep}^i, a_{nf}^i, a_{np}^i>$
s_1	$<40, 160, 0, 0>$
s_2	$<0, 70, 40, 90>$
s_3	$<40, 90, 0, 70>$
s_4	$<0, 30, 40, 130>$
s_5	$<40, 60, 0, 100>$
s_6	$<40, 30, 0, 130>$
s_7	$<0, 30, 40, 130>$
s_8	$<40, 30, 0, 130>$
s_9	$<40, 30, 0, 130>$
s_{10}	$<40, 60, 0, 100>$

Table 3.3 Sets for different combinations of formula and test suite

Scenarios	S_B^R	S_F^R	S_A^R
A	$\emptyset$	$\{s_5, s_8\}$	$\{s_1, s_2, s_3, s_4, s_6, s_7\}$
B	$\{s_6\}$	$\{s_5, s_8\}$	$\{s_1, s_2, s_3, s_4, s_7\}$
C	$\emptyset$	$\{s_1, s_3, s_5, s_8\}$	$\{s_2, s_4, s_6, s_7\}$
D	$\{s_6, s_8, s_9\}$	$\{s_5, s_{10}\}$	$\{s_1, s_2, s_3, s_4, s_7\}$
E	$\emptyset$	$\{s_1, s_3, s_5, s_6, s_8, s_9, s_{10}\}$	$\{s_2, s_4, s_7\}$

formulas among the 30 investigated formulas. In the next chapter, we will give a generalized analysis on the maximality of SBFL, among all potential formulas.

References

1. Wong WE, Debroy V, Choi B (2010) A family of code coverage-based heuristics for effective fault localization. J Syst Softw 83(2):188–208. https://doi.org/10.1016/j.jss.2009.09.037
2. Xie X, Wong WE, Chen TY, Xu B (2011) Spectrum-based fault localization: testing oracles are no longer mandatory. In: Proceedings of the 11th International Conference on Quality Software, pp 1–10. https://doi.org/10.1109/QSIC.2011.20
3. Xie X, Chen TY, Kuo FC, Xu B (2013) A theoretical analysis of the risk evaluation formulas for spectrum-based fault localization. ACM Trans Softw Eng Methodol 22(4):31:1–31:40. https://doi.org/10.1145/2522920.2522924

Chapter 4
On the Maximality of Spectrum-Based Fault Localization

Abstract This chapter will continue to utilize the set-based theoretical framework introduced in Chap. 2, to detailedly explain the process for finding the general theoretical maximal formulas, which was proved by Yoo et al. (ACM Trans Softw Eng Methodol 26(1):4:1–4:30, 2017). In particular, we will introduce a sufficient and necessary condition of general theoretical maximality among the entire space of all possible formulas.

4.1 Definitions

In Chaps. 2 and 3, we introduce the framework and theoretical comparison among a fixed size of risk evaluation formulas. In this section, we will show how to identify the general maximality among all possible formulas [1].

First, we give all definitions used in this chapter. Different from the analysis on individual concrete risk evaluation formulas as shown in Table 2.1, in this chapter, we consider analysis on general formulas, defined as follows.

As introduced in Sect. 1.3, a risk evaluation formula in SBFL accepts a four-dimensional vector as the input ($A_i = <a_{ef}^i, a_{ep}^i, a_{nf}^i, a_{np}^i>$) and one risk score as the output. In fact, for a given pair of program and test suite, the values of F (i.e., total number of failed test cases) and P (i.e., the total number of passed test cases) are constants. Thus for each statement s_i, we have its $A_i = <a_{ef}^i, P - a_{np}^i, F - a_{ef}^i, a_{np}^i>$. In other words, when the program and test suite are fixed, A_i is decided by only two elements, namely, a_{ef}^i and a_{ep}^i.

Let us denote $\bar{A}_i = <a_{ef}^i, a_{ep}^i>$. In this way, the original definition of formula can be formally rephrased as follows.

Part of this chapter ©2017 ACM. Reprinted, with permission from ACM Transactions on Software Engineering and Methodology; June 2017. Vol. 26, No. 1, Article 4, 1–30. DOI: https://doi.org/10. 1145/3078840 (Ref. [1]).

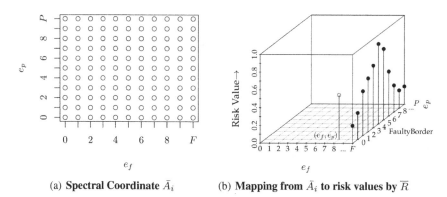

(a) **Spectral Coordinate** $\bar{A}_i$ (b) **Mapping from** $\bar{A}_i$ **to risk values by** $\overline{R}$

Fig. 4.1 Visualizing the SBFL space [1]

Definition 4.1.1 (Risk evaluation formula $\overline{R}$ with two-dimensional input vector)
$\overline{R} : I_f \times I_p \rightarrow Real$, where I_f denotes the set of integers within $[0, F]$ and I_p denotes the set of integers within $[0, P]$, such that $\overline{R}(\bar{A}_i) = R(A_i)$.

Given any values of P and F, the input domain of any formula $\overline{R}$ is shown as the grid in Fig. 4.1a, where both a_{ef} and a_{ep} are nonnegative integers and $0 \leq a^i_{ef} \leq F$ and $0 \leq a^i_{ep} \leq P$. Given a pair of test suite and program, each point (a_{ef}, a_{ep}) on this grid is associated with a group of statements that have the corresponding a_{ef} and a_{ep} values.

A formula $\overline{R}$ maps each point (a^i_{ef}, a^i_{ep}) to a real number that is the risk value of all statements associated with this point, as shown in Fig. 4.1b. Any assignment of risk values is independent of the number of statements associated with each point (a_{ef}, a_{ep}), but solely decided by the definition of $\overline{R}$.

Two components in Fig. 4.1b are critical for the analysis, namely, faulty border and overstepping points, which are defined in following Definitions 4.1.2 and 4.1.3, respectively.

Definition 4.1.2 (Faulty border) We call the sequential points $<(F, 0), (F, 1), \ldots, (F, a_{ep}), \ldots, (F, P)> (0 \leq a_{ep} \leq P)$ the *faulty border*, which is denoted as E.

It can be found that for any $\overline{R}$, the risk values of all points on E are solely decided by their a_{ep}. And in single fault scenario, the faulty statement s_f can only be associated with a point (F, a^f_{ep}) on E. But this point may also be associated with other correct statements s_i having $(F, a^i_{ep})=(F, a^f_{ep})$. These statements always share the same risk values as that of s_f, regardless of the selection of the formula. Points (F, a^i_{ep}) other than (F, a^f_{ep}) must be associated with correct statements. Depending on the adopted formula, the risk values of such points can be either greater than, equal to, or smaller than that of s_f. We can formulate the distribution of risk values on E for $\overline{R}$ in the following way:

Given a formula $\overline{R}$, the distribution of risk values (referred to as $P_{\overline{R}}$) on E can be depicted as a set of $o_p^{i,j}$, where $o_p^{i,j} = \,<a_{np}^i, a_{np}^j, op>$ that indicates the relation between the risk scores of two distinct points (F, a_{np}^i) and (F, a_{np}^j) on E. Given that $a_{np}^i < a_{np}^j$, op can be either ">" (i.e., $\overline{R}(F, a_{np}^i) > \overline{R}(F, a_{np}^j))$, "<" (i.e., $\overline{R}(F, a_{np}^i) < \overline{R}(F, a_{np}^j))$, or "=" (i.e., $\overline{R}(F, a_{np}^i) = \overline{R}(F, a_{np}^j))$.

Definition 4.1.3 (Overstepping points outside E) Let $U_{\overline{R}}$ denote the set of points outside E that have risk scores higher than or equal to those of some points (F, a_{ep}^i) on E, for formula $\overline{R}$. More formally, $U_{\overline{R}} = \{\bar{A} \in I_f \times I_p - E | \exists \bar{A}' \in E$ such that $\overline{R}(\bar{A}) \geq \overline{R}(\bar{A}')\}$

Let us denote the complete set of formulas as $\mathbb{R} = \{\overline{R}\}$. What follows are the definitions for maximal and greatest formula in $\mathbb{R}$.

Definition 4.1.4 (Generalized maximality) A risk evaluation formula $\overline{R}$ is said to be a maximal formula in $\mathbb{R}$ if, for any formula $\overline{R}' \in \mathbb{R}$ such that $\overline{R}' \neq \overline{R} \wedge \overline{R}' \to \overline{R}$, it also holds that $\overline{R}' \leftrightarrow \overline{R}$.

Definition 4.1.5 (Generalized greatest formula) A risk evaluation formula $\overline{R}$ is said to be a *greatest* formula in $\mathbb{R}$ if, for any formula $\overline{R}' \in \mathbb{R} \wedge \overline{R}' \neq \overline{R}$, it holds that $\overline{R} \to \overline{R}'$.

4.2 Theoretical Maximality in $\mathbb{R}$

With the above definitions, it is possible to identify the maximal formulas [1]. To simplify the description, we will use R instead of $\overline{R}$ to represent risk evaluation formula in the following discussion.

4.2.1 Preliminary Propositions

Proposition 4.2.1 *If $U_{R_1} = U_{R_2} = \emptyset$ and $P_{R_1} = P_{R_2}$, it follows that $R_1 \leftrightarrow R_2$.*

Proof Consider the following two cases.

Case 1: statements associated with E. Since $P_{R_1} = P_{R_2}$, then for each pair of these statements, the relation between their risk values is always the same in R_1 and R_2. As a consequence, these statements have the same relative order with respect to s_f (which is associated with one point on E) between R_1 and R_2 and hence belong to the same set division for R_1 and R_2 with any pair of program and test suite.

Case 2: statements associated with points outside E. Since both U_{R_1} and U_{R_2} are empty, these statements always have risk values lower than that of the faulty statement s_f (which is associated with one point on E); therefore, these statements belong to both $S_A^{R_1}$ and $S_A^{R_2}$.

In summary, we have $S_B^{R_1} = S_B^{R_2}$, $S_F^{R_1} = S_F^{R_2}$, and $S_A^{R_1} = S_A^{R_2}$. Following Theorem 2.2.3, $R_1 \leftrightarrow R_2$.   □

Proposition 4.2.2 *If $U_{R_1} = U_{R_2} = \emptyset$ but $P_{R_1} \neq P_{R_2}$, we have $R_1 \nrightarrow R_2$ and $R_2 \nrightarrow R_1$.*

Proof Since $P_{R_1} \neq P_{R_2}$, there must exist at least one pair of points on E, $((F, a_{ep}^i), (F, a_{ep}^j))$ (where $a_{ep}^i < a_{ep}^j$), such that $< a_{ep}^i, a_{ep}^j, op_1 > \in P_{R_1} \wedge < a_{ep}^i, a_{ep}^j, op_2 > \in P_{R_2} \wedge op_1 \neq op_2$. It is sufficient to consider the following two cases because other cases can be transformed to these two cases by swapping R_1 and R_2:

Case 1: $R_1(F, a_{ep}^i) < R_1(F, a_{ep}^j)$ and $R_2(F, a_{ep}^i) > R_2(F, a_{ep}^j)$. With the program shown in Fig. 4.2, it is possible to construct a test suite, such that a_{ef}^4, a_{ef}^5, a_{ef}^9, and a_{ef}^{10} are smaller than F. (As a reminder, it always holds that $a_{ef}^2 = a_{ef}^7 = 0$.) For s_1, s_3, s_6, s_8 (s_f), and s_{11}, whose a_{ef} values are all equal to F, we have $a_{ep}^f = a_{ep}^i < a_{ep}^1 = a_{ep}^3 = a_{ep}^6 = a_{ep}^{11} = a_{ep}^j$. Then, for R_1, we have s_1, s_3, s_6, and s_{11} ranked before s_f and other statements ranked after s_f. However, for R_2, we have s_f ranked at the top of the whole list. Therefore, the *EXAM* score of R_2 is lower than that of R_1.

On the other hand, it is also possible to construct another test suite, such that a_{ef}^4 and a_{ef}^5 are both smaller than F, but a_{ef}^9 is equal to F. (Correspondingly, $a_{ef}^{10} = 0$.) For s_1, s_3, s_6, s_8 (s_f), s_9, and s_{11}, whose a_{ef} values are all equal to F, we have $a_{ep}^9 = a_{ep}^i < a_{ep}^1 = a_{ep}^3 = a_{ep}^6 = a_{ep}^f = a_{ep}^{11} = a_{ep}^j$. Then, for R_1, s_1, s_3 s_6, s_f, and s_{11} are tied together at the top of the whole list, before s_9. However, for R_2, s_9 is ranked at the top, immediately followed by s_1, s_3 s_6, s_f, and s_{11} that are tied together. Therefore, with a consistent tie-breaking scheme, the *EXAM* score of R_1 is lower than that of R_2.

In summary, for the case that $R_1(F, a_{ep}^i) < R_1(F, a_{ep}^j)$ while $R_2(F, a_{ep}^i) > R_2(F, a_{ep}^j)$, it is always possible to find examples to demonstrate $R_1 \nrightarrow R_2$ and $R_2 \nrightarrow R_1$

Case 2: $R_1(F, a_{ep}^i) < R_1(F, a_{ep}^j)$ and $R_2(F, a_{ep}^i) = R_2(F, a_{ep}^j)$. With the program shown in Fig. 4.2, it is possible to construct a test suite, such that $a_{ef}^4 = F$ (correspondingly, $a_{ef}^5 = 0$), while a_{ef}^9 and a_{ef}^{10} are smaller than F. Then, for s_1, s_3, s_4, s_6, s_8 (s_f), and s_{11}, whose a_{ef} values are all equal to F, it follows that $a_{ep}^4 = a_{ep}^i < a_{ep}^1 = a_{ep}^3 = a_{ep}^6 = a_{ep}^f = a_{ep}^{11} = a_{ep}^j$. Then, for R_1, s_1, s_3, s_6, s_f, and s_{11} are tied together at the top of the ranking, before s_4. However, for R_2, s_1, s_3, s_4, s_6, s_f, and s_{11} are tied together at the top of the entire ranking. Since the number of tied statements is different, the *EXAM* score now depends on the tie-breaking scheme, without any guarantee of clear dominance of one formula. For

```
        void foo(double x, double y, double z) {
s1 :        if(z <= 0){
s2 :            // s2
            } else {
s3 :            if (z <= 12) {
s4 :                // s4
                } else {
s5 :                // s5
                }
s6 :            if (z <= 3) {
s7 :                // s7
                } else {
s8 :                if (2 * x − y < 0) { //faulty, should be: if (x
                                                        − y < 0)
s9 :                    // s9
                    } else {
s10 :                   // s10
                    }
                }
            }
s11 :       return; // s11
        }
```

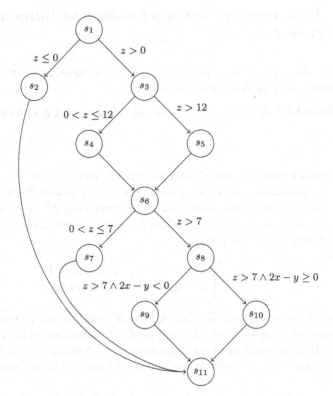

Fig. 4.2 Sample program: the faulty statement s_f is s_8 [1]

example, if the original order of the statements is used as the tie-breaker, R_1 yields a lower *EXAM* score value than R_2; if the reverse of the original order is adopted, the opposite would follow.

On the other hand, it is also possible to construct another test suite, such that a_{ef}^4, a_{ef}^5, a_{ef}^9, and a_{ef}^{10} are smaller than F. Then, for s_1, s_3, s_6, s_8 (s_f), and s_{11} whose a_{ef} values are all equal to F, we have $a_{ep}^f = a_{ep}^i < a_{ep}^1 = a_{ep}^3 = a_{ep}^6 = a_{ep}^{11} = a_{ep}^j$. Then, for R_1, we have s_1, s_3, s_6, and s_{11} tied together at the top of the whole list before s_f and other statements ranked after s_f. However, for R_2, we have s_1, s_3, s_6, s_f, and s_{11} tied together at the top of the whole list. Since the number of tied statements is different, the *EXAM* score now depends on the tie-breaking scheme, without any guarantee of clear dominance of one formula. For example, if the original order of the statements is used as the tie-breaker, R_2 yields a lower *EXAM* score value than R_1; if the reverse of the original order is adopted, the opposite would follow.

In summary, for the case that $R_1(F, a_{ep}^i) < R_1(F, a_{ep}^j)$ while $R_2(F, a_{ep}^i) = R_2(F, a_{ep}^j)$, it is possible to demonstrate that $R_1 \nrightarrow R_2$ and $R_2 \nrightarrow R_1$.

In conclusion, for any two formulas whose U_{R_1} and U_{R_2} are both $\emptyset$, but $P_{R_1} \neq P_{R_2}$, it follows that $R_1 \nrightarrow R_2$ and $R_2 \nrightarrow R_1$.   □

4.2.2 A Necessary and Sufficient Condition for Maximal Formula

With the above preliminary propositions, we now introduce a necessary and sufficient condition for a maximal formula of $\mathbb{R}$.

Proposition 4.2.3 *A formula R is a maximal element of $\mathbb{R}$ **if and only if** U_R is empty.*

Proof

(1) **To prove that if R is a maximal element of $\mathbb{R}$, then $U_R = \emptyset$.**

This is actually equivalent to proving that if $U_R \neq \emptyset$, then R is not a maximal element. In other words, there exists $R' \in \mathbb{R}$ such that $R' \rightarrow R$ but $R \nrightarrow R'$. First, let us construct $R' \in \mathbb{R}$ such that $R' \rightarrow R$. Assume that U_R is non-empty. Let R' be defined as follows:

$$R' = \begin{cases} R & \text{if } a_{ef} = F \\ R - (C_1 - C_2 + 1) & \text{otherwise} \end{cases}$$

where C_1 is the highest risk value of R for all points outside E, while C_2 is the lowest risk value of R for all points on E. By the definition of R', any point outside E has risk value lower than those of the points in E, which means all statements associated with points outside E have risk values lower than that of s_f.

Let $U_{R'}$ denote the sets of points outside E which have risk values higher than or equal to those of some points (F, a^i_{ep}) on E, for formula R'. By definition, R' assigns identical risk values to points on E as R while ensuring that $U_{R'} = \emptyset$.

Case 1: statements associated with E. These statements will be assigned to the same set division by both R and R', for any pair of program and test suite.

Case 2: statements associated with points outside E. For formula R', since these points (including those in U_R) always have risk values lower than that of s_f on E, the corresponding statements belong to $S^{R'}_A$. However, for formula R, since $U_R \neq \emptyset$, some statements corresponding to points outside E belong to either S^R_B, S^R_F, or S^R_A.

Summarizing the above two cases, we have $S^{R'}_B \subseteq S^R_B$ and $S^R_A \subseteq S^{R'}_A$. Following Theorem 2.2.2, $R' \to R$.

Let us now turn to show that $R \not\to R'$, by illustrating that it is possible for R' to produce a smaller *EXAM* score than R. Since $U_R \neq \emptyset$, there exists L, a set of points on E whose risk values evaluated by R are not higher than any point in U_R. To show that R' can produce a smaller *EXAM* score than R, it is sufficient to show that $\bar{A}_f \in L$ while $U_R \neq \emptyset$. However, both L and U_R are specific to the choice of R. In order not to lose generality, therefore, let us show that it is possible to construct a program and a test suite such that $\bar{A}_f$ can be placed anywhere on E and another statement $\bar{A}_i$ can be placed anywhere in $I_f \times I_p - E$, independently from each other. Figure 4.2 illustrates such a program.

With such a program and a test suite, any statement associated with points outside U_R always has the same relative ranking to s_f in R and R'. For all statements associated with U_R, formula R' will rank them below s_f. However, with R:

- statements that are associated with U_R and have risk values higher than that of s_f are always ranked before s_f by R.
- statements that are associated with U_R and have risk values equal to that of s_f will be tied together with s_f by R. However, it is possible to have a consistent tie-breaking scheme which ranks parts or even all of these statements before s_f.   □

It is always possible to have statements associated with U_R ranked before s_f. Consequently, the *EXAM* score of R' is smaller than that of R. Therefore, $R \to R'$ does hold.

In conclusion, if R assigns point (a^j_{ef}, a^j_{ep}) outside E with risk value higher than, or equal to, that of at least one point (F, a^i_{np}) on E, there always exists another formula R' for which $R' \to R$ holds but $R \to R'$ does not hold. Therefore, following Definition 4.1.4, R cannot be a maximal formula.

(2) **To prove that if $U_R = \emptyset$, then R is a maximal element of $\mathbb{R}$.**

Assume that $U_R = \emptyset$. Then, for any distinct formula R', let $P_{R'}$ denote the set of $o^{i,j}_p$ for all pairs of distinct points (F, a^i_{np}) and (F, a^j_{np}) on E (where $a^i_{np} < a^j_{np}$) and $U_{R'}$ denote the sets of points outside E which have risk values higher than or equal to those of some points (F, a_{np}^i) on E, for formula R'. There are following cases.

Case 1: $U_{R'} \neq \emptyset$. As illustrated in the above proof, it is always possible to construct another formula R'', such that $U_{R''} = \emptyset$, $R'' \to R'$, and $R' \nrightarrow R''$. If $P_{R''} = P_R$, after Lemma 4.2.1, $R'' \leftrightarrow R$, and, consequently, $R' \nrightarrow R$. Otherwise, if $P_{R''} \neq P_R$, after Lemma 4.2.2, $R \nrightarrow R''$ and $R'' \nrightarrow R$. As a consequence, $R' \nrightarrow R$.

Case 2: $U_{R'} = \emptyset$. Similar to the above analysis, if $P_{R'} = P_R$, after Lemma 4.2.1, $R' \leftrightarrow R$. Otherwise, if $P_{R'} \neq P_R$, after Lemma 4.2.2, $R \nrightarrow R'$ and $R' \nrightarrow R$.

In summary, if $U_R = \emptyset$, then for any formula R', we have either $R' \leftrightarrow R$ or $R' \nrightarrow R$. After Definition 4.1.4, R is a maximal element of $\mathbb{R}$. □

4.2.3 Non-existence of the Greatest Formula

All the above analysis actually imply a very important conclusion, as follows.

Proposition 4.2.4 *There is no greatest formula in* $\mathbb{R}$.

Proof Assume that there exists a greatest formula R_g. After Proposition 4.2.3, $U_{R_g} = \emptyset$ and R_g is a maximal element of $\mathbb{R}$. Consider the two maximal groups of formulas ER_1 and ER_5 proved in Chap. 2. It is not difficult to prove that $U_{ER_1} = U_{ER_5} = \emptyset$ and $P_{ER_1} \neq P_{ER_5}$. Thus, there are three possible cases for P_{R_g}, as follows:

Case 1: $P_{R_g} = P_{ER_1}$. Then it follows that, for ER_5, $U_{ER_5} = U_{R_g} = \emptyset \wedge P_{ER_5} \neq P_{R_g}$.

Case 2: $P_{R_g} = P_{ER_5}$. Then it follows that, for ER_1, $U_{ER_1} = U_{R_g} = \emptyset \wedge P_{ER_1} \neq P_{R_g}$.

Case 3: $P_{R_g} \neq P_{ER_1}$ and $P_{R_g} \neq P_{ER_5}$. Then it follows that, both for ER_1 and ER_5, $U_{ER_1} = U_{R_g} = \emptyset \wedge P_{ER_1} \neq P_{R_g} \wedge U_{ER_5} = U_{R_g} = \emptyset$ but $P_{ER_5} \neq P_{R_g}$.

For any of the above cases, it is possible to construct another formula R' such that $U_{R'} = U_{R_g} = \emptyset$ and $P_{R'} \neq P_{R_g}$. After Proposition 4.2.2, we have $R' \nrightarrow R_g$ and $R_g \nrightarrow R'$. After Definition 4.1.5, R_g cannot be the greatest formula. □

As a reminder, the above proposition shows the non-existence of the theoretical greatest element. However, there are also observations that in large-scaled experiments, formulas from ER1 show significant advantage over other formulas, in practice [1].

Reference

1. Yoo S, Xie X, Kuo FC, Chen TY, Harman M (2017) Human competitiveness of genetic programming in spectrum-based fault localisation: theoretical and empirical analysis. ACM Trans Softw Eng Methodol 26(1):4:1–4:30. https://doi.org/10.1145/3078840

Chapter 5
A Generalized Theoretical Framework for Hybrid Spectrum-Based Fault Localization

Abstract Combining SBFL with other techniques is generally regarded as a feasible approach, as advantages from both techniques may be preserved. SENDYS, which combines SBFL with slicing-hitting-set-computation, is one of the promising techniques. In this chapter, we will extend the theoretical framework introduced in Chap. 2 to make the framework applicable to such combined methods (Tu et al. J Syst Softw 147:106–123, 2019.). With this extended framework, we provide an in-depth theoretical analysis, which patches a loophole of SENDYS and proposes an enhancement of SENDYS that is proved to be even better than traditional SBFL maximal formulas.

5.1 A Hybrid Spectrum-Based Fault Localization: SENDYS

Combining SBFL with other techniques is generally regarded as a feasible approach, as advantages from both techniques may be preserved. One of the promising techniques was developed by Hofer and Wotawa, namely, SENDYS [1] which is a combination of SBFL and slicing-hitting-set-computation (SHSC) [5]. First, let us discuss some definitions in SHSC.

Definition 5.1.1 (Conflict in SHSC) In SHSC, a conflict is a set of components (e.g., statements) in a system causing the misbehavior. The incorrectness of components leads to the inconsistency between observations and expectations.

In other words, the components in a conflict cannot be correct simultaneously. For example, the set of all statements in a failed dynamic slice is responsible for a program failure and reveals the detected program misbehavior. Thus, this statement set forms a conflict which means that these statements cannot be correct simultaneously [4, 5]. Note that the faults in a program are non-omission faults which are faulty statements not related with missing code.

Part of this chapter ©Reprinted from The Journal of Systems and Software; January 2019, Vol. 147, Tu J, Xie X, Chen TY, Xu B, On the analysis of spectrum based fault localization using hitting sets, 106–123, DOI: https://doi.org/10.1016/j.jss.2018.10.013 (Ref. [3]), Copyright (2019), with permission from Elsevier.

Definition 5.1.2 (Diagnose) A diagnosis is a **possible** root cause for the failure.

For example, given two failed dynamic slices, $\{1, 3\}$ and $\{2, 3, 4\}$, each failed dynamic slice forms a conflict where the equivalence of slices and conflicts has been proved in [4]. From the two conflicts, we know that statements 1, 3 cannot be correct simultaneously and neither are statements 2, 3, 4. If we select a statement from each conflict such as $\{1, 4\}$, then $\{1, 4\}$ is a diagnosis which is a **possible** root cause for the failures.

To depict the relationship between diagnoses and conflicts, there is another concept, namely, **hitting set**, which is formally defined as follows:

Definition 5.1.3 (Hitting set) For a set of sets DS, a set H is a hitting set if and only if the intersection between H and any element x of DS is not empty, i.e., $\forall x \in DS, x \bigcap H \neq \emptyset$.

The hitting set H is minimal if none of its subsets is a hitting set. In the context of program debugging, a minimal diagnosis is a minimal hitting set of all conflicts that correspond to all failed dynamic slices. For example, the minimal hitting sets for the two failed dynamic slices are $\{3\}$, $\{1, 2\}$, and $\{1, 4\}$. As a reminder, all possible minimal hitting sets can be divided into two categories: single-element minimal hitting sets which contain only one statement and multiple-element minimal hitting sets which contain more than one statement.

SENDYS combines SBFL and SHSC. Given a program PG, a test suite TS, the risk formula, and minimal hitting sets H^m, SENDYS is shown in Algorithm 1 (SENDYS): First, they collect spectra matrix O, and based on the spectra matrix, the initial risk value $R(s)$ for each statement is computed using Ochiai and the initial risk values are also normalized; then, compute the risk value $Pr(H_i)$ of each minimal hitting set based on the normalized statement risk values; finally, derive the risk value $R_{\text{new}}(s)$ of each statement being faulty associated with the minimal hitting set risk values, and return the final statements ranking in the descending order of the normalized statement risk value $R_{\text{norm}}(s)$.

Algorithm 1: Algorithm SENDYS [3]

Input: Program PG, risk formula Ochiai, minimal hitting sets H^m, and test suite TS
Output: Statements ranking

1 Compute the matrix O for program PG after the execution of test suite TS:
   $O = Matrix(PG, TS)$
2 Compute the risk value $R(s)$ for each statement of program PG: $R(s) = Ochiai(s, O)$
3 Compute the normalized risk value $R_{\text{norm}}(s)$ for each statement of program PG:
   $R_{\text{norm}}(s) = R(s) \div \sum_i^{|PG|} R(s_i)$
4 Compute the risk value for each minimal hitting set H_i:
   $Pr(H_i) = \prod_{s \in H_i} R_{\text{norm}}(s) \times \prod_{s' \in PG \backslash H_i} (1 - R_{\text{norm}}(s'))$
5 Derive the risk of each statement being faulty based on H^s:
   $R_{\text{new}}(s) = \sum_{H_i \in H^s} Pr(H_i), \forall H_i \text{ such that } s \in H_i$
6 Normalize the computed risk value of each statement:
   $R_{\text{norm}}(s) = R_{\text{new}}(s) \div \sum_i^{|PG|} R_{\text{new}}(s_i)$
7 Return the risk value ranking of each statement in the descending order of $R_{\text{norm}}(s)$

The minimal hitting sets can be divided into two types: (i) single-element minimal hitting set (denoted as H_S), which contains one and only one statement which is involved in all the dynamic slices, and (ii) multiple-element minimal hitting set (denoted as H_M), which contains more than one statement.

5.2 Addressing the *NOR* Problem in SENDYS

As a reminder, SENDYS is not restricted to any particular risk formula. Algorithm 1 is configured with formula Ochiai. However, by configuring Algorithm 1 with other formulas, this original SENDYS has overlooked some possible scenarios. Without giving consideration to these scenarios, the original SENDYS may lead to unreasonable results.

5.2.1 Issue About Negative Values

First, many risk formulas (such as Op1, Goodman, etc.) may produce negative initial risk values. But simply normalizing these negative values based on Step 3 could lead to unreasonable results and a series of problems in the subsequent steps.

Let us consider a sample scenario where two failed dynamic slices from Sect. 5.1: $\{1, 3\}$ and $\{2, 3, 4\}$. All possible minimal hitting sets are $\{3\}$, $\{1, 2\}$, and $\{1, 4\}$. Assume that statement 3 is faulty and the initial risk values of statements from 1 to 4 are -0.3, -0.1, $n0.2$, and -0.4, respectively. By simply applying Step 3 in Algorithm 1, the initial risk values for statements 1 to 4 are normalized as 0.3, 0.1, 0.2, and 0.4, which obviously does not make any sense. Thus, it is necessary to explicitly specify an appropriate strategy to handle such cases.

5.2.2 Issue About Zero Values

Secondly, in Algorithm 1, initial risk values may be also assigned as zero by some formulas. Then the minimal hitting sets including such statements are assigned zero risk values. In principle, the risk value computation of a minimal hitting set needs to consider the contribution of each statement in this minimal hitting set. Unfortunately, the contributions of other statements having non-zero risk values in this minimal hitting set are overlooked. To investigate the influence of zero initial risk values, let us consider the two possible types of formulas: The first type of formulas (such as Jaccard, Tarantula, Ochiai, etc.) produces zero or positive risk values and assigns zero values only to statements with $a_{ef} = 0$. Though we can never assert that such statements are fault-free, at least we know that they can never be the faults that trigger the currently observed failures [6]. In such a case, the performance of SENDYS is not affected, since these statements can be viewed as "correct" in terms of the fault under discussion. According to Algorithm 1 Step 4, diagnoses containing such statements are assigned zero risk values, and it is reasonable to assign any diagnosis containing correct statements zero risk values. On the other hand, diagnoses which only contain faulty statements are assigned positive values. From the above, the performance of SENDYS is not affected by such zero risk values.

However, there exists another type of formulas, such as Op1, CBI, Wong3, etc., which may assign zero risk values to statements with $a_{ef} \neq 0$, and these statements cannot be excluded from potential faulty statements under discussion. In this case, zero initial risk values may give rise to a poor risk prediction. For example, consider two failed dynamic slices from Sect. 5.1: $\{1, 3\}$ and $\{2, 3, 4\}$. All possible minimal hitting sets are $\{3\}$, $\{1, 2\}$, and $\{1, 4\}$. Assume that statement 3 is faulty and the initial risk values of statements from 1 to 4 are $0, -0.3, -0.2$, and -0.5, respectively. The initial rank of the faulty statement is 2. Directly following Algorithm 1 Step 3, the computed normalized risk values of the four statements are the same as their initial ones. Furthermore, according to Algorithm 1 Step 4, the risk values $Pr(H_i)$ of the three minimal hitting sets are $-0.39, 0$, and 0. Actually, from Algorithm 1 Step 5, final risk values become $-0.39, 0, 0$, and 0 for statements 1 to 4, respectively. The final rank of the faulty statement decreases to 4 due to the zero initial risk values.

5.2.3   Addressing the NOR Problem in the Original SENDYS

Let us denote the above two issues in the original SENDYS as the *NOR* problem. In order to conduce a generalized theoretical analysis, this problem must be addressed first. To this end, a slight modification in the normalization process (Step 3) of Algorithm 1 will help, which is given in Algorithm 2.

Algorithm 2: Algorithm M_1 [3]

Input: Program PG, risk formula $Formula$, minimal hitting sets H^m, and test suite TS
Output: Statements ranking

1   Compute the matrix O for program PG after the execution of test suite TS:
$O = Matrix(PG, TS)$
2   Compute the risk value $R(s)$ for each statement of program PG: $R(s) = Formula(s, O)$
3   Get minimum risk value p of all the initial risk values: $p = Min(R(s))$
4   If the minimum risk value p is nonpositive or zero, then add $-p$ and a small real number to the risk value of each statement: $R(s) = R(s) - p + 0.00000001$
5   Compute the refined normalized risk value $R_{norm}(s)$ for each statement of program PG:
$R_{norm}(s) = R(s) \div \sum_i^{|PG|} R(s_i)$
6   Compute the final statements ranking with Algorithm 1 (SENDYS). Start with Step 4 in Algorithm 1 (SENDYS)

During normalizing the initial risk values, in order to have a consistent performance, it is necessary to keep the relative order of the statements ranking. Given a statements ranking, applying addition mathematical operation to the risk value of each statement should not change the relative order of each statement, and addition operation is an order-preserving operation. Hence, if there exist nonpositive risk values in statements ranking, we can add an appropriate positive value to the initial risk value of each statement.

As a consequence, M_1 has patched the loophole of the original SENDYS after a few corrections. It can be found that M_1 delivers identical performance with the original SENDYS if the adopted formula has no *NOR* problem.

5.3 Theoretical Analysis in Single-Fault Scenario

In this section, we will discuss a theoretical analysis on SENDYS, in single-fault scenario [3].

First, we introduce a simple generalization of the framework in Chap. 2 to make it applicable to the context of SENDYS. Next we will discuss some properties of M_1 and propose enhanced SENDYS (M_2). Then we show the superiority of M_2 over M_1 and the basic SBFL (denoted as M_0) and further reformulate this complicated algorithm M_2 into a simple conversion G. This conversion gives a shortcut explanation to M_2. Finally, we show the proof that the enhanced SENDYS can even outperform traditional SBFL maximal formulas.

5.3.1 Preliminary: Generalized Set Theory-Based Framework

The theoretical framework in Chap. 2 is designed to compare different risk formulas only, where the fault localization method is fixed to SBFL. However, in the analysis on SENDYS, objects for comparison become the entire methods that integrate fault localization algorithm and risk formula. As a consequence, the previous framework is not applicable here. Thus, it is necessary to generalize the framework by substituting the "formula" in the framework with "the entire fault localization method." After the generalization, all the definitions and theorems become applicable to current context. First, Definition 2.2.1 can be rewritten in the following way.

Definition 5.3.1 (Set division: generalized) Given a program with n statements $PG = \{s_1, s_2, \ldots, s_n\}$, a test suite of m test cases $TS = \{t_1, t_2, \ldots, t_m\}$, one faulty statement $s_f \in PG$, and a fault localization method M which gives a whole ranking list to all the statements in PG, let $M(s_i)$ denote the risk value assigned by M to a statement s_i. With respect to the faulty statement s_f, we have the three following subsets.

$$S_B^M = \{s_i \in PG \mid M(s_i) > M(s_f), 1 \le i \le n\}$$

$$S_F^M = \{s_i \in PG \mid M(s_i) = M(s_f), 1 \le i \le n\}$$

$$S_A^M = \{s_i \in PG \mid M(s_i) < M(s_f), 1 \le i \le n\}$$

Similar to the basic version of SBFL (introduced in Chap. 1), after applying method M, all statements will finally be ranked according to their risk values $M(s_i)$. Hence all statements of S_B^M will be ranked before s_f, all statements of S_F^M will be tied with s_f, and all statements of S_A^M will be ranked after s_f.

When adopting *EXAM* as the performance metric, the ranking of s_f, which is decided by its relative $M(s_f)$ to other s_i in the statements ranking, is the determinant of method $M's$ performance. It is not difficult to find that, by replacing formula R with method M in theoretical framework introduced in Chap. 2, we can rephrase the theorems of "Better" and "Equivalent" in Chap. 2 to context correspondingly.

Theorem 5.3.1 *Given any two methods M_i and M_j, if we have $S_B^{M_i} \subseteq S_B^{M_j}$ and $S_A^{M_j} \subseteq S_A^{M_i}$ for any program, faulty statement s_f, and test suite, then $M_i \to M_j$.*

Theorem 5.3.2 *Given any two methods M_i and M_j, if we have $S_B^{M_i} = S_B^{M_j}$, $S_F^{M_i} = S_F^{M_j}$, $S_A^{M_i} = S_A^{M_j}$ for any program, faulty statement s_f, and test suite, then $M_i \leftrightarrow M_j$.*

Based on Theorems 5.3.1 and 5.3.2, it becomes possible to compare the performance of different methods and furthermore analyze the performance of different risk formulas being combined in M_1 in the single-fault scenario theoretically.

5.3.2   Properties of M_1 in the Single-Fault Scenario

From Sect. 5.1, we know that each minimal hitting set is computed based on failed relevant dynamic slices. In this theoretical analysis, we consider all the possible minimal hitting sets. Let us denote the union of all the possible H_S (i.e., single-element minimal hitting set) as U_S and the union of all the possible H_M (i.e., multiple-element minimal hitting set) as U_M.

Lemma 5.3.1 *Given any statement $s_i \in U_S$, $M_1(s_i) = Pr(H_{S_i})$ where $Pr(H_{S_i})$ is the risk value of single-element hitting set H_{S_i} that consists of s_i and $M_1(s_i)$ is the updated risk value of s_i computed by M_1.*

Proof Given any statement $s_i \in U_S$, let H_{S_i} denote the single-element minimal hitting set including s_i. Referring to Algorithm 2 (M_1) in Sect. 5.2, the risk value of

s_i is the sum of risk values of all the minimal hitting sets containing s_i. Hence, the risk value of s_i is the risk value of H_{S_i}. □

Then, let us discuss about the computation of risk values for single-element hitting sets. Referring to Algorithm 2 (M_1), for each H_S, we have $Pr(H_S) = R_{\text{norm}}(s_i) \times \prod_{s' \in PG \setminus H_S}(1 - R_{\text{norm}}(s'))$ where $s_i \in H_S$. We define such mathematical operation as τ (Hitting Set Mathematical Operation).

Definition 5.3.2 (τ) *Given n real numbers* $S = \{p_1, p_2, \ldots, p_n\}$ *where* $0 < p_i \leq 1$ $(1 \leq i \leq n)$ *and* $\sum_{i=1}^{n} p_i = 1$, τ *is defined as* $p_i \times \prod_{j \neq i}(1 - p_j)$ *where* $1 \leq i \leq n$ *and* $1 \leq j \leq n$.

In the following, we can prove that τ is an order-preserving mathematical operation for the normalized statements ranking.

Lemma 5.3.2 *Given any normalized statements ranking* γ, *after applying* τ *on each statement in* γ, *the relative order of each statement in the ranking* γ *still remains the same.*

Proof Given a program with n statements set $PG = \{s_1, s_2, \ldots, s_n\}$, the risk value of any statement s_i is denoted as $R(s_i)$, and the statements in γ are ranked in the descending order of risk value. Given any two statements s_i and s_j where $1 \leq i \leq n$, $1 \leq j \leq n$, and s_j is ranked before s_i, we have $R(s_i) = R(s_j)$ or $R(s_i) < R(s_j)$. After applying operation τ on the two statements, we have $\tau(s_i) = R(s_i) \times (1 - R(s_j)) \times \prod_k(1 - R(s_k))$ and $\tau(s_j) = R(s_j) \times (1 - R(s_i)) \times \prod_k(1 - R(s_k))$ where $k \neq i, k \neq j$ and $1 \leq k \leq n$.

(a) For $R(s_i) = R(s_j)$. Immediately, we have $\tau(s_i) = \tau(s_j)$. If the tie-breaking scheme is consistent, after applying τ, statement s_j is still ranked before s_i.
(b) For $R(s_i) < R(s_j)$. We have $R(s_i) < R(s_j)$ and $(1 - R(s_j)) < (1 - R(s_i))$. $\prod_k(1 - R(s_k))$ is the common part of $\tau(s_i)$ and $\tau(s_j)$. Thus, $\tau(s_i) < \tau(s_j)$. After applying τ, statement s_j is still ranked before s_i.

In summary, after applying τ, s_j is still ranked before s_i. Hence, τ is an order-preserving operation for the statement ranking. □

5.3.3 Enhanced M_1 in the Single-Fault Scenario

When focusing on the single-fault scenario, the faulty statement s_f is covered by all failed test executions. It is not difficult to conclude that s_f is covered by all failed relevant dynamic slices as well. Referring to the definition of hitting sets, U_S is the intersection of all the failed relevant dynamic slices. Hence, we can immediately conclude that for the faulty statement s_f, we have $s_f \in U_S$.

Accordingly, it is possible to have an enhanced M_1 algorithm in the single-fault scenario (denoted as M_2), which assigns the lowest risk values (negative or zero value) to each multiple-element hitting set. Following Algorithm 2 (M_1), the risk

---

Algorithm 3: Algorithm M_2 [3]

Input: Program PG, risk formula $Formula$, minimal hitting sets H^m, and test suite TS
Output: Statements ranking
1 Normalize the initial risk values with Algorithm 2 (M_1). Stop at Step 5 in Algorithm 2 (M_1)
2 Compute the risk value for minimal hitting set H_i which is a single-element hitting set,
   $H_i = \{s_i\}: Pr_s(H_i) = R_{\text{norm}}(s_i) \times \prod_{s' \in PG \setminus H_i}(1 - R_{\text{norm}}(s'))$
3 Assign zero risk value to each minimal hitting set H_i which is a multiple-element hitting set:
   $Pr_m(H_i) = 0$
4 Compute the final statements ranking with Algorithm 1 (SENDYS). Start with Step 5 in
   Algorithm 1 (SENDYS)

---

value of any minimal hitting set must be positive; hence, the assignment of negative or zero value can be the lowest risk value. Algorithm 3 illustrates the process of M_2.

Since Lemmas 5.3.1 and 5.3.2 are properties of focusing on single-fault diagnoses, it is not difficult to find that the properties of M_1 in the single-fault scenario are also held for M_2.

5.3.4 Comparison Among the M_i Algorithms with Execution Slice

We use notation M_i^R to represent the entire fault localization method which integrates the risk formula R and the localization algorithm M_i (M_0, M_1 or M_2).

In the following, according to the generalized set theory-based framework, referring to Definition 5.3.1, we divide statements ranking of M_0, M_1, and M_2 into three subsets, respectively. Based on the divided subsets, we prove that given any risk formula R, M_2^R performs better than M_1^R and M_0^R. Moreover, we will introduce a simple formula conversion G which is proved to be equivalent to the process of Algorithm M_2. Analysis on conversion G will be given.

Let U_D^f denote the union of all the failed relevant dynamic slices. In M_1 and M_2, risk values returned by a risk formula will be updated based on the obtained minimal hitting sets. Referring to Algorithm 2 (M_1), only these statements belonging to U_D^f ($U_S \bigcup U_M$) are assigned with new positive risk values, while others are assigned with new risk values of 0. Therefore, statements outside U_D^f (i.e., $PG \setminus U_D^f$) having lower risk values than the ones within U_D^f belong to $S_A^{M_1}$. Referring to Algorithm 3 (M_2), not only the statements outside U_D^f but also the statements in U_M are reassigned with the lowest value (zero value) because each H_M is assigned the lowest risk value 0 according to Step 3. On the other hand, statements in U_S are reassigned with new positive risk values. Thus statements outside U_S having lower risk values than the ones within U_S belong to $S_A^{M_2}$.

Notice that for both M_1 and M_2, the faulty statement is always reassigned with a positive value (but may not necessarily be the highest one in U_S). Therefore, we have the following statement subsets division for M_1 and M_2.

Corollary 5.3.1 *Given any risk formula R, let PG denote the program statements set. For M_1, we have the following three subsets:*

$$S_B^{M_1} = \{s_i \mid M_1(s_i) > M_1(s_f) \text{ and } s_i \in U_D^f\}$$

$$S_F^{M_1} = \{s_i \mid M_1(s_i) = M_1(s_f) \text{ and } s_i \in U_D^f\}$$

$$S_A^{M_1} = \{s_i \mid (M_1(s_i) < M_1(s_f) \text{ and } s_i \in U_D^f)$$
$$\text{or } s_i \in PG \setminus U_D^f\}$$

Corollary 5.3.2 *Given any risk formula R, let PG denote the program statements set. For M_2, we have the following three subsets*

$$S_B^{M_2} = \{s_i \mid M_2(s_i) > M_2(s_f), \text{ and } s_i \in U_S\}$$

$$S_F^{M_2} = \{s_i \mid M_2(s_i) = M_2(s_f), \text{ and } s_i \in U_S\}$$

$$S_A^{M_2} = \{s_i \mid (M_2(s_i) < M_2(s_f), \text{ and } s_i \in U_S)$$
$$\text{or } s_i \in U_M \text{ or } s_i \in PG \setminus U_D^f\}$$

Based on the properties of Algorithm M_1 in the single-fault scenario (Lemmas 5.3.1 and 5.3.2), we can obtain Lemma 5.3.3 that is the basis upon which M_2^R performs better than M_0^R and M_1^R for any risk formula R (see Propositions 5.3.1 and 5.3.2).

Lemma 5.3.3 *Given any risk formula R, statements in U_S have the same relative order in M_0^R, M_1^R, and M_2^R.*

Proof For any two distinct statements s_k and s_j belonging to U_S, given any risk formula R, assume $R(s_j) \geq R(s_k)$. Obviously, we have $M_0^R(s_j) \geq M_0^R(s_k)$. Besides we have two single-element s_k and s_j constitute $H_{S_1} = \{s_k\}$ and $H_{S_2} = \{s_j\}$, respectively. Let $Pr(H_{S_1})$ and $Pr(H_{S_2})$ denote the risk values of H_{S_1} and H_{S_2}, respectively. Referring to Lemma 5.3.1, we have $M_1^R(s_k) = Pr(H_{S_1})$ and $M_1^R(s_j) = Pr(H_{S_2})$ and $M_2^R(s_k) = Pr(H_{S_1})$ and $M_2^R(s_j) = Pr(H_{S_2})$.

Referring to Lemma 5.3.2, after computing the risk value of each single-element minimal hitting set, we still have $Pr(H_{S_2}) \geq Pr(H_{S_1})$. Consequently, we have $M_1^R(s_j) \geq M_1^R(s_k)$ and $M_2^R(s_j) \geq M_2^R(s_k)$. If the tie-breaking scheme is consistent, s_j and s_k still have the same relative order in M_0^R, M_1^R, and M_2^R.

From the above, we obtain that statements in U_S have the same relative order in M_0^R, M_1^R, and M_2^R.   □

Proposition 5.3.1 *For any given risk formula R, in the single-fault scenario, we have* $M_2^R \rightarrow M_0^R$.

Proof Given any risk evaluation formula R, for the convenience of illustration, we use M_0 and M_2 to represent M_0^R and M_2^R, respectively, in this proof.

For M_0, referring to Definition 5.3.1, we have:

$$S_B^{M_0} = \{s_i \mid M_0(s_i) > M_0(s_f) \text{ and } s_i \in PG\}$$

$$S_F^{M_0} = \{s_i \mid M_0(s_i) = M_0(s_f) \text{ and } s_i \in PG\}$$

$$S_A^{M_0} = \{s_i \mid M_0(s_i) < M_0(s_f) \text{ and } s_i \in PG\}$$

For M_2, referring to Corollary 5.3.2, we have:

$$S_B^{M_2} = \{s_i \mid M_2(s_i) > M_2(s_f) \text{ and } s_i \in U_S\}$$

$$S_F^{M_2} = \{s_i \mid M_2(s_i) = M_2(s_f) \text{ and } s_i \in U_S\}$$

$$S_A^{M_2} = \{s_i \mid (M_2(s_i) < M_2(s_f) \text{ and } s_i \in U_S)$$

$$\text{or } s_i \in U_M \text{ or } s_i \in PG \setminus U_D^f\}$$

(a) To prove that $S_B^{M_2} \subseteq S_B^{M_0}$.

   Assume statement $s_i \in S_B^{M_2}$. Referring to Lemma 5.3.3, the statements in U_S have the same relative order in both M_0 and M_2. Since $U_S \subset PG$, we have $S_B^{M_2} \subseteq S_B^{M_0}$.

(b) To prove that $S_A^{M_0} \subseteq S_A^{M_2}$.

   $S_A^{M_0}$ and $S_A^{M_2}$ can be expressed using another form: $S_A^{M_0} = PG \setminus S_B^{M_0} \setminus S_F^{M_0}$; $S_A^{M_2} = PG \setminus S_B^{M_2} \setminus S_F^{M_2}$.

   Similar to (a), we can also prove that $S_F^{M_2} \subseteq S_F^{M_0}$. Referring to (a), we have $S_B^{M_2} \subseteq S_B^{M_0}$; thus, $S_A^{M_0} \subseteq S_A^{M_2}$.

In conclusion, we have $S_B^{M_2} \subseteq S_B^{M_0}$ and $S_A^{M_0} \subseteq S_A^{M_2}$. Immediately after Theorem 5.3.1, $M_2^R \rightarrow M_0^R$.   □

Proposition 5.3.2 *For any given risk formula R, in the single-fault scenario, we have* $M_2^R \rightarrow M_1^R$.

Proof Given any risk evaluation formula R, for the convenience of illustration, we use M_1 and M_2 to represent M_1^R and M_2^R, respectively, in this proof.

For M_1, referring to Corollary 5.3.1, we have:

$$S_B^{M_1} = \{s_i \mid M_1(s_i) > M_1(s_f) \text{ and } s_i \in U_D^f\}$$

$$S_F^{M_1} = \{s_i \mid M_1(s_i) = M_1(s_f) \text{ and } s_i \in U_D^f\}$$

$$S_A^{M_1} = \{s_i \mid (M_1(s_i) < M_1(s_f) \text{ and } s_i \in U_D^f)$$

$$\text{or } s_i \in PG \setminus U_D^f\}$$

For M_2, referring to Corollary 5.3.2, we have:

$$S_B^{M_2} = \{s_i \mid M_2(s_i) > M_2(s_f) \text{ and } s_i \in U_S\}$$

$$S_F^{M_2} = \{s_i \mid M_2(s_i) = M_2(s_f) \text{ and } s_i \in U_S\}$$

$$S_A^{M_2} = \{s_i \mid (M_2(s_i) < M_2(s_f) \text{ and } s_i \in U_S)$$

$$\text{or } s_i \in U_M \text{ or } s_i \in PG \setminus U_D^f\}$$

(a) To prove that $S_B^{M_2} \subseteq S_B^{M_1}$.

Since $U_S \subset U_D^f$, besides, referring to Lemma 5.3.3, the relative order of statements in U_S is the same in M_1 and M_2. Therefore, $S_B^{M_2} \subseteq S_B^{M_1}$.

(b) To prove that $S_A^{M_1} \subseteq S_A^{M_2}$.

From the above, we have

$$S_A^{M_1} = \{s_i \mid M_2(s_i) < M_2(s_f) \text{ and } s_i \in U_D^f\}$$

$$\cup \{s_i \mid s_i \in PG \setminus U_D^f\}$$

$$S_A^{M_2} = \{s_i \mid M_2(s_i) < M_2(s_f) \text{ and } s_i \in U_S\}$$

$$\cup \{s_i \mid s_i \in U_M\} \cup \{s_i \mid s_i \in PG \setminus U_D^f\}$$

Besides, referring to Lemma 5.3.3, the relative order of statements in U_S is the same in M_1 and M_2.

Hence, we have $S_A^{M_1} \subseteq S_A^{M_2}$.

In conclusion, we have $S_B^{M_2} \subseteq S_B^{M_1}$ and $S_A^{M_1} \subseteq S_A^{M_2}$. Immediately after Theorem 5.3.1, $M_2^R \rightarrow M_1^R$. □

Propositions 5.3.1 and 5.3.2 tell us that in single-fault scenario, M_2 (i.e., the enhanced SENDYS) never gives worse performance than M_1 (i.e., the correction of SENDYS) and M_0 (i.e., the original SBFL).

The proof of Proposition 4.2.3 implies a simple maximal conversion. In this chapter, we denote this maximal conversion as conversion $C_{\max}$. Any non-maximal risk formula R can be converted into a maximal formula through the process of conversion C_{max} which is defined as follows.

Definition 5.3.3 (Conversion C_{max}) Given any risk formula R, conversion C_{max} assigns identical risk values to points on the faulty border as R and to all points outside the faulty border smaller risk values than that of any point on the faulty border.

By applying C_{max} on any formula, we can transform this formula into a maximal one. We illustrated this conversion by visualizing the landscape of a formula in 3D figure (shown in Fig. 4.1b), which has given the first explanation to maximal formulas in traditional SBFL. Here, we will introduce a similar conversion on formulas, denoted as G and presented in Algorithm 4, such that the basic SBFL (i.e., M_0) with this transformed formula has equally good performance as M_2 that has shown definite superiority over other two methods. With G, the complicated M_2 algorithm can be easily and vividly reformulated.

Algorithm 4 first computes O_d, which includes both passed and failed dynamic slices. From O_d, we know F that is the number of failed dynamic slices and d_{ef}^i that is the number of failed dynamic slices including statement s_i. Then, for each statement with $d_{ef}^i = F$, define the output of $G^R(s_i)$ as $R(s_i)$ (i.e., the original risk value computed by formula R); while for all the remaining statements, define their $G^R(s_i)$ outputs as a constant lower than p which is the minimum of risk values $R(s_i)$ among all s_i with $d_{ef}^i = F$.

Actually, this G conversion is very similar to C_{max} defined in Definition 5.3.3. The difference is that C_{max} only decreases the risk values of statements outside the faulty border (shown in Fig. 4.1b), but G decreases the risk values of statements both outside the fault border and on the faulty border but having $d_{ef}^i < F$.

Algorithm 4: Conversion G [3]

Input: Program PG, risk formula R, and test suite TS
Output: A transformed R (denoted as G^R)
1 Compute the matrix of relevant dynamic slices O_d for PG after the execution of TS
2 Denote the number of failed test cases as F, which is also the number of failed dynamic slices
3 Compute d_{ef}^i from O_d for each statement s_i
4 For each s_i with $d_{ef}^i = F$: define $G^R(s_i) = R(s_i)$
5 Get minimum risk value p of all s_i with $d_{ef}^i = F$: $p = Min(R(s_i))$ ($\forall s_i$ with $d_{ef}^i = F$)
6 For each s_i with $d_{ef}^i < F$: define $G^R(s_i)$ as a constant value lower than p

---

Given any risk formula R, we denote G^R as the transformed formula by using G conversion. Next we will prove that M_0 with G^R has equal superiority to the complicated algorithm M_2. In other words, G actually reformulates M_2 by providing a shortcut to achieve the same goal. Given any risk formula R, we use $M_0^{C_{max}}$ to represent SBFL with the maximal version of any formula R transformed by C_{max}.

Lemma 5.3.4 *Given any* M_2^R *where* R *belongs to* $\mathscr{F}$, *the points associated with any statement in* U_S *are on the faulty border.*

Proof Referring to the definition of minimal hitting sets, we have U_S as the intersection of all the failed relevant dynamic slices. Hence, given any statement $s_i \in U_S$, s_i is executed by all the failed executions. As a consequence, we have $a_{ef} = F$. Therefore, the points associated with all the statements in U_S are on the faulty border. $\square$

Lemma 5.3.5 *For any statement* $s_i \in U_S$, *let* d_{ef}^i *denote the number of failed relevant dynamic slices including* s_i, *we have* $d_{ef}^i = F$.

Proof Referring to the definition of minimal hitting sets, we have U_S as the intersection of all failed relevant dynamic slices; hence for any statement $s_i \in U_S$, we have $d_{ef}^i = F$. $\square$

Let $M_0^{G^R}$ denote the basic SBFL configuring with the transformed formula G^R. Then, we have the following propositions.

Proposition 5.3.3 *For any given risk formula* R, *in the single-fault scenario, we have* $M_0^{G^R} \leftrightarrow M_2^R$.

Proof Given any risk formula R, for the convenience of illustration, we use M_2 to denote M_2^R in the proof. Consider the points outside the faulty border and on the faulty border in G^R, respectively.

For M_2, referring to Corollary 5.3.2, we have:

$$S_B^{M_2} = \{s_i \mid M_2(s_i) > M_2(s_f) \text{ and } s_i \in U_S\}$$

$$S_F^{M_2} = \{s_i \mid M_2(s_i) = M_2(s_f) \text{ and } s_i \in U_S\}$$

$$S_A^{M_2} = \{s_i \mid (M_2(s_i) < M_2(s_f) \text{ and } s_i \in U_S)$$

$$\text{or } s_i \in U_M \text{ or } s_i \in PG \setminus U_D^f\}$$

Referring to Algorithm 4 (conversion G), for the points outside the faulty border, risk values of these statements are always lower than that of faulty statement; thus, these statements belong to S_A^G which denotes the set of statement having smaller risk values than that of the faulty statement in G^R. Notice that we can have the notations of S_B^G and S_F^G for G^R similarly. The corresponding d_{ef} values of these statements are smaller than F; referring to Lemma 5.3.5, these statements do not belong to U_S. Thus, these statements belong to $S_A^{M_2}$. Thus $S_A^{M_2} = S_A^G$.

For the points on the faulty border, in G^R, all these points are associated with statements having $d_{ef} = F$; referring to Lemma 5.3.5, the set of these statements is equal to U_S. These statements have the same relative order in M_0^R and G^R. Referring to Lemma 5.3.3, the relative order of these statements is the same in M_0^R and M_2^R.

Thus, in both M_2^R and G^R, the relative order of these statements is the same. If the tie-breaking is consistent, we can have $S_B^{M_2} = S_B^G$, $S_F^{M_2} = S_F^G$.

Following immediately from Theorem 5.3.2, we have proved $M_0^{G^R} \leftrightarrow M_2^R$. $\square$

Referring to Proposition 5.3.3, we prove that given any risk formula R, M_2^R is equivalent to the variant of formula R after applying conversion G. Besides, from Propositions 5.3.1 and 5.3.2, we have that for any risk formula R, M_2^R performs better than M_1^R and M_0^R. It indicates that in the single-fault scenario, the updated risk values of statements through the computation of single-element minimal hitting set in Algorithm 3 can be substituted for a simple formula conversion G. Hence, in the following, we focus on the analysis of conversion G.

As defined in Sect. 4.1, let us denote the distribution of risk values on the faulty border as P_R. Through investigating different risk formulas being applied conversion G, we have the following proposition.

Proposition 5.3.4 *For any two risk formulas R_1 and R_2, in the single-fault scenario, if R_1 and R_2 have the same P_R, then $M_0^{G^{R_1}} \leftrightarrow M_0^{G^{R_2}}$.*

Proof Firstly, we prove that $M_2^{R_1} \leftrightarrow M_2^{R_2}$ is held.

Let s_f denote the faulty statement and (F, a_{ep}^f) denote the corresponding point on the faulty border. Referring to Lemma 5.3.3, these statements in U_S have the same relative order in both R_1 and $M_2^{R_1}$ and R_2 and $M_2^{R_2}$. From the known condition, R_1 and R_2 have the same P_R; thus, $M_2^{R_1}$ and $M_2^{R_2}$ also have the same P_R. We use M_2^1 to denote $M_2^{R_1}$ and M_2^2 to denote $M_2^{R_2}$ for illustrating conveniently.

For M_2^1, referring to Corollary 5.3.2, we have:

$$S_B^{M_2^1} = \{s_i \mid M_2^1(s_i) > M_2^1(s_f) \text{ and } s_i \in U_S\}$$

$$S_F^{M_2^1} = \{s_i \mid M_2^1(s_i) = M_2^1(s_f) \text{ and } s_i \in U_S\}$$

$$S_A^{M_2^1} = \{s_i \mid (M_2^1(s_i) < M_2^1(s_f) \text{ and } s_i \in U_S)$$
$$\text{or } s_i \in U_M \text{ or } s_i \in PG \setminus U_D^f\}$$

For M_2^2, referring to Corollary 5.3.2, we have:

$$S_B^{M_2^2} = \{s_i \mid M_2^2(s_i) > M_2^2(s_f) \text{ and } s_i \in U_S\}$$

$$S_F^{M_2^2} = \{s_i \mid M_2^2(s_i) = M_2^2(s_f) \text{ and } s_i \in U_S\}$$

$$S_A^{M_2^2} = \{s_i \mid (M_2^2(s_i) < M_2^2(s_f) \text{ and } s_i \in U_S)$$
$$\text{or } s_i \in U_M \text{ or } s_i \in PG \setminus U_D^f\}$$

(a) To prove that $S_B^{M_2^1} = S_B^{M_2^2}$.

Assume statement $s_i \in S_B^{M_2^1}$. Referring to Lemma 5.3.4, the point associated with s_i is on the faulty border which is denoted as (F, a_{ep}^i). Whatever $a_{ep}^i > a_{ep}^f$ and $a_{ep}^i < a_{ep}^f$, the risk value of the point associated with s_i is larger than that of the point associated with s_f for $M_2^{R_1}$. Besides, $M_2^{R_1}$ and $M_2^{R_2}$ have the same P_R; then, for $M_2^{R_2}$, the risk value of s_i is still higher than that of s_f. Thus, we have $s_i \in S_B^{M_2^2}$. Therefore, $S_B^{M_2^1} \subseteq S_B^{M_2^2}$. In a similar way, we can prove that $S_B^{M_2^2} \subseteq S_B^{M_2^1}$.

In summary, we have proved $S_B^{M_2^1} = S_B^{M_2^2}$.

(b) To prove that $S_F^{M_2^1} = S_F^{M_2^2}$.

Assume statement $s_i \in S_F^{M_2^1}$; referring to Lemma 5.3.4, the point associated with s_i is on the faulty border which is denoted as (F, a_{ep}^i). Whatever $a_{ep}^i > a_{ep}^f$ and $a_{ep}^i < a_{ep}^f$, the risk value of the point associated with s_i is equal to that of the point associated with s_f for $M_2^{R_1}$. Besides, $M_2^{R_1}$ and $M_2^{R_2}$ have the same P_R; if the tie-breaking is consistent, the relative order of s_i and s_f is still the same for $M_2^{R_2}$. Thus, we have $s_i \in S_F^{M_2^2}$. Therefore, $S_F^{M_2^1} \subseteq S_F^{M_2^2}$. In a similar way, we can prove that $S_F^{M_2^2} \subseteq S_F^{M_2^1}$.

In summary, we have proved $S_F^{M_2^1} = S_F^{M_2^2}$.

From the above, it is not difficult to get $S_A^{M_2^1} = S_A^{M_2^2}$. Following immediately Theorem 5.3.2, we have proved $M_2^{R_1} \leftrightarrow M_2^{R_2}$. Finally, referring to Proposition 5.3.3, we have $M_0^{G^{R_1}} \leftrightarrow M_0^{G^{R_2}}$. □

Proposition 5.3.4 provides a sufficient condition for the equivalence of any two formulas being applied conversion G. In other words, formulas which have the same P_R after applying conversion G constitute their own maximal groups. We take the 30 risk formulas in Chap. 2 as examples to illustrate Proposition 5.3.4:

- Formulas that are **not** from $ER5$ have the same P_R: given any two points on the faulty border which are denoted as (F, a_{ep}^i) and (F, a_{ep}^j), respectively, if $a_{ep}^i < a_{ep}^j$, then the risk value of (F, a_{ep}^i) is higher than that of (F, a_{ep}^j). We refer to such P_R as "descending P_R." Given any R_1 and R_2 having descending P_R, G^{R_1} and G^{R_2} are equivalent to each other.
- Formulas from $ER5$ have the same P_R: the risk values of any two points on the faulty border are equal which we refer to as equal P_R. Given any two formulas having equal P_R, G^{R_1} and G^{R_2} are equivalent to each other.

Next, let us compare the performance between the transformed formula G^R and the traditional maximal formula proved in Chap. 4. Due to the equivalence between

$M_0^{G^R}$ and M_2^R, this comparison also reveals the relation between the enhanced SENDYS (M_2) and basic SBFL (M_0) with maximal formulas. Given any formula R, denote G^R and $C_{\max}^R$ as the transformed formula via G and $C_{\max}$, respectively. According to the proof in Chap. 4, the latter one is maximal formula in basic SBFL. We denote $M_0^{C_{\max}}$ as basic SBFL working on execution slice with maximal formula $C_{\max}^R$.

Proposition 5.3.5 *For any given risk formula R, in the single-fault scenario, we have $M_0^{G^R}(M_2^R) \rightarrow M_0^{C_{\max}}$.*

Proof Referring to Algorithm 4, we have that after applying conversion G on R, points associated with statements having $a_{ef} = F$ and $d_{ef} \neq F$ which have higher risk values than that of the faulty statement can be removed. Thus, we can obtain that $M_0^{G^R}(M_2^R) \rightarrow M_0^{C_{\max}}$.   □

As discussed after Algorithm 4, G further removes noises on the faulty border left by $C_{\max}$. That is, any point associated with statements having $a_{ef} = F$ but $d_{ef} < F$ is assigned with a risk value lower than that of the faulty statement. Such statements cannot be faulty in the single-fault scenario. As a reminder, to what extent $M_0^{G^R}$ can improve $M_0^{C_{\max}}$ depends on the number of statements with $d_{ef} < F$ and $a_{ef} = F$, which varies in different scenarios.

5.3.5   Comparison Among the M_i Algorithms with Dynamic Slice

Note that in the above analysis, $M_0^{G^R}$ and $M_0^{C_{\max}}$ are applied on execution slice. It is known that M_0 (i.e., basic SBFL) can be applied on various types of spectra. For example, Lei et al. [2] showed that by applying M_0 on dynamic slices, the fault localization performance can be improved.

For each statement s_i, the results of relevant dynamic slices can be represented as a tuple $d = <d_{ef}^i, d_{ep}^i, d_{nf}^i, d_{np}^i>$, where d_{ef}^i and d_{ep}^i represent the number of failed and passed relevant dynamic slices including s_i, respectively; d_{nf}^i and d_{np}^i represent the number of failed and passed relevant dynamic slices not including s_i, respectively. Given any risk formula R, we denote the $C_{\max}$ version of R applied on relevant dynamic slices as $\widetilde{M_0^{C_{\max}}}$. In the following, we will introduce the comparison of performance between $M_0^{G^R}$ and $\widetilde{M_0^{C_{\max}}}$.

Proposition 5.3.6 *For any given risk formula R, in the single-fault scenario, we have $M_0^{G^R}(M_2^R) \nleftrightarrow \widetilde{M_0^{C_{\max}}}$.*

Proof We prove this proposition by constructing a counterexample to show neither $M_0^{G^R}(M_2^R) \rightarrow \widetilde{M_0^{C_{\max}}}$ nor $\widetilde{M_0^{C_{\max}}} \rightarrow M_0^{G^R}(M_2^R)$ holds.

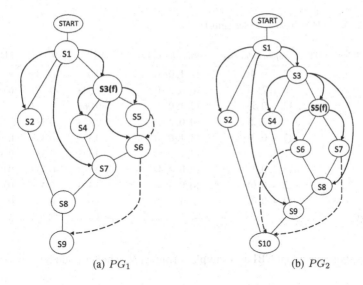

Fig. 5.1 Control flow graphs with dependency [3]

Let us consider the two sample programs PG_1 and PG_2, whose control flow graphs with dependency information are shown in Fig. 5.1. *In Fig. 5.1, the dashed arrows represent data dependency, the solid arrows represent control dependency, and the solid lines indicate control flow relations.* The faulty statements of PG_1 and PG_2 are S_3 and S_5, respectively.

- **Scenario 1:** Suppose we have a test suite TS_1 executed on PG_1, whose results are shown in Table 5.1. The testing results include two failed test cases and four passed test cases (i.e., $F = 2$). The execution slices and dynamic slices (by considering both control and data dependency) are listed in the second and third columns, respectively. Accordingly, we have $(a_{ef}, a_{ep}, a_{nf}, a_{np})$ and $(d_{ef}, d_{ep}, d_{nf}, d_{np})$ shown in Table 5.2.

Table 5.1 TS_1 executed on PG_1 (Scenario 1)

Pass or fail	Execution slices	Dynamic slices
Fail	$(S_1, S_3, S_5, S_6, S_7, S_8, S_9)$	$(S_1, S_3, S_5, S_6, S_9)$
Fail	$(S_1, S_3, S_5, S_6, S_7, S_8, S_9)$	$(S_1, S_3, S_5, S_6, S_9)$
Pass	(S_1, S_2, S_8, S_9)	(S_9)
Pass	$(S_1, S_3, S_5, S_6, S_7, S_8, S_9)$	$(S_1, S_3, S_5, S_6, S_9)$
Pass	$(S_1, S_3, S_4, S_7, S_8, S_9)$	(S_9)
Pass	$(S_1, S_3, S_4, S_7, S_8, S_9)$	(S_9)

Table 5.2 $M_0^{G^R}(M_2^R) \nrightarrow \widetilde{M_0^{C_{\max}}}$ (Scenario 1)

Statements of PG_1	$(a_{ef}, a_{ep}, a_{nf}, a_{np})$	$(d_{ef}, d_{ep}, d_{nf}, d_{np})$	$M_0^{G^R}$	$\widetilde{M_0^{C_{\max}}}$	(M_2^R)
S_1	(2, 4, 0, 0)	(2, 1, 0, 3)	0.0	0.333	0.112
S_2	(0, 1, 2, 3)	(0, 0, 2, 4)	−0.333	−0.333	0.0
$S_3(f)$	(2, 3, 0, 1)	(2, 1, 0, 3)	0.067	0.333	0.143
S_4	(0, 2, 2, 2)	(0, 0, 2, 4)	−0.333	−0.333	0.0
S_5	(2, 1, 0, 3)	(2, 1, 0, 3)	0.333	0.333	0.317
S_6	(2, 1, 0, 3)	(2, 1, 0, 3)	0.333	0.333	0.317
S_7	(2, 3, 0, 1)	(0, 0, 2, 4)	−0.333	−0.333	0.0
S_8	(2, 4, 0, 0)	(0, 0, 2, 4)	−0.333	−0.333	0.0
S_9	(2, 4, 0, 0)	(2, 4, 0, 0)	0.0	0.0	0.112
Ranking	—	—	**3**	**2**	**3**

Suppose we adopt CBI as a sample formula [7], which should be

$$\frac{a_{ef}}{a_{ef} + a_{ep}} - \frac{a_{ef} + a_{nf}}{a_{ef} + a_{nf} + a_{ep} + a_{np}} \text{(for } M_0 \text{ that uses execution slices);}$$

$$\frac{d_{ef}}{d_{ef} + d_{ep}} - \frac{d_{ef} + d_{nf}}{d_{ef} + d_{nf} + d_{ep} + d_{np}} \text{(for } \widetilde{M_0} \text{ that uses dynamic slices).}$$

As a consequence, we have $M_0^{G^R}$ assign risk values to statements with $d_{ef}=2$ as $\frac{a_{ef}}{a_{ef}+a_{ep}} - \frac{a_{ef}+a_{nf}}{a_{ef}+a_{nf}+a_{ep}+a_{np}}$ and assign "min_G - constant" to the remaining statements (where "min_G" is the minimum among all the above risk values with $d_{ef}=2$ in $M_0^{G^R}$). Similarly, we have $\widetilde{M_0^{C_{\max}}}$ assign risk values to statements with $d_{ef}=2$ as $\frac{d_{ef}}{d_{ef}+d_{ep}} - \frac{d_{ef}+d_{nf}}{d_{ef}+d_{nf}+d_{ep}+d_{np}}$ and assign "min_C - constant" to the remaining statements (where "min_C" is the minimum among all the risk values with $d_{ef}=2$ in $\widetilde{M_0^{C_{\max}}}$).[1]

Accordingly, the risk values are shown in Table 5.2. By adopting the *Original Order* tie-breaking scheme [7], we have the ranking shown in Table 5.2, which demonstrates the possibility of "$\widetilde{M_0^{C_{\max}}}$ performing better than $M_0^{G^R}$." As a reminder, we also list the risk values and ranking given by M_2^R for illustrating the equivalence between M_2^R and $M_0^{G^R}$. But we don't repeat the calculation of M_2^R here, since it is not necessary to this proof, and the equivalence between M_2^R and $M_0^{G^R}$ has been theoretically proved in Proposition 5.3.3.

In summary, we have proved $M_0^{G^R}(M_2^R) \nrightarrow \widetilde{M_0^{C_{\max}}}$.

---

[1] According to the definition, the constant can be any value. In Table 5.2, we have constant as 0.333.

- **Scenario 2:** Suppose we have a test suite TS_2 executed on PG_2, whose results are shown in Table 5.3. The testing results include two failed test cases and six passed test cases (i.e., $F = 2$). The execution slices and dynamic slices (by considering both control and data dependency) are listed in the second and third columns, respectively. Accordingly, we have $(a_{ef}, a_{ep}, a_{nf}, a_{np})$ and $(d_{ef}, d_{ep}, d_{nf}, d_{np})$ shown in Table 5.4.

  Again, suppose we adopt CBI as illustration. The risk values are shown in Table 5.4.[2] By adopting the "*Original Order*" tie-breaking scheme, we have the ranking shown in Table 5.4, which demonstrates the possibility of "$M_0^{G^R}$ outperforming $\widetilde{M_0^{C\max}}$." Thus, we have proved $\widetilde{M_0^{C\max}} \nrightarrow M_0^{G^R}(M_2^R)$.

  From the above two examples, we can have $M_0^{G^R}(M_2^R) \nleftrightarrow \widetilde{M_0^{C\max}}$.   □

Table 5.3 TS_2 for PG_2 (Scenario 2)

Pass or fail	Execution slices	Dynamic slices
Fail	$(S_1, S_3, S_5, S_6, S_8, S_9, S_{10})$	$(S_1, S_3, S_5, S_6, S_{10})$
Fail	$(S_1, S_3, S_5, S_7, S_8, S_9, S_{10})$	$(S_1, S_3, S_5, S_7, S_{10})$
Pass	(S_1, S_2, S_{10})	(S_{10})
Pass	$(S_1, S_3, S_4, S_9, S_{10})$	(S_{10})
Pass	$(S_1, S_3, S_5, S_6, S_8, S_9, S_{10})$	$(S_1, S_3, S_5, S_6, S_{10})$
Pass	$(S_1, S_3, S_5, S_7, S_8, S_9, S_{10})$	$(S_1, S_3, S_5, S_7, S_{10})$
Pass	$(S_1, S_3, S_4, S_9, S_{10})$	(S_{10})
Pass	$(S_1, S_3, S_5, S_7, S_8, S_9, S_{10})$	$(S_1, S_3, S_5, S_7, S_{10})$

Table 5.4 $\widetilde{M_0^{C\max}} \nrightarrow M_0^{G^R}(M_2^R)$ (Scenario 2)

Statements of PG_1	$(a_{ef}, a_{ep}, a_{nf}, a_{np})$	$(d_{ef}, d_{ep}, d_{nf}, d_{np})$	$M_0^{G^R}$	$\widetilde{M_0^{C\max}}$	(M_2^R)
S_1	$(2, 6, 0, 0)$	$(2, 3, 0, 3)$	0.0	0.15	0.146
S_2	$(0, 1, 2, 5)$	$(0, 0, 2, 6)$	-0.15	-0.15	0.0
S_3	$(2, 5, 0, 1)$	$(2, 3, 0, 3)$	0.036	0.15	0.173
S_4	$(0, 2, 2, 4)$	$(0, 0, 2, 6)$	-0.15	-0.15	0.0
$S_5(f)$	$(2, 3, 0, 3)$	$(2, 3, 0, 3)$	0.15	0.15	0.272
S_6	$(1, 1, 1, 5)$	$(1, 1, 1, 5)$	-0.15	-0.15	0.0
S_7	$(1, 2, 1, 4)$	$(1, 2, 1, 4)$	-0.15	-0.15	0.0
S_8	$(2, 3, 0, 3)$	$(0, 0, 2, 6)$	-0.15	-0.15	0.0
S_9	$(2, 5, 0, 1)$	$(0, 0, 2, 6)$	-0.15	-0.15	0.0
S_{10}	$(2, 6, 0, 0)$	$(2, 6, 0, 0)$	0.0	0.0	0.146
Ranking	—	—	**1**	**3**	**1**

---

[2]We have 0.15 as the constant in Table 5.4.

References

1. Hofer B, Wotawa F (2012) Spectrum enhanced dynamic slicing for better fault localization. In: Proceedings of the 20th European conference on artificial intelligence, pp 420–425. https://doi.org/10.3233/978-1-61499-098-7-420
2. Lei Y, Mao X, Dai Z, Wang C (2012) Effective statistical fault localization using program slices. In: Proceedings of the 36th annual international computers, software and applications conference, pp 1–10. https://doi.org/10.1109/COMPSAC.2012.9
3. Tu J, Xie X, Chen TY, Xu B (2019) On the analysis of spectrum based fault localization using hitting sets. J Syst Softw 147:106–123. https://doi.org/10.1016/j.jss.2018.10.013
4. Wotawa F (2002) On the relationship between model-based debugging and program slicing. Artif Intell 135(1–2):125–143. https://doi.org/10.1016/s0004-3702(01)00161-8
5. Wotawa F (2010) Fault localization based on dynamic slicing and hitting-set computation. In: Proceedings of the 10th international conference on quality software, pp 161–170. https://doi.org/10.1109/QSIC.2010.51
6. Xie X, Chen TY, Xu B (2010) Isolating suspiciousness from spectrum-based fault localization techniques. In: Proceedings of the 10th international conference on quality software, pp 385–392. https://doi.org/10.1109/QSIC.2010.45
7. Xie X, Chen TY, Kuo FC, Xu B (2013) A theoretical analysis of the risk evaluation formulas for spectrum-based fault localization. ACM Trans Softw Eng Methodol 22(4):31:1–31:40. https://doi.org/10.1145/2522920.2522924

Chapter 6
Practicality of the Theoretical Frameworks

Abstract In the previous chapters, we have introduced several theoretical frameworks for analyzing SBFL performance. It can be found that there are several assumptions when adopting the frameworks. In this chapter, we will be further discussing about the practicality of the theoretical frameworks with some potential concerns of "ideal assumptions" (Chen et al. A revisit of a theoretical analysis on spectrum-based fault localization. In: Proceedings of the 39th annual computer software and applications conference, vol 1, pp 17–22, 2015).

6.1 100% Coverage and Omission Fault

There are concerns from the assumptions of 100% coverage and non-omission fault. It is true that in real life, it is very common that a test suite cannot achieve a 100% coverage on the whole program. And omission faults are also not rare. However, these will not hinder the application of the theoretical frameworks in practice.

As a coverage-based debugging technique, SBFL utilizes coverage profiles and testing results to perform a risk assessment, with intuitions of "higher a_{ef}/lower a_{ep} should lead to higher risk value." In other words, SBFL is actually designed for locating non-omission fault, that is, its responsibility is to find the root faulty statement, of which the execution will trigger failure. This is also explicitly indicated in "the assumptions of SBFL" by Steimann et al. [5] – "Every failed test case executes at least one fault whose execution causes the failure." Obviously, this implies that only the risk assessment on those **covered** statements is meaningful, because statements that are **not** covered by **any** test case can **never** be the root non-omission fault of the observed failures. As a consequence, it is unreasonable to investigate statements that are not covered by any test case. This is supported by Steimann et al. [5] – "However, searching the explanation for failed test cases in

Part of this chapter ©2015 IEEE. Reprinted, with permission from Proceedings of the 39th IEEE Annual International Computers, Software and Applications Conference; 2015, Vol. 1, 17–22. DOI: https://doi.org/10.1109/COMPSAC.2015.196 (Ref. [1]).

code that is not covered by any test case, or even not covered by any failed test case, not only makes little sense per se."

In the theoretical frameworks, the assumptions of 100% coverage are **never** equivalent to "having a test suite that can achieve a 100% coverage on the **whole** program." Instead, the 100% coverage means that the risk assessment and theoretical analysis are only performed on the covered statements while those statements without being covered by any test case are excluded from consideration. It should be very clear that the introduced frameworks are applicable to **any** test suite with **any** coverage level, because we can simply focus on the **covered subset** of the given program, for which the test suite effectively achieves 100% coverage, regardless what level of coverage it really achieves for the whole program. Since the above intuitions and principles are the basis of SBFL, it should be always followed by both theoretical and empirical studies.

In fact, there are two commonly adopted methods in dealing with non-100% coverage in empirical studies:

- Method A: Exclude the non-covered statements, and focus on the covered ones for SBFL.
- Method B: Simply calculate the risk values for an uncovered statement in the same way as we do for a covered statement, by ignoring the coverage level.

It is obvious that Method A complies with the SBFL's nature and should be adopted in reasonable studies. This is consistent with the theoretical assumption and has been suggested by Steimann et al. [5]. On the other hand, Method B may introduce noises [5]. It may not affect some formulas with which the risk values of uncovered statements are no higher than those of the covered statements, especially lower than those of the statements with $a_{ef}^i = F$, such as Jaccard. However, for some formulas, it is possible that the risk values of uncovered statements are higher than those of the covered statements, for example, Wong2 ($a_{ef} - a_{ep}$). In the latter formulas, noises from the uncovered statements may affect the performance. Actually, things may be even more complicated in some formulas, such as Ochiai and Tarantula, where uncovered statements become undefined due to the zero denominator. Then, how to define these statements will affect the performance of the formula. Two extreme cases can be (i) ranking these statements at the top of the lists or (ii) ranking them at the bottom. Obviously, these two strategies may give totally different results, while the latter one gives better performance and is essentially the same as the above Method A. (Note that it provides the same absolute ranking for the faulty statement as Method A, but lower *EXAM* score because more statements are considered and hence a larger denominator. But the comparison results between formulas are the same as the ones with Method A.)

As mentioned above some empirical studies have suggested to use Method A [5] to avoid the potential noises. Steimann et al. [5] also suggested to further exclude the statements with $a_{ef} = 0$, which has actually been suggested earlier by Xie et al. [7, 8].

6.2 Tie-Breaking Scheme

Another concern on the theoretical analysis is about the "consistent tie-breaking scheme."

It is very common that SBFL assigns the same risk values to different statements. In such a case, a tie-breaking scheme is required to further distinguish these statements. Therefore, given a program and a test suite, the *EXAM* score is co-determined by formula R and the adopted tie-breaking scheme. In other words, a tie-breaking scheme is **not** a component of a risk evaluation formula. Instead, it is a component of a SBFL technique. Thus, for a fair comparison between various risk evaluation formulas R, the tie-breaking scheme should be the same across different R, which must therefore be applicable to any formula. For example, it is obviously not meaningful to bind formula R_1 with tie-breaking scheme B_1 while binding R_2 with a different tie-breaking scheme B_2 and then treat the comparison between $R_1 + B_1$ and $R_2 + B_2$ equally as the comparison between R_1 and R_2.

Therefore, the theoretical frameworks require different formulas to use a common tie-breaking scheme. Moreover, we have chosen a general family of tie-breaking schemes, namely, consistent tie-breaking scheme, as a representative in the previous theoretical analysis. We use it because of the following reasons.

- Instead of being one particular single scheme, consistent tie-breaking scheme actually covers **a large family** of schemes. Based on Definition 2.2.2, as long as a tie-breaking scheme always gives the same relative order to any set of tied statements, it is said to be consistent. In other words, such a tie-breaking scheme **does not** care about what particular order should be used for tied statements in one formula. Instead, it only requires the same relative order for the common set of tied statements in different formulas. There can be a wide variety of relative orders, such as the sequential order in the source code or control flow graph, order decided by other information, user-defined order based on their debugging habits or experience, or even a fixed random order.[1] Obviously, all of these particular schemes can be practically applied in real life, of course in empirical studies as well.
- Consistent tie-breaking scheme that always provides identical relative order to tied statements is the most straightforward and intuitive way to be totally independent of the risk formulas. With such a scheme, any noises from the tie-breaking schemes can be excluded such that a fair comparison between formulas can be guaranteed.

As a reminder, choosing the consistent tie-breaking scheme in the theoretical frameworks does **not** mean that the frameworks are inapplicable with other tie-breaking schemes. In the following discussion, we will prove that the propositions in Chap. 3 still hold with other commonly adopted tie-breaking schemes, such as

---

[1] Same random order in different formulas.

"Best", "Worst," and "Average." However, we must also point out that strictly speaking, such tie-breaking schemes are **not realistic** solutions when performing SBFL in practice. Instead, they are just laboratory strategies to estimate the performance of SBFL technique. That is, such tie-breaking schemes cannot be applied in practice simply because we do not know which statement is faulty.

Theorem 6.2.1 *If R_1 and R_2 satisfy the corresponding subset relations required by Theorem 2.2.2 or 2.2.3, then by adopting "**Best** tie-breaking scheme," we still have $R_1 \rightarrow R_2$ and $R_1 \leftrightarrow R_2$, respectively, for any program and test suite.*

Proof "Best tie-breaking scheme" ranks s_f at the top among all statements in S_F^R. Thus, have $E = |S_B^R| + 1$. Let us denote the difference between E_1 and E_2 as $\delta = E_1 - E_2$. It follows immediately that $\delta = |S_B^{R_1}| - |S_B^{R_2}|$.

1. If $S_B^{R_1} \subseteq S_B^{R_2}$ and $S_A^{R_2} \subseteq S_A^{R_1}$, we have $|S_B^{R_1}| - |S_B^{R_2}| \leq 0$. As a consequence, $\delta \leq 0$, that is, $E_1 \leq E_2$.
2. If $S_B^{R_1} = S_B^{R_2}$ and $S_A^{R_2} = S_A^{R_1}$, we have $|S_B^{R_1}| - |S_B^{R_2}| = 0$. As a consequence, $\delta = 0$, that is, $E_1 = E_2$.

After Definitions 2.2.3 and 2.2.4, the theorem is proved. $\square$

Theorem 6.2.2 *If R_1 and R_2 satisfy the corresponding subset relations required by Theorem 2.2.2 or 2.2.3, then by adopting "Worst tie-breaking scheme," we still have $R_1 \rightarrow R_2$ and $R_1 \leftrightarrow R_2$, respectively, for any program and test suite.*

Proof "Worst tie-breaking scheme" ranks s_f at the bottom among all statements in S_F^R. Thus, we have

$$E = |S_B^R| + |S_F^R| = |S| - |S_A^R|$$

Let us denote $\delta = E_1 - E_2$, and then we have $\delta = |S_A^{R_2}| - |S_A^{R_1}|$.

1. If $S_B^{R_1} \subseteq S_B^{R_2}$ and $S_A^{R_2} \subseteq S_A^{R_1}$, we have $|S_A^{R_2}| - |S_A^{R_1}| \leq 0$. As a consequence, $\delta \leq 0$, that is, $E_1 \leq E_2$.
2. If $S_B^{R_1} = S_B^{R_2}$ and $S_A^{R_2} = S_A^{R_1}$, we have $|S_A^{R_2}| - |S_A^{R_1}| = 0$. As a consequence, $\delta = 0$, that is, $E_1 = E_2$.

After Definitions 2.2.3 and 2.2.4, the theorem is proved. $\square$

Actually, conclusions in the above two theorems have also been discussed in [6]. As a reminder, it can be found from the above proofs that, with "Best" or "Worst" tie-breaking schemes, comparing two formulas does not require the subset relations for both S_B^R and S_A^R. With "Best" tie-breaking scheme, $S_B^{R_1} \subseteq S_B^{R_2}$ implies $E_1 \leq E_2$, and $S_B^{R_1} = S_B^{R_2}$ implies $E_1 = E_2$, regardless of the relations for the other two subsets, while with "Worst" tie-breaking scheme, $S_A^{R_2} \subseteq S_A^{R_1}$ implies $E_1 \leq E_2$, and $S_A^{R_1} = S_A^{R_2}$ implies $E_1 = E_2$, regardless of the relations for the other two subsets. However, even though the adoption of these two tie-breaking schemes can simplify the theorem, they were not included in [8] because neither "Best" nor "Worst" is applicable in real life.

Theorem 6.2.3 *If R_1 and R_2 satisfy $S_B^{R_1} \subseteq S_B^{R_2}$ and $S_A^{R_2} \subseteq S_A^{R_1}$, then by adopting "Average" tie-breaking scheme, we still have $R_1 \rightarrow R_2$, for any program and test suite.*

Proof "Average" tie-breaking scheme ranks s_f at the medium position among all statements in S_F^R. If $|S_F^R|$ is odd, we always have $E = |S_B^R| + \frac{|S_F^R|+1}{2}$. If $|S_F^R|$ is even, there are two possible definitions of the medium position, and correspondingly, we have (i) $E = |S_B^R| + \frac{|S_F^R|}{2}$ or (ii) $E = |S_B^R| + \frac{|S_F^R|}{2} + 1$. Since the proofs with definitions (i) and (ii) are very similar, due to the page limitation, we will adopt (i) for even $|S_F^R|$.

Let us denote $\delta = E_1 - E_2$, $\delta_B = |S_B^{R_1}| - |S_B^{R_2}|$, and $\delta_A = |S_A^{R_1}| - |S_A^{R_2}|$. Given R_1 and R_2, since $S_B^{R_1} \subseteq S_B^{R_2}$ and $S_A^{R_2} \subseteq S_A^{R_1}$, we have

$$\delta_B = |S_B^{R_1}| - |S_B^{R_2}| \leq 0$$

$$\delta_A = |S_A^{R_1}| - |S_A^{R_2}| \geq 0$$

Then,

$$|S| = |S_B^{R_1}| + |S_F^{R_1}| + |S_A^{R_1}| = |S_B^{R_2}| + |S_F^{R_2}| + |S_A^{R_2}|$$

can be rewritten as

$$(|S_B^{R_1}| - |S_B^{R_2}|) + (|S_A^{R_1}| - |S_A^{R_2}|) = \delta_B + \delta_A = |S_F^{R_2}| - |S_F^{R_1}| \tag{6.1}$$

There are following possible cases.

1. Consider the case that both $S_F^{R_1}$ and $S_F^{R_2}$ are even or odd. Then, we have $\delta = (|S_B^{R_1}| + \frac{|S_F^{R_1}|}{2}) - (|S_B^{R_2}| + \frac{|S_F^{R_2}|}{2})$. After Equation (6.1), we have $\delta = \frac{1}{2}(\delta_B - \delta_A)$. Since $\delta_B \leq 0$ and $\delta_A \geq 0$, we have $\delta \leq 0$. In other words, we have $E_1 \leq E_2$.

2. Consider the case that $S_F^{R_1}$ is odd while $S_F^{R_2}$ is even. Then, we have

$$\delta = \left(|S_B^{R_1}| + \frac{|S_F^{R_1}|+1}{2}\right) - \left(|S_B^{R_2}| + \frac{|S_F^{R_2}|}{2}\right)$$

After Equation (6.1), we have $\delta = \frac{1}{2}(\delta_B - \delta_A + 1)$. In this case, since $S_F^{R_1}$ is odd while $S_F^{R_2}$ is even, then δ_B and δ_A cannot be 0 at the same time. Thus, we must have $\delta_B - \delta_A \leq -1$ and hence $\delta \leq 0$. In other words, we also have $E_1 \leq E_2$.

3. Consider the case that $S_F^{R_1}$ is even while $S_F^{R_2}$ is odd. Then, we have

$$\delta = \left(|S_B^{R_1}| + \frac{|S_F^{R_1}|}{2} \right) - \left(|S_B^{R_2}| + \frac{|S_F^{R_2}|+1}{2} \right)$$

After Equation (6.1), we have $\delta = \frac{1}{2}(\delta_B - \delta_A - 1)$. Similar to the second case, δ_B and δ_A cannot be 0 at the same time. Thus, we must have $\delta_B - \delta_A \leq -1$ and hence $\delta < 0$. In other words, we have $E_1 < E_2$.

In summary, if $S_B^{R_1} \subseteq S_B^{R_2}$ and $S_A^{R_2} \subseteq S_A^{R_1}$, then by adopting "Average" tie-breaking scheme, we also have $E_1 \leq E_2$, for any program and test suite. After Definition 2.2.3, the theorem is proved. $\square$

Theorem 6.2.4 *If R_1 and R_2 satisfy $S_B^{R_1} = S_B^{R_2}$, $S_F^{R_1} = S_F^{R_2}$, and $S_A^{R_2} = S_A^{R_1}$, then by adopting any "Average tie-breaking scheme," we still have $R_1 \leftrightarrow R_2$, for any program and test suite.*

Proof Since $S_B^{R_1} = S_B^{R_2}$, $S_F^{R_1} = S_F^{R_2}$, and $S_A^{R_2} = S_A^{R_1}$, then we have $\delta_B = 0$ and $\delta_A = 0$, and $S_F^{R_1}$ and $S_F^{R_2}$ must both be either even or odd. Thus, we have $\delta = \frac{1}{2}(\delta_B - \delta_A) = 0$, which means $E_1 = E_2$. After Definition 2.2.4, the theorem is proved. $\square$

6.3   Single-Fault Scenario

The third concern comes from the assumption of "single fault." As discussed above, SBFL formulas are designed based on intuition of "higher e_f/lower e_p should lead to higher risk value." It is not difficult to find out that such an intuition is only meaningful for single (non-omission)-fault scenario [2]. Fortunately, DiGiuseppe and Jones [2] also have demonstrated that "in terms of localizing at least one, most prominent, fault, the performance of SBFL is not adversely affected by the increasing number of faults, even in the presence of fault localization interference." Such an evidence implies that the conclusions of the introduced theoretical analysis are equally useful for multiple faults.

On the other hand, an attractive idea was proposed to assist the application of SBFL in multiple-fault scenario, namely, parallel debugging approaches [3, 4, 9]. As introduced in Sect. 1.4.2, in parallel debugging, test cases are first clustered into several specialized test suites based on various execution information, and each of the test suites targets an individual single fault. In practice, each specialized test suite is dispatched to a particular developer, who is supposed to focus on the corresponding single fault. In other words, by properly clustering the test suite, the multiple-fault scenario can be transformed into single-fault scenario, in which the introduced theoretical frameworks can be applied. For more details about parallel debugging, please refer to the following Sect. 8.3.

References

1. Chen TY, Xie X, Kuo FC, Xu B (2015) A revisit of a theoretical analysis on spectrum-based fault localization. In: Proceedings of the 39th annual computer software and applications conference, vol 1, pp 17–22. https://doi.org/10.1109/COMPSAC.2015.196
2. DiGiuseppe N, Jones JA (2011) On the influence of multiple faults on coverage-based fault localization. In: Proceedings of ACM international symposium on software testing and analysis, pp 199–209. https://doi.org/10.1145/2001420.2001446
3. Jones JA, Bowring JF, Harrold MJ (2007) Debugging in parallel. In: Proceedings of ACM SIGSOFT international symposium on software testing and analysis, pp 16–26. https://doi.org/10.1145/1273463.1273468
4. Liu C, Han J (2006) Failure proximity: a fault localization-based approach. In: Proceedings of the 14th ACM SIGSOFT international symposium on foundations of software engineering, pp 46–56. https://doi.org/10.1145/1181775.1181782
5. Steimann F, Frenkel M, Abreu R (2013) Threats to the validity and value of empirical assessments of the accuracy of coverage-based fault locators. In: Proceedings of international symposium on software testing and analysis, pp 314–324. https://doi.org/10.1145/2483760.2483767
6. Wong WE, Debroy V, Gao R, Li Y (2014) The DStar method for effective software fault localization. IEEE Trans Reliab 63(1):290–308. https://doi.org/10.1109/TR.2013.2285319
7. Xie X, Chen TY, Xu B (2010) Isolating suspiciousness from spectrum-based fault localization techniques. In: Proceedings of the 10th international conference on quality software, pp 385–392. https://doi.org/10.1109/QSIC.2010.45
8. Xie X, Chen TY, Kuo FC, Xu B (2013) A theoretical analysis of the risk evaluation formulas for spectrum-based fault localization. ACM Trans Softw Eng Methodol 22(4):31:1–31:40. https://doi.org/10.1145/2522920.2522924
9. Zheng AX, Jordan MI, Liblit B, Naik M, Aiken A (2006) Statistical debugging: simultaneous identification of multiple bugs. In: Proceedings of the 23rd international conference on machine learning, pp 1105–1112. https://doi.org/10.1145/1143844.1143983

Chapter 7
Tackling the Oracle Problem in Spectrum-Based Fault Localization

Abstract Currently, all existing SBFL techniques have assumed the existence of a test oracle; otherwise, the program spectrum will not be associated with the testing result of failed or passed. As a consequence, a program with no test oracle will have no sufficient information to perform SBFL. However, in many real-world applications, it is very common that test oracles do not exist, and hence SBFL cannot be applied in such situations. In this chapter, we will introduce a technique proposed by us Xie et al. (Inf Softw Technol 55(5):866–879, 2013), namely, metamorphic slice to alleviate this problem. Metamorphic slice is resulted from the integration of metamorphic testing and program slicing. Instead of using the program slice and the testing result of failed or passed for an individual test case, metamorphic slice and the testing result of violation or non-violation of a metamorphic relation are used. Then, the existence of test oracle is no longer a prerequisite to SBFL, and hence the application domain of SBFL can be significantly extended.

7.1 The Oracle Problem in SBFL

As discussed in Chap. 1, in order to evaluate the risk values for the program statements, SBFL requires information of program spectrum that associated with testing results of *failed* or *passed*. For instance, when adopting the statement binary coverage as the program spectrum, coverage of each test execution must be associated with the testing result of the corresponding individual test case, in terms of *failed* or *passed* (as shown in Fig. 1.1). In other words, the SBFL procedure has assumed **the existence of a test oracle.**

However, such assumption is not always true. Many real-life programs, including complex computational programs, bioinformatics applications, machine learning algorithms, etc. [1, 7], do not have test oracles (known as "an oracle problem").

Part of this chapter ©Reprinted from Information and Software Technology; May 2013, Vol. 55, No. 5, Xie X, Wong WE, Chen TY, Xu B, Metamorphic slice: An application in spectrum-based fault localization, 866–879, DOI: https://doi.org/10.1016/j.infsof.2012.08.008 (Ref. [8]), Copyright (2013), with permission from Elsevier.

Thus, this assumption has severely restricted the application of SBFL. In this chapter, we will introduce a solution to alleviate such an oracle problem in SBFL [8].

7.2 A Solution to General Oracle Problem: Metamorphic Testing

"Oracle problem" means it is impossible or too expensive to verify the correctness of the computed outputs [5]. For example, in programs computing multiple precision arithmetic, the operands involved are very large numbers, and hence, the computed results are very expensive to check. When testing a compiler, it is not easy to verify whether the generated object code is equivalent to the source code or not. Other examples include testing programs involving machine learning algorithms, simulations, combinatorial calculations, graph display in the monitor, etc. [6, 7].

Actually, the oracle problem has been one of the biggest difficulties in software testing in the past decades, and several attempts have been conducted to alleviate it. One attempt is to use a "pseudo-oracle," in which multiple implementations of an algorithm process the same test case input and the outputs are compared; if the outputs are not the same, then one or both of the implementations contain a fault. But this is not always feasible, since multiple implementations may not exist, or they may have been created by the same developers or by groups of developers who are prone to making the same types of mistakes. However, even without multiple implementations, these applications often exhibit properties such that given a test case input and its output, if the input is modified in a certain way, it should be possible to predict some characteristics of the new output. This approach is known as metamorphic testing.

Metamorphic testing (MT) [2, 3] uses some specific properties of the problem domain, namely, metamorphic relations (MRs), to verify the relationship between multiple but related test cases and their outputs, rather than verifying the correctness of the output for each individual test case. Generally speaking, when conducting MT, we first need to identify the MRs of the program under testing and choose a test case selection strategy to generate the source test cases, from which the corresponding follow-up test cases are constructed based on the MRs. Then, we execute both the source and the follow-up test cases on the program and check whether their outputs satisfy the corresponding MRs.

Consider a program that searches for the shortest path between any two nodes in an undirected graph and reports its length. Given a weighted graph G, a start node x, and a destination node y in G, the target program is to output the shortest path and its length. Let us denote the length of the shortest path by $d(x, y, G)$. Suppose that the computed value of $d(x, y, G)$ is 12345. It is very expensive to check whether 12345 is correct due to the combinatorially large number of possible paths between x and y. Therefore, such a program is said to have the oracle problem. When applying

MT to this program, we first need to define an MR based on some well-known properties in graph theory. One possible MR (referred to as MR1) is that the length of the shortest path will remain unchanged if we swap the start node and destination node, that is, $d(x, y, G)=d(y, x, G)$. Another possible MR (referred to as MR2) is that suppose w is any node in the shortest path with x as the start node and y as the destination node, then the sum of the length of the shortest path from x to w and the length of the shortest path from w to y shall be equal to the length of the shortest path from x to y, that is, $d(x, y, G)=d(x, w, G)+d(w, y, G)$.

The core idea is that although it is difficult to verify the correctness of the individual output, namely, $d(x, y, G)$, $d(y, x, G)$, $d(x, w, G)$, and $d(w, y, G)$, it is easy to verify whether the MR1 and MR2 are satisfied or not, that is, whether $d(x, y, G)=d(y, x, G)$ and $d(x, y, G)=d(x, w, G)+d(w, y, G)$. In other words, for MR1, we can run the program using y as the start node and x as the destination node; if $d(y, x, G)$ is not equal to 12345, test cases (x, y, G) and (y, x, G) are said to *violate* MR1. Then, we can conclude that the program is incorrect. As a reminder, if $d(y, x, G)$ is also 12345, we can neither conclude the program is correct nor incorrect. This is due to the limitation of software testing. And the similar conclusion can be obtained by using MR2. In this example, (x, y, G) is referred to as the source test case, (y, x, G) is the follow-up test case of MR1, and (x, w, G) and (w, y, G) are the follow-up test cases of MR2. As shown, follow-up test cases could be multiple and dependent on both the source test case and the relevant MR. As a reminder, the source test case involved in an MR need not be a single test case, and it can be selected according to any test case selection strategies.

For convenience of reference, we will refer a source test case (or a group of source test cases if appropriate) and its corresponding follow-up test cases as a metamorphic test group. As a reminder, a metamorphic test group *violating* its corresponding MR implies an incorrect program, but a satisfaction of the corresponding MR does not imply the correctness of the program [2, 3].

7.3 *Metamorphic Slice*: A Property-Based Program Slice

In this section, we introduce a concept of program slice, namely, *metamorphic slice* [8]. It is based on the integration of metamorphic testing and program slicing. Different from the traditional program slice, *metamorphic slice* is not only data-based but also property-based. Intuitively speaking, a *metamorphic slice* is a group of slices which are bound together with a specific program property (known as MR).

Corresponding to the traditional *static slice*, *dynamic slice*, and *execution slice*, we can have *static metamorphic slice*, *dynamic metamorphic slice*, and *execution metamorphic slice*, respectively. As introduced in Chap. 1, the most adopted spectrum is the statement binary coverage, which is essentially *execution slice*. Thus here we give the definition of *execution metamorphic slice* as an illustration.

Definition 7.3.1 (Execution metamorphic slice) For a metamorphic relation MR, suppose $T^S=\{t_1^S, t_2^S, \ldots, t_{ks}^S\}$ and $T^F=\{t_1^F, t_2^F, \ldots, t_{kf}^F\}$ are its respective set of source test cases and set of follow-up test cases, such that T^S and T^F constitute a metamorphic test group g. The *execution metamorphic slice*, $e\_mslice(MR, T^S)$, is the union of all $e\_slice(t)$, where $t \in (T^S \cup T^F)$. That is,

$$e\_mslice(MR, T^S) = \left(\bigcup_{i=1}^{ks} e\_slice(t_i^S)) \cup (\bigcup_{i=1}^{kf} e\_slice(t_i^F) \right)$$

Technically speaking, a *metamorphic slice* has bound the $e\_slice(t)$ of all test cases belonging to a metamorphic test group of MR. For a given MR, each e_mslice must be associated with a metamorphic testing result of *violation* or *non-violation*. More importantly, regardless of the availability of the testing result of *failure* or *pass* associated with each individual e_slice, such metamorphic testing result is always available. Thus, if we replace the application of e_slice in SBFL with the application of e_mslice, respectively, it is always feasible to obtain sufficient information for fault localization, no matter whether the test oracle is available or not.

7.4 SBFL with e_mslice

With the above preliminary knowledge, we now can formally introduce the alleviation of oracle problem in SBFL, that is, SBFL with e_mslice [8].

In SBFL with e_mslice, the coverage information is provided by the e_mslice of each metamorphic test group g_i. Suppose there are m metamorphic test groups in the current metamorphic test suite. Then, there are m $e\_mslices$ and m metamorphic testing results in total. With this information, as shown in Fig. 7.1, we can construct the counterparts for the matrix and vectors in the conventional SBFL.

Fig. 7.1 Essential information for SBFL with e_mslice [8]

$$MTS : (\ g_1 \quad g_2 \quad \cdots \quad g_m\ )$$

$$PG : \begin{pmatrix} s_1 \\ s_2 \\ \cdot \\ \cdot \\ \cdot \\ s_n \end{pmatrix} \quad MS : \begin{pmatrix} 1/0 & 1/0 & \cdots & 1/0 \\ 1/0 & 1/0 & \cdots & 1/0 \\ & \cdot & & \\ & \cdot & & \\ 1/0 & 1/0 & \cdots & 1/0 \end{pmatrix}$$

$$RE : (\ v/n \quad v/n \quad \cdots \quad v/n\ )$$

In Fig. 7.1, the vector *MTS* is the test suite containing *m* metamorphic test groups. The *j*th column of matrix *MS* represents the corresponding e_mslice of g_j, in which the binary value of "1" in the *i*th line denotes the membership of statement s_i in this e_mslice and 0 otherwise. Besides, the *j*th element in vector *RE* records the corresponding metamorphic testing result for g_i, with "*v*" indicating *violated* and "*n*" indicating *non-violated*.

The transformation from Fig. 1.1 (essential information for SBFL with e_slice) to Fig. 7.1 (essential information for SBFL with e_mslice) basically consists of the following replacements. Each individual test case t_j is replaced by a metamorphic test group g_j; the e_slice for each t_j is replaced by e_mslice for each g_j; and the testing result of *failure* or *pass* is replaced by the metamorphic testing result of *violation* or *non-violation*, respectively. After such replacements, the same procedure can be applied to reformulate the collected information into vector A_i or each s_i and to evaluate the risk value r_i of s_i using a formula.

In the conventional SBFL using e_slice, a *failed* test case implies that a faulty statement is definitely included in the corresponding e_slice, while a *passed* test case does not provide a definite conclusion whether the corresponding e_slice is free of faulty statement. Similarly, a *violated* metamorphic test group implies that there is at least one *failed* test case within it. Even though it is impossible to know which test cases are actually the *failed* ones, we still can conclude that a faulty statement must be included in the union of all the corresponding e_slices, that is, the e_mslice. On the other hand, a *non-violated* metamorphic test group does not provide a definite conclusion that all the involved test cases are *passed*, and the correctness of all statements in the current e_mslice is not guaranteed.

7.5 Illustrative Examples

To conduct SBFL with *metamorphic slices*, MRs should be first generated for the program under testing. In this section, we show MRs for two programs, namely, *grep* and *SeqMap* [8].

(1) **Program *grep* and its MRs.**
    grep is a well-known UNIX utility written in C to perform pattern matching. Given a pattern to be matched and some input files for searching, *grep* searches these files for lines containing a match to the specified pattern. It supports three different versions of syntax for regular expression, namely, "Basic," "Extended," and "Perl." By default, *grep* follows the "Basic" version, and when a match in a line is found, the whole line is printed to standard output. For example, *grep* can be invoked by command: *grep "[Gg]r?ep" myfile.txt*, where expression "*[Gg]r?ep*" is the specified regular expression to be matched and "*myfile.txt*" is the input file. *grep* searches "*myfile.txt*" for lines containing a match to pattern "*[Gg]r?ep*" and prints all lines containing "*grep*," "*Grep*," "*gep*," or "*Gep*."

However, testing *grep* is not an easy task, because it may be very difficult to verify the correctness of its output. As shown in the above example command, though we can check whether all the printed lines actually contain matches to the specified pattern, it is almost impossible to know whether *grep* has printed all the matched lines, unless we do an exhaustive examination through the entire file (namely, inspecting every single line of "*myfile.txt*"). Therefore, *grep* has the oracle problem, which makes it impossible to be applied with traditional SBFL algorithms.

Given the same input file to be scanned, the regular expressions in the source and follow-up test cases are denoted as r_s and r_f, respectively. All the three MRs construct r_f that is equivalent to r_s. As a consequence, the output of the follow-up test case (denoted as O_f) should be the same as the output of the source test case (denoted as O_s).

- **MR1: Completely decomposing the bracketed sub-expression**
  In a bracketed regular expression "$[x_1 \ldots x_n]$," where x_i is a single character, if these characters "$x_1, \ldots, x_n$" are continuous for the current locale,[1] they can be presented in a compressed way "$[x_1-x_n]$." For such a bracketed regular expression, one of its equivalents is the complete decomposition of the bracket, by using the symbol "|" that means "or." In MR1, we construct r_f by completely decomposing such bracketed sub-expressions in r_s. For example, if r_s contains a sub-expression "$[abcdef]$" or "$[a-f]$," then we have "$a|b|c|d|e|f$" instead in r_f.
- **MR2: Splitting the bracketed structure**
  Consider the bracketed regular expression "$[x_1 \ldots x_n]$" or "$[x_1-x_n]$" again. Another equivalent format is to split the bracket into two brackets, by using symbol "|." In MR2, r_f is constructed by replacing such sub-expression in r_s with this equivalent. For example, if r_s contains a sub-expression "$[abcdef]$" or "$[a-f]$," then we have "$[ab]|[c-f]$" instead in r_f.
- **MR3: Bracketing simple characters**
  Apart from the reserved words with special meanings, any simple character in a regular expression should be equivalent to itself enclosed by the brackets, that is, "a" is equivalent to "$[a]$" if a is not a reserved word. In MR3, r_f is constructed by replacing some simple characters in r_s with their bracketed formats. For example, if r_s contains a sub-expression "abc," then we have "$[a][b][c]$" instead in r_f.

(2) **Program *SeqMap* and its MRs.**

SeqMap is a Short Sequence Mapping Tool in bioinformatics [4]. Given a long reference string t and a set of short strings $P=\{p_1, \ldots, p_k\}$, which consist of characters taken from the set of alphabets $\{A, T, G, C\}$, as well as a maximum number of mismatches e, *SeqMap* finds all substrings in t such that

---

[1]In our experiments, we consider the default C locale, where characters are sorted according to their ASCII codes.

each substring has an edit distance equal to or less than e against some $p_i \in P$. Here edit distance refers to the number of operations required to transform one string to another. The valid edit operations include substitution, insertion, and deletion. If a p_i matches any substring in t with not more than e edit distance, it is said to be mappable, otherwise unmappable. *SeqMap* outputs all the mappable p_i with optional information including the mapped location in t, the mapped substring of t, the edit distance of this mapping, etc.

Obviously, for each mappable p_i, it may be not difficult to verify the correctness of the printed mapping information. However, it is very expensive to check whether *SeqMap* has printed all the possible matching positions in t, or whether all the unmappable p_i are indeed truly unmappable to t. In other words, soundness of the output is easy to verify, but not the completeness of the output. Therefore, *SeqMap* also has the oracle problem.

For this program, we construct MRs by modifying t and e while keeping P unchanged. Given a set of short strings $P=\{p_1, \ldots, p_k\}$, a long reference string t_s, and the specified maximum of mismatches e_s as a source test case, the output of the set of all mappable p_i is denoted as M_s. Obviously, $M_s \subseteq P$. And the set of unmappable p_i is $U_s=(P \backslash M_s)$. Let us denote the long reference string and the specified maximum of mismatches in the follow-up test case as t_f and e_f, respectively. The sets of mappable and unmappable short strings produced by the follow-up test case are referred to as M_f and U_f, respectively.

- **MR1: Concatenating some elements of P to t_s** Suppose P_1 is a non-empty subset of P. t_f is constructed by concatenating all elements in P_1 to the end of t_s one by one. As a consequence,

  - For any $p_i \in M_s$, we have $p_i \in M_f$. Thus, $M_s \subseteq M_f$.
  - For each $p_i \in (M_s \cap P_1)$, the follow-up test case should have at least one additional mapping location in t_f.
  - Each $p_i \in (U_s \cap P_1)$ should be mapped at least once in t_f, that is, we have $p_i \in M_f$.

- **MR2: Deleting a substring in t_s**
  In this MR, t_f is constructed from t_s by deleting an arbitrary portion of strings at either the head or the end of t_s. As a consequence, for any $p_i \in U_s$, we have $p_i \in U_f$. Therefore, $U_s \subseteq U_f$.

- **MR3: Changing of e_s**
  In this MR, $t_f=t_s$. And e_f can be set to either greater or smaller than e_s.

  - Consider the case that $0 \leq e_f < e_s$. Then, we have $M_f \subseteq M_s$.
  - Consider the case that $0 \leq e_s < e_f$. Then, we have $M_s \subseteq M_f$.

Given n source test cases $T^S=\{t_1^S, t_2^S, \ldots, t_n^S\}$, it is easy to obtain follow-up test cases through each of the above MRs (denoted as $T^{MR_i}=\{t_1^{MR_i}, t_2^{MR_i}, \ldots, t_n^{MR_i}\}$ for MR_i). By executing both T^S and T^{MR_i}, we are able to collect the $e\_slice(t_j^S)$ and $e\_slice(t_j^{MR_i})$ for each pair of source and follow-up test cases. By following

Definition 7.3.1, it is always possible to obtain the *e_mslice* for each pair of source of follow-up test cases. Furthermore, by checking their outputs against MR_i, we are able to have their metamorphic testing results as *violation* or *non-violation*.

Up to now, it will be straightforward to form the matrix shown in Fig. 7.1, as well as to finish the remained steps for ranking all program statements.

References

1. Baker J, Thornton J (2004) Software engineering challenges in bioinformatics. In: Proceedings of the 26th international conference on software engineering, pp 12–15. https://doi.org/10.1109/ICSE.2004.1317409
2. Chen TY, Cheung SC, Yiu SM (1998) Metamorphic testing: a new approach for generating next test cases. Techncal Report HKUST-CS98-01, Department of Computer Science, Hong Kong University
3. Chen TY, Kuo FC, Tse TH, Zhou Z (2003) Metamorphic testing and beyond. In: Proceedings of the 11th annual international workshop on software technology and engineering practice, pp 94–100. https://doi.org/10.1109/STEP.2003.18
4. Jiang H, Wong WH (2008) SeqMap: mapping massive amount of oligonucleotides to the genome. Bioinformatics 24(20):2395–2396, https://doi.org/10.1093/bioinformatics/btn429
5. Weyuker EJ (1982) On testing non-testable programs. Comput J 25(4):465–470. https://doi.org/10.1093/comjnl/25.4.465
6. Xie X, Ho JWK, Murphy C, Kaiser G, Xu B, Chen TY (2009) Application of metamorphic testing to supervised classifiers. In: Proceedings of the 9th international conference on quality software, pp 135–144. https://doi.org/10.1109/QSIC.2009.26
7. Xie X, Ho JWK, Murphy C, Kaiser G, Xu B, Chen TY (2011) Testing and validating machine learning classifiers by metamorphic testing. J Syst Softw 84(4):544–558
8. Xie X, Wong WE, Chen TY, Xu B (2013) Metamorphic slice: an application in spectrum-based fault localization. Inf Softw Technol 55(5):866–879. https://doi.org/10.1016/j.infsof.2012.08.008

Chapter 8
Spectrum-Based Fault Localization for Multiple Faults

Abstract Currently, SBFL for multi-fault scenario has received more and more attention. In general, there are two common ways to perform multiple fault localization, namely, sequential debugging (SD) and parallel debugging (PD). SD executes the program against all failed test cases and all passed test cases in test suite and achieves the goal of eliminating all faults through localizing one fault at a time iteratively. PD separates failed test cases and forms a number of fault-focused clusters (each cluster is aimed at one fault); each fault-focused cluster merged with passed cases can be executed simultaneously for parallel fault localization. Because of the lower cost and higher efficiency, PD is more widely investigated. This chapter will introduce two important techniques of PD, namely, P2 and MSeer.

8.1 Challenge in SBFL: Dealing with Multiple Faults

A lot of studies around spectrum-based fault localization (SBFL) have been carried out by a significant number of researchers in recent years, but many of them are based on single-fault environment, that is, assuming that there is only one fault in the program, which is obviously inconsistent with reality. In single-fault environment, all failed executions are unquestionably caused by one fault in the program; however, in multiple-fault environment, various failed executions have different origins, i.e., the due-to relationship between a failure and its corresponding fault(s) is not defined in advance, which would decrease the effectiveness of the fault localization technique.

In general, there are two common ways to solve the problem of multiple-fault localization: sequential debugging (SD) and parallel debugging (PD). SD executes the program PG against all failed test cases and all passed test cases in test suite TS and achieves the goal of eliminating all faults through localizing one fault at a time iteratively. PD separates failed test cases and forms a number of fault-focused clusters (each cluster is aimed at one fault); each fault-focused cluster merged with passed cases can be executed simultaneously for parallel fault localization.

8.2 Sequential Debugging

Sequential debugging is also known as One-Bug-at-A-time (OBA) method. It is one of the easiest methods for solving software multiple-fault localization. OBA starts working when the failures of PG are observed through a given TS. After localizing and fixing the first fault according to the ranking, the debugger will continue to execute fixed PG against TS and observe the execution result of TS and then re-localize and move faults again until no execution failure has been detected. Figure 8.1 demonstrates the OBA process using SBFL technique.

The detailed steps for OBA using SBFL are as follows:

- Step 1: Execute PG against TS and collect spectrum information simultaneously;
- Step 2: Input the spectrum information into the risk evaluation formula, and then generate the statement risk value ranking;
- Step 3: Localize and fix one fault according to the ranking;
- Step 4: Repeat Step 1 - Step 3 until no execution failure can be observed.

It is obvious that One-Bug-at-a-time is actually a sequential debugging method that starts the next localization process only after the current fault has been fixed. Its evident drawbacks are high costs of time and low efficiency. In addition, OBA is often used for fault localization based on Bayesian reasoning. However, Wong et al. pointed out that this is equivalent to assuming that multiple faults existing in the program are independent of one another [12]; in other words, the possible correlation between the various faults is disregarded, which is certainly incompatible with the actual situation. Debroy and Wong investigated the interaction between multiple faults and found that there were mainly two conditions: destructive interference and constructive interference [2]. The former refers to the execution failure, which is triggered when a fault exists on its own, while the execution result becomes correct when another fault is injected. The latter means that if there is a certain fault on its own, the execution failure will not be triggered; only if there are two faults at the same time, the program will show abnormality. The conclusion

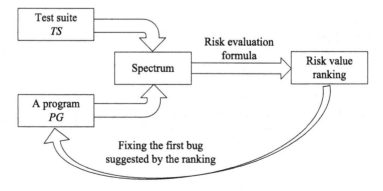

Fig. 8.1 An overview of OBA using SBFL technique

in [2] confirms that destructive interference is more common than constructive interference.

In summary, OBA not only has the disadvantages of high cost and low efficiency, but is also often inconsistent with the practice. In order to overcome these drawbacks of sequential debugging, many researchers are focusing on parallel debugging and proposing a series of new methods.

8.3 Parallel Debugging

The basic principle of multiple-fault parallel localization is to separate failed cases in TS according to the similarity measure, so that the failed cases in the same cluster are triggered by the same fault, and different faults cause the failed cases between different clusters. That is, the multiple-fault is isolated into multiple single-faults by generating a number of $fault\text{-}focused$ clusters, which reduces the complexity of the problem.

Clustering is a recognized scheme for separating failed test cases in TS. A proper representation of failed cases is the prerequisite for a high-quality clustering process. There are mainly two types of vectors widely used to represent failed test cases. One is the path of execution coverage, which is a binary vector transformed from the trace of execution of a failed test case on PG (similar to the representation used to compute T-proximity). Another is the risk value ranking, which is a statement risk value list generated by the risk evaluation formula using spectrum information gathered from a failed case and all passed cases on PG (similar to the representation used to compute R-proximity). Liu et al. have proved that the latter has higher efficiency than the former [7], because the fault could trigger execution failure in various ways. In other words, even failed cases caused by the same fault can have different paths of execution, which is obviously ignored by the representation using execution path coverage.

Several researchers have proposed a series of SBFL techniques for multiple-fault based on R-proximity accordingly, such as P2 proposed by Jones et al. [5] and MSeer proposed by Gao et al. [3].

8.3.1 Approach: P2

In [5], two parallel debugging techniques for multiple-fault were proposed: P1 based on behavior models and fault localizing results and P2 based on fault localizing results only. However, [1, 3, 4] all pointed out that Jones et al. did not provide technical details for the clustering process of P1 in [5], so P1 was hard to reproduce. In contrast, P2 has been used by many researchers for experimental comparison. The detail of P2 is shown in Fig. 8.2.

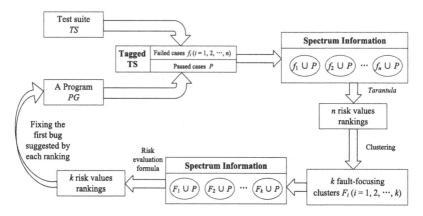

Fig. 8.2 An overview of P2

The detailed steps for P2 are as follows:

- Step 1: Execute PG against TS and gather coverage information, and then divide the test cases in TS into failed cases and passed cases by comparing between expected outputs and target outputs;
- Step 2: Merge n failed cases with all passed cases to obtain n sub-TSs;
- Step 3: Input spectrum information of n sub-TSs into $Tarantula$ to generate n rankings;
- Step 4: Conduct hierarchical clustering on n rankings according to Jaccard distance to generate k fault-focused clusters;
- Step 5: Merge the failed cases in k clusters with all passed cases, respectively, to obtain k fault-focused TSs;
- Step 6: Input the spectrum information of these fault-focused TSs into the risk evaluation formula to generate k rankings;
- Step 7: Localize and fix the first fault suggested by each ranking;
- Step 8: Repeat Step 1 - Step7 until there is no detectable execution failure.

The distance measure and clustering algorithm in Step 4 is the core of P2 and will directly affect the effectiveness of this technique. The following describes the Jaccard distance metric and hierarchical clustering algorithm involved in P2.

For rankings r_i and r_j that represent two failed test cases, Jaccard computes the distance (between 0 and 1) by taking the ratio of the intersection of the two rankings to the union.

$$Jaccard(r_i, r_j) = 1 - \frac{|r_i \cap r_j|}{|r_i \cup r_j|}$$

where $|r_i \cap r_j|$ and $|r_i \cup r_j|$ are the size of the intersection and the union of r_i and r_j, respectively. To determine whether the relationship between two rankings is $similar$ or $not\ similar$, P2 sets the $threshold = 0.5$; r_i and r_j are not considered to be *similar* unless the distance between them is smaller than the *threshold*. It should be noted that when measuring Jaccard distance, P2 only considers the top *MostSusp* part of the rankings and the rest are deemed *not of interest*.

Jones et al. first presented the definition of *Expense* to evaluate the effectiveness of P2.

$$Expense = \frac{rank\ of\ fault}{size\ of\ program} \times 100\%$$

Based on *Expense*, Jones et al. further proposed two metrics, *total developer expense* (denote as *D*) and *critical expense to a failure-free program* (denote as *FF*), to conduct a more comprehensive evaluation of P2.

$$D = \sum_{i=1}^{|faults|} Expense_i$$

$$FF = \sum_{i=1}^{|iterations|} max\{Expense_f | f \text{ is a subtask at iteration } i\}$$

D is used to evaluate total costs paid by all debuggers to localize all faults in the program in a sequential or parallel manner and captures essential quantities such as employee-hours and payroll-expense; *FF* is used to evaluate the cost to deliver a failure-free program and can be used to calculate the time required to complete the multiple-fault localization task. Jones et al. also pointed out that the failure-free program does not mean the program has no fault, only that it does not present abnormalities against the current TS.

8.3.2   Approach: MSeer

Gao et al., who are also interested in SBFL for multiple faults, argue that P2 has two apparent disadvantages. Firstly, all statements are assigned the same weight by Jaccard distance metric; in other words, no attention is paid to enhancing the contribution of high-risk value statements when measuring the distance between rankings, so that the distance between rankings cannot be measured accurately. Secondly, the hierarchical clustering algorithm does not have strong effectiveness in the process of multiple-fault localization. Thus, Gao et al. proposed a parallel debugging method [3], MSeer, which is shown in Fig. 8.3.

There are three fundamental differences in MSeer compared with P2: the use of Crosstab in ranking generation, the revised Kendall tau metric in distance metric, and the K-medoids algorithm based on the estimated number of clusters and the initial medoids.

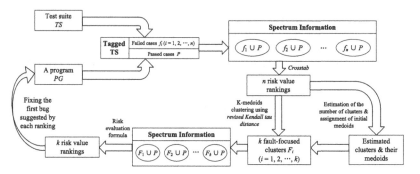

Fig. 8.3 An overview of MSeer

(1) **Crosstab: A risk evaluation formula.** Crosstab is a risk evaluation technique proposed by Wong et al. [11], which uses spectrum information to construct a crosstab for each statement by computing the chi-square statistic and the coefficient of contingency [8]. Crosstab is given by

$$\chi^2 = \frac{(a_{ef} - E_{ef})^2}{E_{ef}} + \frac{(a_{ep} - E_{ep})^2}{E_{ep}} + \frac{(a_{nf} - E_{nf})^2}{E_{nf}} + \frac{(a_{np} - E_{np})^2}{E_{np}}$$

Crosstab will first calculate φ for each statement to determine its association with failed and passed execution and then use φ to decide if the statement should be assigned χ^2, $-\chi^2$, or 0. Please refer to [11] for more details on this technique.

(2) **Revised Kendall tau distance.** By counting the number of discordant pairs between two rankings of the same size [6], Kendall tau computes distance between them directly. Gao et al. pointed out that although Kendall tau distance has been successfully used in other research such as information retrieval [10] and bioengineering [9], it cannot be directly applied to SBFL since it assigns identical weight to all statements. Kendall tau distance metric is given by

$$D(x, y) = \sum_{1 \leq i < j \leq m} K\left(s_i, s_j\right)$$

where x and y are two rankings to be compared and m is the number of statements included in each ranking. In the original Kendall tau, $K(s_i, s_j)$ is defined as follows:

- If $(x(s_i) - x(s_j)) \times (y(s_i) - y(s_j)) < 0$, $K(s_i, s_j) = 1$;
- Otherwise, $K(s_i, s_j) = 0$

where $x(s_i)$, $x(s_j)$, $y(s_i)$, $y(s_j)$ represent the positions of statement s_i and statement s_j in ranking x and ranking y, respectively. Thus, even though s_i and s_j are at a very low position in the ranking, their contribution to the distance would still be the same as that of the statement at a high position in the ranking, which is contrary to Gao et al.'s viewpoint. To solve this problem, Gao et al. proposed a revised Kendall tau distance:

$$D'(x, y) = \sum_{1 \leq i < j \leq N} K'\left(s_i, s_j\right)$$

where x and y are two rankings to be compared and N is the number of statements included in each ranking. In the revised Kendall tau, $K'(s_i, s_j)$ is defined as follows:

- If $(x(s_i) - x(s_j)) \times (y(s_i) - y(s_j)) < 0$, $K'(s_i, s_j) = x(s_i)^{-1} + x(s_j)^{-1} + y(s_i)^{-1} + y(s_j)^{-1}$;
- Otherwise, $K'(s_i, s_j) = 0$

Obviously, the greater is the risk value of s_i and s_j, the higher the value of $K'(s_i, s_j)$, which met Gao et al.'s preceding concept.

(3) **Estimation of the number of clusters and assignment of initial medoids.** As a mainstream clustering algorithm, K-medoids is applied in many fields including software fault localization. One limitation of K-medoids is that the number of clusters must be determined in advance. Gao et al. argue that in software multiple-fault localization, the number of clusters generated by clustering is expected to be the same as the number of faults in PG; however, the latter is often not known by the debugger, which limits the application of K-medoids in SBFL for multiple-fault. On the other hand, Gao et al. also mention that K-medoids has another obvious drawback, i.e., in the process of minimizing the cost function, K-medoids has to examine each individual possible combination of rankings as initial medoids, which will make the cost significantly higher. To eliminate this limitation, Gao et al. proposed an approach for estimating the number of clusters and determining the initial medoids simultaneously for K-medoids [3], as mentioned below.

Execute PG against TS, supposing there are n failed test cases in TS. Merge these n failed cases and all passed cases P respectively to form n sub-TSs, then input sub-TSs into Crosstab to generate n rankings $\{r_1, r_2, r_3, \ldots, r_n\}$.

- Step 1: Compute the revised Kendall tau distance between r_i and r_j ($1 \leq i, j \leq n$);
- Step 2: Assign the potential value P_i^0 for each ranking r_i ($1 \leq i \leq n$);

$$P_i^0 = \sum_{j=1}^{n} e^{-\alpha D'(r_i, r_j)^2}$$

where $\alpha = 4 / \psi^2$ and ψ equals to half of the 5 percent winsorized mean of the distance between two distinct rankings.

- Step 3: Once P_i^θ is computed, select the ranking with the highest potential value as R^θ, and set its potential value as M^θ (randomly choose one when multiple rankings share the same highest potential value). Set R^0 as the first cluster medoid and then proceed to Step 4. The criterion for determining the number of clusters is provided by the algorithm in Algorithm 5.[1]

Algorithm 5: A criterion to determine the number of clusters [3]

---

if $M^\theta > \bar{\varepsilon} M^0$ ($\bar{\varepsilon} = 0.5$ and $\underline{\varepsilon} = 0.15$)
  Accept R^θ as a cluster medoid and go to Step 4
else if $M^\theta < \underline{\varepsilon} M^0$
  Reject R^θ and stop
else
  Let D'_{min} = [shortest of the revisited Kendall-tau distance between R^θ and all previously found cluster medoids]
  if $\frac{D'_{min}}{\psi} + \frac{M^\theta}{M^0} \geq 1$
    Accept R^θ as a cluster medoid and go to Step 4
  else
    (1) Reject R^θ and set the potential value of M^θ to 0
    (2) Select the ranking with the next highest potential value as R^θ and assign its potential value as the new M^θ
    (3) Repeat the stopping criterion from the beginning
  end if
end if

- Step 4: Update the potential value of each ranking, and then go back to Step 3.

$$P_i^{\theta+1} = P_i^\theta - M^\theta \times e^{-\beta D'(r_i, R^\theta)^2}$$

where $\beta = 16 / 9\psi^2$.

It follows that MSeer primarily improves Step 3 and Step 4 of P2. The detailed process of MSeer is not described here due to the remaining steps of these two techniques being essentially identical.

References

1. Abreu R, Zoeteweij P, Gemund AJV (2009) Spectrum-based multiple fault localization. In: Proceedings of the 24th IEEE/ACM international conference on automated software engineering, pp 88–99. https://doi.org/10.1109/ASE.2009.25

---

2. Debroy V, Wong WE (2009) Insights on fault interference for programs with multiple bugs. In: Proceedings of the 20th international symposium on software reliability engineering, pp 165–174. https://doi.org/10.1109/ISSRE.2009.14

3. Gao R, Wong WE (2019) Mseer-an advanced technique for locating multiple bugs in parallel. IEEE Trans Softw Eng 45(3):301–318. https://doi.org/10.1109/TSE.2017.2776912

4. Hogerle W, Steimann F, Frenkel M (2014) More debugging in parallel. In: Proceedings of the 25th international symposium on software reliability engineering, pp 133–143. https://doi.org/10.1109/ISSRE.2014.29

5. Jones JA, Bowring JF, Harrold MJ (2007) Debugging in parallel. In: Proceedings of ACM SIGSOFT international symposium on software testing and analysis, pp 16–26. https://doi.org/10.1145/1273463.1273468

6. Kendall MG, Gibbons J (1990) Rank correlation method. Biometrika 11 en 12. https://doi.org/10.2307/2333282

7. Liu C, Zhang X, Han J (2008) A systematic study of failure proximity. IEEE Trans Softw Eng 34(6):826–843. https://doi.org/10.1109/TSE.2008.66

8. Sahoo S, Criswell J, Geigle C, Adve V (2013) Using likely invariants for automated software fault localization. ACM SIGPLAN Not 48(4):139–152. https://doi.org/10.1145/2490301.2451131

9. Sengupta D, Bandyopadhyay S, Maulik U (2010) A novel measure for evaluating an ordered list: application in microrna target prediction. In: Proceedings of the international symposium on biocomputing, pp 1–7. https://doi.org/10.1145/1722024.1722067

10. Teevan J, Dumais S, Horvitz E (2007) Characterizing the value of personalizing search. In: Proceedings of the 30th international ACM sigir conference on research & development in information retrieval, pp 757–758. https://doi.org/10.1145/1277741.1277894

11. Wong WE, Debroy V, Xu D (2012) Towards better fault localization: a crosstab-based statistical approach. IEEE Trans Syst Man Cybern 42(3):378–396. https://doi.org/10.1109/TSMCC.2011.2118751

12. Wong WE, Gao R, Li Y, Abreu R, Wotawa F (2016) A survey on software fault localization. IEEE Trans Softw Eng 42(8):707–740. https://doi.org/10.1109/TSE.2016.2521368

Chapter 9
Conclusion

Abstract This chapter concludes the entire book. This book provides the first comprehensive guide to fundamental theories in SBFL while addressing some emerging challenges in this area. We believe that these contents will be helpful to readers who want to gain deep understanding of SBFL.

SBFL has been extensively investigated, due to its simplicity and effectiveness. There exist a large number of studies that design new risk evaluation formulas. But in this book, instead of introducing various formulas, we choose to cover some fundamental and essential theories, as well as some emerging and challenging research directions, in SBFL.

The first part of this book (from Chaps. 2, 3, 4, 5, and 6) is about the essential theories of SBFL. In fact, with the emerging of many risk evaluation formulas, it is very important to know which one should be used when SBFL is applied. Most of the related studies have adopted an empirical approach, and hence the reported results are strongly dependent on the experimental setup. Though researchers used various approaches to control the threats to validity in order to provide a more fair comparison of various formulas, the empirical investigations can hardly be considered as sufficiently comprehensive due to the huge number of possible combinations of various factors in SBFL.

To tackle this problem, we have proposed the first theoretical framework that reveals the intrinsic and definite relations among any arbitrary formulas, without any empirical analysis [5]. Further, we worked together with Prof. Shin Yoo from Korea Advanced Institute of Science and Technology, Prof. Mark Harman from University College London, and Prof. Tsong Yueh Chen and Dr. Fei-Ching Kuo from Swinburne University, to prove the sufficient and necessary condition to the general maximality [6]. Besides, we have extended the framework to analyze hybrid SBFL methods [4]. These theories have been elaborated in detail in this book. An ACM Computing Review on our framework [5] points out that:

> There is an unhealthy tendency toward empirical studies in software testing and debugging research. Researchers use hypothesis testing to determine whether their proposal is better than that of their predecessors. Reviewers demand more subject programs and larger test pools for further validation. It is refreshing to see that the authors of this paper do not

X. Xie, B. Xu, *Essential Spectrum-based Fault Localization*,
https://doi.org/10.1007/978-981-33-6179-9_9

simply rely on empirical studies, but prove mathematically whether various proposals have hit their mark. [3]

The second part of this book (from Chaps. 7 to 8) introduces some emerging challenges in SBFL. The first challenge is known as the "oracle problem." We have proposed a concept of "metamorphic slice" to address this problem in SBFL, and this technique is introduced in Chap. 7. The second challenge is to deal with multiple faults. In this book, we introduce two approaches, namely, P2 (proposed by Jones et al. [2]) and Mseer (proposed by Gao et al. [1]), in Chap. 8.

References

1. Gao R, Wong WE (2019) Mseer-an advanced technique for locating multiple bugs in parallel. IEEE Trans Softw Eng 45(3):301–318. https://doi.org/10.1109/TSE.2017.2776912
2. Jones JA, Bowring JF, Harrold MJ (2007) Debugging in parallel. In: Proceedings of ACM SIGSOFT international symposium on software testing and analysis, pp 16–26. https://doi.org/10.1145/1273463.1273468
3. THTse (2013) Review on "a theoretical analysis of the risk evaluation formulas for spectrum-based fault localization". Technical Report CR141805 (1402-0139), ACM Comput Rev.
4. Tu J, Xie X, Chen TY, Xu B (2019) On the analysis of spectrum based fault localization using hitting sets. J Syst Softw 147:106–123. https://doi.org/10.1016/j.jss.2018.10.013
5. Xie X, Chen TY, Kuo FC, Xu B (2013) A theoretical analysis of the risk evaluation formulas for spectrum-based fault localization. ACM Trans Softw Eng Methodol 22(4):31:1–31:40. https://doi.org/10.1145/2522920.2522924
6. Yoo S, Xie X, Kuo FC, Chen TY, Harman M (2017) Human competitiveness of genetic programming in spectrum-based fault localisation: theoretical and empirical analysis. ACM Trans Softw Eng Methodol 26(1):4:1–4:30. https://doi.org/10.1145/3078840

Appendix A
S_B^R, S_F^R, and S_A^R for All Formulas

In Chap. 2, we have presented the set divisions for all formulas in Table 2.1, in the form of propositions. In this appendix, we will demonstrate and prove the complete construction process of S_B^R, S_F^R, and S_A^R in these propositions.

(1) **Op2**

As stated in Table 2.1, formula Op2 is defined as follows.

$$R_{Op2}(s_i) = a_{ef}^i - \frac{a_{ep}^i}{a_{ep}^i + a_{np}^i + 1}$$

It follows from Lemmas 2.3.1 and 2.3.2 that

$$R_{Op2}(s_i) = a_{ef}^i - \frac{a_{ep}^i}{P+1}$$

$$R_{Op2}(s_f) = F - \frac{a_{ep}^f}{P+1}$$

Then, after Definition 2.2.1, we have

$$S_B^{Op2} = \{s_i | a_{ef}^i - \frac{a_{ep}^i}{P+1} > F - \frac{a_{ep}^f}{P+1}, 1 \le i \le n\} \tag{A.1}$$

$$S_F^{Op2} = \{s_i | a_{ef}^i - \frac{a_{ep}^i}{P+1} = F - \frac{a_{ep}^f}{P+1}, 1 \le i \le n\} \tag{A.2}$$

$$S_A^{Op2} = \{s_i | a_{ef}^i - \frac{a_{ep}^i}{P+1} < F - \frac{a_{ep}^f}{P+1}, 1 \le i \le n\} \tag{A.3}$$

© The Author(s), under exclusive license to Springer Nature Singapore Pte Ltd. 2021
X. Xie, B. Xu, *Essential Spectrum-based Fault Localization*,
https://doi.org/10.1007/978-981-33-6179-9

We are going to prove that S_B^{Op2}, S_F^{Op2}, and S_A^{Op2} are equal to the above sets X^1 in (2.1), Y^1 in (2.2), and Z^1 in (2.3), respectively.

First, we will prove $S_B^{Op2}=X^1$. For any s_i, we have either $(a_{ef}^i<F)$ or $(a_{ef}^i=F)$. Therefore, S_B^{Op2} defined in (A.1) can be rewritten as

$$S_B^{Op2}=\{s_i\,|\,a_{ef}^i<F \text{ and } a_{ef}^i-\frac{a_{ep}^i}{P+1} > F-\frac{a_{ep}^f}{P+1}, 1\leq i\leq n\}$$

$$\cup\{s_i\,|\,a_{ef}^i=F \text{ and } a_{ef}^i-\frac{a_{ep}^i}{P+1} > F-\frac{a_{ep}^f}{P+1}, 1\leq i\leq n\}$$

Consider the case that $a_{ef}^i<F$. Then, we have $F-a_{ef}^i\geq 1$. Since $a_{ep}^i-a_{ep}^f\leq P$ after Lemma 2.3.1, we have $\frac{a_{ep}^f-a_{ep}^i}{P+1}<1$. Thus,

$$\left(a_{ef}^i-\frac{a_{ep}^i}{P+1}\right)-\left(F-\frac{a_{ep}^f}{P+1}\right)=\frac{a_{ep}^f-a_{ep}^i}{P+1}-\left(F-a_{ef}^i\right)<0$$

Therefore, we have

$$a_{ef}^i-\frac{a_{ep}^i}{P+1}<F-\frac{a_{ep}^f}{P+1}$$

which is contradictory to

$$a_{ef}^i-\frac{a_{ep}^i}{P+1}>F-\frac{a_{ep}^f}{P+1}$$

Thus,

$$\{s_i\,|\,a_{ef}^i<F \text{ and } a_{ef}^i-\frac{a_{ep}^i}{P+1}>F-\frac{a_{ep}^f}{P+1}, 1\leq i\leq n\}=\emptyset$$

Hence, we have

$$S_B^{Op2}=\{s_i\,|\,a_{ef}^i=F \text{ and } a_{ef}^i-\frac{a_{ep}^i}{P+1} > F-\frac{a_{ep}^f}{P+1}, 1\leq i\leq n\} \qquad (A.4)$$

- Assume that $s_i\in S_B^{Op2}$. After (A.4), we have

$$a_{ef}^i=F \text{ and } a_{ef}^i-\frac{a_{ep}^i}{P+1}>F-\frac{a_{ep}^f}{P+1}$$

Since $a_{ef}^i = F$, $a_{ef}^i - \frac{a_{ep}^i}{P+1} > F - \frac{a_{ep}^f}{P+1}$ becomes $\frac{a_{ep}^f - a_{ep}^i}{P+1} > 0$. Since $P+1 > 0$,

then $\frac{a_{ep}^f - a_{ep}^i}{P+1} > 0$ implies $a_{ep}^f - a_{ep}^i > 0$. Thus, $s_i \in X^1$ after (2.1). Therefore,

$S_B^{Op2} \subseteq X^1$.

- Assume that $s_i \in X^1$. After (2.1), we have

$$a_{ef}^i = F \text{ and } a_{ep}^f - a_{ep}^i > 0$$

Since $a_{ef}^i = F$, we have

$$a_{ep}^f - a_{ep}^i = (a_{ep}^f - a_{ep}^i) - (P+1)(F - a_{ef}^i) > 0$$

Since $P+1 > 0$, $(a_{ep}^f - a_{ep}^i) - (P+1)(F - a_{ef}^i) > 0$ implies $a_{ef}^i - \frac{a_{ep}^i}{P+1}$

$> F - \frac{a_{ep}^f}{P+1}$. Thus, $s_i \in S_B^{Op2}$ after (A.4). Therefore, $X^1 \subseteq S_B^{Op2}$.

In summary, we have proved that $S_B^{Op2} = X^1$.

Similarly, we can prove that $S_F^{Op2} = Y^1$.

Next, we are going to prove $S_A^{Op2} = Z^1$. S_A^{Op2} defined in (A.3) can be rewritten as

$$S_A^{Op2} = \{s_i \mid a_{ef}^i < F \text{ and } a_{ef}^i - \frac{a_{ep}^i}{P+1} < F - \frac{a_{ep}^f}{P+1}, 1 \le i \le n\}$$

$$\cup \{s_i \mid a_{ef}^i = F \text{ and } a_{ef}^i - \frac{a_{ep}^i}{P+1} < F - \frac{a_{ep}^f}{P+1}, 1 \le i \le n\}$$

Consider the case that $a_{ef}^i < F$. As shown in the above proof of $S_B^{Op2} = X^1$,

$a_{ef}^i < F$ implies $a_{ef}^i - \frac{a_{ep}^i}{P+1} < F - \frac{a_{ep}^f}{P+1}$. Thus, $(a_{ef}^i < F$ and $a_{ef}^i - \frac{a_{ep}^i}{P+1} < F - \frac{a_{ep}^f}{P+1})$

is logically equivalent to $a_{ef}^i < F$. Therefore, S_A^{Op2} becomes

$$\{s_i \mid a_{ef}^i < F, 1 \le i \le n\} \cup \{s_i \mid a_{ef}^i = F \text{ and } a_{ef}^i - \frac{a_{ep}^i}{P+1} < F - \frac{a_{ep}^f}{P+1}, 1 \le i \le n\}$$

Similar to the proof of $S_B^{Op2} = X^1$, $\{s_i \mid a_{ef}^i = F$ and $a_{ef}^i - \frac{a_{ep}^i}{P+1} < F - \frac{a_{ep}^f}{P+1}, 1 \le i \le n\}$

can be proved to be equivalent to $\{s_i \mid a_{ef}^i = F$ and $a_{ep}^f - a_{ep}^i < 0, 1 \le i \le n\}$.

Therefore,

$$S_A^{Op2} = \{s_i \mid (a_{ef}^i < F) \text{ or } (a_{ef}^i = F \text{ and } a_{ep}^f - a_{ep}^i < 0), 1 \le i \le n\} = Z^1$$

In conclusion, we have proved that $S_B^{Op2} = X^1$, $S_F^{Op2} = Y^1$, and $S_A^{Op2} = Z^1$.

(2) **Jaccard**

As stated in Table 2.1, formula Jaccard is defined as follows.

$$R_J(s_i) = \frac{a_{ef}^i}{a_{ef}^i + a_{nf}^i + a_{ep}^i}$$

It follows from Lemmas 2.3.1 and 2.3.2 that $R_J(s_i)=\frac{a_{ef}^i}{F+a_{ep}^i}$ and $R_J(s_f)=\frac{F}{F+a_{ep}^f}$. Then, after Definition 2.2.1, we have

$$S_B^J=\{s_i\,|\,\frac{a_{ef}^i}{F+a_{ep}^i} > \frac{F}{F+a_{ep}^f}, 1\leq i\leq n\} \tag{A.5}$$

$$S_F^J=\{s_i\,|\,\frac{a_{ef}^i}{F+a_{ep}^i} = \frac{F}{F+a_{ep}^f}, 1\leq i\leq n\} \tag{A.6}$$

$$S_A^J=\{s_i\,|\,\frac{a_{ef}^i}{F+a_{ep}^i} < \frac{F}{F+a_{ep}^f}, 1\leq i\leq n\} \tag{A.7}$$

We are going to prove that the above sets S_B^J, S_F^J, and S_A^J are equal to the following sets, X^2, Y^2, and Z^2, respectively.

$$X^2=\{s_i\,|\,a_{ef}^i > 0 \text{ and } 1+\frac{a_{ep}^f}{F} - \frac{F}{a_{ef}^i} - \frac{a_{ep}^i}{a_{ef}^i} > 0, 1\leq i\leq n\} \tag{A.8}$$

$$Y^2=\{s_i\,|\,a_{ef}^i > 0 \text{ and } 1+\frac{a_{ep}^f}{F} - \frac{F}{a_{ef}^i} - \frac{a_{ep}^i}{a_{ef}^i} = 0, 1\leq i\leq n\} \tag{A.9}$$

$$Z^2=\{s_i\,|\,(a_{ef}^i = 0) \text{ or } (a_{ef}^i > 0 \text{ and } 1+\frac{a_{ep}^f}{F} - \frac{F}{a_{ef}^i} - \frac{a_{ep}^i}{a_{ef}^i} < 0), 1\leq i\leq n\} \tag{A.10}$$

First, we will prove $S_B^J=X^2$. For any s_i, we have either $(a_{ef}^i=0)$ or $(a_{ef}^i>0)$. Therefore, S_B^J in (A.5) can be rewritten as

$$S_B^J=\{s_i\,|\,a_{ef}^i=0 \text{ and } \frac{a_{ef}^i}{F+a_{ep}^i} > \frac{F}{F+a_{ep}^f}, 1\leq i\leq n\}$$

$$\cup\{s_i\,|\,a_{ef}^i>0 \text{ and } \frac{a_{ef}^i}{F+a_{ep}^i} > \frac{F}{F+a_{ep}^f}, 1\leq i\leq n\}$$

Consider the case that $(a_{ef}^i=0)$. Since $F>0$ and $(F+a_{ep}^f)>0$ after Lemma 2.3.1, we have $\dfrac{a_{ef}^i}{F+a_{ep}^i}=\dfrac{0}{F+a_{ep}^i}=0<\dfrac{F}{F+a_{ep}^f}$, which is contradictory to $\dfrac{a_{ef}^i}{F+a_{ep}^i}>\dfrac{F}{F+a_{ep}^f}$. Thus,

$$\{s_i\,|\,a_{ef}^i=0 \text{ and } \frac{a_{ef}^i}{F+a_{ep}^i}>\frac{F}{F+a_{ep}^f},\ 1\le i\le n\}=\emptyset$$

Hence, we have

$$S_B^J = \{s_i\,|\,a_{ef}^i>0 \text{ and } \frac{a_{ef}^i}{F+a_{ep}^i}>\frac{F}{F+a_{ep}^f},\ 1\le i\le n\} \qquad (\text{A}.11)$$

- Assume that $s_i\in S_B^J$. It follows from (A.11) that $(a_{ef}^i>0$ and $\dfrac{a_{ef}^i}{F+a_{ep}^i}>\dfrac{F}{F+a_{ep}^f})$. Since $a_{ef}^i>0$, $F>0$, $(F+a_{ep}^i)>0$ (after Lemma 2.3.1), and $(F+a_{ep}^f)>0$ (after Lemma 2.3.1), $\dfrac{a_{ef}^i}{F+a_{ep}^i}>\dfrac{F}{F+a_{ep}^f}$ implies $\dfrac{F+a_{ep}^i}{a_{ef}^i}<\dfrac{F+a_{ep}^f}{F}$. After rearranging the terms, we have $1+\dfrac{a_{ep}^f}{F}-\dfrac{F}{a_{ef}^i}-\dfrac{a_{ep}^i}{a_{ef}^i}>0$. Thus, $s_i\in X^2$ after (A.8). Therefore, $S_B^J\subseteq X^2$.

- Assume that $s_i\in X^2$. After (A.8), we have $(a_{ef}^i>0$ and $1+\dfrac{a_{ep}^f}{F}-\dfrac{F}{a_{ef}^i}-\dfrac{a_{ep}^i}{a_{ef}^i}>0)$. After rearranging the terms, $1+\dfrac{a_{ep}^f}{F}-\dfrac{F}{a_{ef}^i}-\dfrac{a_{ep}^i}{a_{ef}^i}>0$ becomes $\dfrac{F+a_{ep}^i}{a_{ef}^i}<\dfrac{F+a_{ep}^f}{F}$, which implies $\dfrac{a_{ef}^i}{F+a_{ep}^i}>\dfrac{F}{F+a_{ep}^f}$ after $a_{ef}^i>0$, $F>0$, $(F+a_{ep}^i)>0$, and $(F+a_{ep}^f)>0$. It follows from (A.11) that $s_i\in S_B^J$. Therefore, $X^2\subseteq S_B^J$.

In summary, we have proved that $S_B^J=X^2$.
Similarly, we can prove that $S_F^J=Y^2$.
Next, we are going to prove $S_A^J=Z^2$. S_A^J in (A.7) can be rewritten as

$$S_A^J=\{s_i\,|\,a_{ef}^i=0 \text{ and } \frac{a_{ef}^i}{F+a_{ep}^i}<\frac{F}{F+a_{ep}^f},\ 1\le i\le n\}$$

$$\cup\{s_i\,|\,a_{ef}^i>0 \text{ and } \frac{a_{ef}^i}{F+a_{ep}^i}<\frac{F}{F+a_{ep}^f},\ 1\le i\le n\}$$

Consider the case $(a_{ef}^i=0)$, which implies $\dfrac{a_{ef}^i}{F+a_{ep}^i}=0<\dfrac{F}{F+a_{ep}^f}$. Thus, $(a_{ef}^i=0$ and $\dfrac{a_{ef}^i}{F+a_{ep}^i}<\dfrac{F}{F+a_{ep}^f})$ is logically equivalent to $(a_{ef}^i=0)$. Therefore, S_A^J becomes

$$\{s_i|a_{ef}^i=0, 1\le i\le n\}\cup\{s_i|a_{ef}^i>0 \text{ and } \dfrac{a_{ef}^i}{F+a_{ep}^i}<\dfrac{F}{F+a_{ep}^f}, 1\le i\le n\}$$

Similar to the proof of $S_B^J=X^2$, we can prove

$$\{s_i|a_{ef}^i>0 \text{ and } \dfrac{a_{ef}^i}{F+a_{ep}^i}<\dfrac{F}{F+a_{ep}^f}, 1\le i\le n\}$$

$$=\{s_i|a_{ef}^i>0 \text{ and } 1+\dfrac{a_{ep}^f}{F}-\dfrac{F}{a_{ef}^i}-\dfrac{a_{ep}^i}{a_{ef}^i}<0, 1\le i\le n\}$$

Therefore,

$$S_A^J=\{s_i|(a_{ef}^i=0) \text{ or } (a_{ef}^i>0 \text{ and } 1+\dfrac{a_{ep}^f}{F}-\dfrac{F}{a_{ef}^i}-\dfrac{a_{ep}^i}{a_{ef}^i}<0), 1\le i\le n\}$$

$$=Z^2$$

In conclusion, we have proved that $S_B^J=X^2$, $S_F^J=Y^2$, and $S_A^J=Z^2$.

(3) **Anderberg**

As stated in Table 2.1, formula Anderberg is defined as

$$R_{An}(s_i) = \dfrac{a_{ef}^i}{a_{ef}^i + 2(a_{nf}^i + a_{ep}^i)}$$

It follows from Lemmas 2.3.1 and 2.3.2 that $R_{An}(s_i)=\dfrac{a_{ef}^i}{2F-a_{ef}^i+2a_{ep}^i}$ and $R_{An}(s_f)=\dfrac{F}{F+2a_{ep}^f}$. Then, after Definition 2.2.1, we have

$$S_B^{An} = \{s_i|\dfrac{a_{ef}^i}{2F - a_{ef}^i + 2a_{ep}^i} > \dfrac{F}{F + 2a_{ep}^f}, 1\le i\le n\} \qquad (A.12)$$

$$S_F^{An} = \{s_i|\dfrac{a_{ef}^i}{2F - a_{ef}^i + 2a_{ep}^i} = \dfrac{F}{F + 2a_{ep}^f}, 1\le i\le n\} \qquad (A.13)$$

$$S_A^{An} = \{s_i|\dfrac{a_{ef}^i}{2F - a_{ef}^i + 2a_{ep}^i} < \dfrac{F}{F + 2a_{ep}^f}, 1\le i\le n\} \qquad (A.14)$$

We are going to prove that S_B^{An}, S_F^{An}, and S_A^{An} are equal to the above sets X^2 in (A.8), Y^2 in (A.9), and Z^2 in (A.10), respectively.

First, we will prove $S_B^{An}=X^2$. For any s_i, we have either $(a_{ef}^i=0)$ or $(a_{ef}^i>0)$. Therefore, S_B^{An} in (A.12) can be rewritten as

$$S_B^{An}=\{s_i\,|\,a_{ef}^i=0 \text{ and } \frac{a_{ef}^i}{2F-a_{ef}^i+2a_{ep}^i}>\frac{F}{F+2a_{ep}^f}, 1\leq i\leq n\}$$

$$\cup\{s_i\,|\,a_{ef}^i>0 \text{ and } \frac{a_{ef}^i}{2F-a_{ef}^i+2a_{ep}^i}>\frac{F}{F+2a_{ep}^f}, 1\leq i\leq n\}$$

Consider the case that $(a_{ef}^i=0)$. Since $F>0$ and $(F+2a_{ep}^f)>0$ after Lemma 2.3.1, we have $\frac{a_{ef}^i}{2F-a_{ef}^i+2a_{ep}^i}=0<\frac{F}{F+2a_{ep}^f}$, which is contradictory to $\frac{a_{ef}^i}{2F-a_{ef}^i+2a_{ep}^i}>\frac{F}{F+2a_{ep}^f}$. Thus,

$$\{s_i\,|\,a_{ef}^i=0 \text{ and } \frac{a_{ef}^i}{2F-a_{ef}^i+2a_{ep}^i}>\frac{F}{F+2a_{ep}^f}, 1\leq i\leq n\}=\emptyset$$

Hence we have

$$S_B^{An} = \{s_i\,|\,a_{ef}^i>0 \text{ and } \frac{a_{ef}^i}{2F - a_{ef}^i + 2a_{ep}^i} > \frac{F}{F + 2a_{ep}^f}, 1\leq i\leq n\} \qquad \text{(A.15)}$$

- Assume that $s_i\in S_B^{An}$. After (A.15), we have

$$a_{ef}^i>0 \text{ and } \frac{a_{ef}^i}{2F - a_{ef}^i + 2a_{ep}^i} > \frac{F}{F + 2a_{ep}^f}$$

Since $a_{ef}^i>0$, $F>0$, $(2F-a_{ef}^i+2a_{ep}^i)>0$, and $(F+2a_{ep}^f)>0$ (after Lemma 2.3.1), $\frac{a_{ef}^i}{2F-a_{ef}^i+2a_{ep}^i}>\frac{F}{F+2a_{ep}^f}$ implies $\frac{2F-a_{ef}^i+2a_{ep}^i}{a_{ef}^i}<\frac{F+2a_{ep}^f}{F}$. After rearranging the terms, we have

$$1+\frac{a_{ep}^f}{F}-\frac{F}{a_{ef}^i}-\frac{a_{ep}^i}{a_{ef}^i}>0$$

It follows from (A.8) that $s_i\in X^2$. Therefore, $S_B^{An}\subseteq X^2$.

- Assume that $s_i \in X^2$. After (A.8), we have ($a_{ef}^i > 0$ and $1 + \frac{a_{ep}^f}{F} - \frac{F}{a_{ef}^i} - \frac{a_{ep}^i}{a_{ef}^i} > 0$).

  After rearranging the terms, $1 + \frac{a_{ep}^f}{F} - \frac{F}{a_{ef}^i} - \frac{a_{ep}^i}{a_{ef}^i} > 0$ becomes $\frac{2F - a_{ef}^i + 2a_{ep}^i}{a_{ef}^i} < \frac{F + 2a_{ep}^f}{F}$, which implies $\frac{a_{ef}^i}{2F - a_{ef}^i + 2a_{ep}^i} > \frac{F}{F + 2a_{ep}^f}$ after $a_{ef}^i > 0$, $F > 0$, $(F + 2a_{ep}^f) > 0$, and $(2F - a_{ef}^i + 2a_{ep}^i) > 0$. Then, we have $s_i \in S_B^{An}$ after (A.15). Therefore, $X^2 \subseteq S_B^{An}$.

In summary, we have proved that $S_B^{An} = X^2$.

Similarly, we can prove that $S_F^{An} = Y^2$.

Next, we are going to prove $S_A^{An} = Z^2$. S_A^{An} defined in (A.14) can be rewritten as follows.

$$S_A^{An} = \{s_i \mid a_{ef}^i = 0 \text{ and } \frac{a_{ef}^i}{2F - a_{ef}^i + 2a_{ep}^i} < \frac{F}{F + 2a_{ep}^f}, 1 \le i \le n\}$$

$$\cup \{s_i \mid a_{ef}^i > 0 \text{ and } \frac{a_{ef}^i}{2F - a_{ef}^i + 2a_{ep}^i} < \frac{F}{F + 2a_{ep}^f}, 1 \le i \le n\}$$

Consider the case ($a_{ef}^i = 0$), which implies $\frac{a_{ef}^i}{2F - a_{ef}^i + 2a_{ep}^i} = 0 < \frac{F}{F + 2a_{ep}^f}$. Thus, $\left(a_{ef}^i = 0 \text{ and } \frac{a_{ef}^i}{2F - a_{ef}^i + 2a_{ep}^i} < \frac{F}{F + 2a_{ep}^f}\right)$ is logically equivalent to ($a_{ef}^i = 0$). Therefore, S_A^{An} becomes

$$\{s_i \mid a_{ef}^i = 0, 1 \le i \le n\} \cup \{s_i \mid a_{ef}^i > 0 \text{ and } \frac{a_{ef}^i}{2F - a_{ef}^i + 2a_{ep}^i} < \frac{F}{F + 2a_{ep}^f}, 1 \le i \le n\}$$

Similar to the proof of $S_B^{An} = X^2$, we can prove

$$\{s_i \mid a_{ef}^i > 0 \text{ and } \frac{a_{ef}^i}{2F - a_{ef}^i + 2a_{ep}^i} < \frac{F}{F + 2a_{ep}^f}, 1 \le i \le n\}$$

$$= \{s_i \mid a_{ef}^i > 0 \text{ and } 1 + \frac{a_{ep}^f}{F} - \frac{F}{a_{ef}^i} - \frac{a_{ep}^i}{a_{ef}^i} < 0, 1 \le i \le n\}$$

Therefore, we have

$$S_A^{An} = \{s_i \mid (a_{ef}^i = 0) \text{ or } (a_{ef}^i > 0 \text{ and } 1 + \frac{a_{ep}^f}{F} - \frac{F}{a_{ef}^i} - \frac{a_{ep}^i}{a_{ef}^i} < 0), 1 \le i \le n\}$$

$$= Z^2$$

In conclusion, we have proved that $S_B^{An} = X^2$, $S_F^{An} = Y^2$, and $S_A^{An} = Z^2$.

(4) Sørensen-Dice

As stated in Table 2.1, formula Sørensen-Dice is defined as follows.

$$R_{SD}(s_i) = \frac{2a_{ef}^i}{2a_{ef}^i + a_{nf}^i + a_{ep}^i}$$

It follows from Lemmas 2.3.1 and 2.3.2 that $R_{SD}(s_i)=\frac{2a_{ef}^i}{a_{ef}^i+a_{ep}^i+F}$ and $R_{SD}(s_f)=\frac{2F}{2F+a_{ep}^f}$. Then, after Definition 2.2.1, we have

$$S_B^{SD} = \{s_i \mid \frac{2a_{ef}^i}{a_{ef}^i+a_{ep}^i + F} > \frac{2F}{2F+a_{ep}^f}, 1\leq i \leq n\} \tag{A.16}$$

$$S_F^{SD} = \{s_i \mid \frac{2a_{ef}^i}{a_{ef}^i+a_{ep}^i + F} = \frac{2F}{2F+a_{ep}^f}, 1\leq i \leq n\} \tag{A.17}$$

$$S_A^{SD} = \{s_i \mid \frac{2a_{ef}^i}{a_{ef}^i+a_{ep}^i + F} < \frac{2F}{2F+a_{ep}^f}, 1\leq i \leq n\} \tag{A.18}$$

We are going to prove that S_B^{SD}, S_F^{SD}, and S_A^{SD} are equal to the above sets X^2 in (A.8), Y^2 in (A.9), and Z^2 in (A.10), respectively.

First, we will prove $S_B^{SD}=X^2$. For any s_i, we have either $(a_{ef}^i=0)$ or $(a_{ef}^i>0)$. Therefore, S_B^{SD} in (A.16) can be rewritten as

$$S_B^{SD}=\{s_i \mid a_{ef}^i=0 \text{ and } \frac{2a_{ef}^i}{a_{ef}^i + a_{ep}^i + F} > \frac{2F}{2F + a_{ep}^f}, 1\leq i \leq n\}$$

$$\cup\{s_i \mid a_{ef}^i>0 \text{ and } \frac{2a_{ef}^i}{a_{ef}^i + a_{ep}^i + F} > \frac{2F}{2F + a_{ep}^f}, 1\leq i \leq n\}$$

Consider the case that $(a_{ef}^i=0)$. Since $F>0$ and $(2F+a_{ep}^f)>0$ after Lemma 2.3.1, we have $\frac{2a_{ef}^i}{a_{ef}^i+a_{ep}^i+F}=0<\frac{2F}{2F+a_{ep}^f}$, which is contradictory to $\frac{2a_{ef}^i}{a_{ef}^i+a_{ep}^i+F}>\frac{2F}{2F+a_{ep}^f}$. Thus,

$$\{s_i \mid a_{ef}^i=0 \text{ and } \frac{2a_{ef}^i}{a_{ef}^i + a_{ep}^i + F} > \frac{2F}{2F + a_{ep}^f}, 1\leq i \leq n\}=\emptyset$$

Hence, we have

$$S_B^{SD} = \{s_i \,|\, a_{ef}^i > 0 \text{ and } \frac{2a_{ef}^i}{a_{ef}^i + a_{ep}^i + F} > \frac{2F}{2F + a_{ep}^f}, 1 \le i \le n\} \qquad (A.19)$$

- Assume that $s_i \in S_B^{SD}$. After (A.19), we have

$$a_{ef}^i > 0 \text{ and } \frac{2a_{ef}^i}{a_{ef}^i + a_{ep}^i + F} > \frac{2F}{2F + a_{ep}^f}$$

Since $a_{ef}^i > 0$, $F > 0$, $(a_{ef}^i + a_{ep}^i + F) > 0$, and $(2F + a_{ep}^f) > 0$ (after Lemma 2.3.1), $\frac{2a_{ef}^i}{a_{ef}^i + a_{ep}^i + F} > \frac{2F}{2F + a_{ep}^f}$ implies $\frac{a_{ef}^i + a_{ep}^i + F}{a_{ef}^i} < \frac{2F + a_{ep}^f}{F}$, which can be rearranged as $1 + \frac{a_{ep}^f}{F} - \frac{F}{a_{ef}^i} - \frac{a_{ep}^i}{a_{ef}^i} > 0$. Then, we have $s_i \in X^2$ after (A.8). Therefore, $S_B^{SD} \subseteq X^2$.

- Assume that $s_i \in X^2$. After (A.8), we have $(a_{ef}^i > 0$ and $1 + \frac{a_{ep}^f}{F} - \frac{F}{a_{ef}^i} - \frac{a_{ep}^i}{a_{ef}^i} > 0)$. Obviously, $1 + \frac{a_{ep}^f}{F} - \frac{F}{a_{ef}^i} - \frac{a_{ep}^i}{a_{ef}^i} > 0$ can be rearranged as $\frac{a_{ef}^i + a_{ep}^i + F}{a_{ef}^i} < \frac{2F + a_{ep}^f}{F}$, which implies $\frac{2a_{ef}^i}{a_{ef}^i + a_{ep}^i + F} > \frac{2F}{2F + a_{ep}^f}$ after $a_{ef}^i > 0$, $F > 0$, $(a_{ef}^i + a_{ep}^i + F) > 0$, and $(2F + a_{ep}^f) > 0$. Then, we have $s_i \in S_B^{SD}$ after (A.19). Therefore, $X^2 \subseteq S_B^{SD}$.

In summary, we have proved that $S_B^{SD} = X^2$.
Similarly, we can prove that $S_F^{SD} = Y^2$.
Next, we are going to prove $S_A^{SD} = Z^2$. S_A^{SD} in (A.18) can be rewritten as follows.

$$S_A^{SD} = \{s_i \,|\, a_{ef}^i = 0 \text{ and } \frac{2a_{ef}^i}{a_{ef}^i + a_{ep}^i + F} < \frac{2F}{2F + a_{ep}^f}, 1 \le i \le n\}$$

$$\cup \{s_i \,|\, a_{ef}^i > 0 \text{ and } \frac{2a_{ef}^i}{a_{ef}^i + a_{ep}^i + F} < \frac{2F}{2F + a_{ep}^f}, 1 \le i \le n\}$$

Consider the case $(a_{ef}^i = 0)$, which implies $\frac{2a_{ef}^i}{a_{ef}^i + a_{ep}^i + F} = 0 < \frac{2F}{2F + a_{ep}^f}$. Thus, $(a_{ef}^i = 0$ and $\frac{2a_{ef}^i}{a_{ef}^i + a_{ep}^i + F} < \frac{2F}{2F + a_{ep}^f})$ is logically equivalent to $(a_{ef}^i = 0)$.

Therefore, S_A^{SD} becomes

$$\{s_i | a_{ef}^i = 0,\ 1 \leq i \leq n\} \cup \{s_i | a_{ef}^i > 0 \text{ and } \frac{2a_{ef}^i}{a_{ef}^i + a_{ep}^i + F} < \frac{2F}{2F + a_{ep}^f},\ 1 \leq i \leq n\}$$

Similar to the proof of $S_B^{SD} = X^2$, we can prove

$$\{s_i | a_{ef}^i > 0 \text{ and } \frac{2a_{ef}^i}{a_{ef}^i + a_{ep}^i + F} < \frac{2F}{2F + a_{ep}^f},\ 1 \leq i \leq n\}$$

$$= \{s_i | a_{ef}^i > 0 \text{ and } 1 + \frac{a_{ep}^f}{F} - \frac{F}{a_{ef}^i} - \frac{a_{ep}^i}{a_{ef}^i} < 0,\ 1 \leq i \leq n\}$$

Therefore, we have

$$S_A^{SD} = \{s_i | (a_{ef}^i = 0) \text{ or } (a_{ef}^i > 0 \text{ and } 1 + \frac{a_{ep}^f}{F} - \frac{F}{a_{ef}^i} - \frac{a_{ep}^i}{a_{ef}^i} < 0),\ 1 \leq i \leq n\}$$

$$= Z^2$$

In conclusion, we have proved that $S_B^{SD} = X^2$, $S_F^{SD} = Y^2$, and $S_A^{SD} = Z^2$.

(5) **Dice**

As stated in Table 2.1, formula Dice is defined as

$$R_D(s_i) = \frac{2a_{ef}^i}{a_{ef}^i + a_{nf}^i + a_{ep}^i}$$

It follows from Lemmas 2.3.1 and 2.3.2 that $R_D(s_i) = \frac{2a_{ef}^i}{F + a_{ep}^i}$ and $R_D(s_f) = \frac{2F}{F + a_{ep}^f}$. Then, after Definition 2.2.1, we have

$$S_B^D = \{s_i | \frac{2a_{ef}^i}{F + a_{ep}^i} > \frac{2F}{F + a_{ep}^f},\ 1 \leq i \leq n\} \tag{A.20}$$

$$S_F^D = \{s_i | \frac{2a_{ef}^i}{F + a_{ep}^i} = \frac{2F}{F + a_{ep}^f},\ 1 \leq i \leq n\} \tag{A.21}$$

$$S_A^D = \{s_i | \frac{2a_{ef}^i}{F + a_{ep}^i} < \frac{2F}{F + a_{ep}^f},\ 1 \leq i \leq n\} \tag{A.22}$$

We are going to prove that S_B^D, S_F^D, and S_A^D are equal to the above sets X^2 in (A.8), Y^2 in (A.9), and Z^2 in (A.10), respectively.

First, we will prove $S_B^D = X^2$. For any s_i, we have either $(a_{ef}^i = 0)$ or $(a_{ef}^i > 0)$. Therefore, S_B^D defined in (A.20) can be rewritten as

$$S_B^D = \{s_i \,|\, a_{ef}^i = 0 \text{ and } \frac{2a_{ef}^i}{F + a_{ep}^i} > \frac{2F}{F + a_{ep}^f}, 1 \le i \le n\}$$

$$\cup \{s_i \,|\, a_{ef}^i > 0 \text{ and } \frac{2a_{ef}^i}{F + a_{ep}^i} > \frac{2F}{F + a_{ep}^f}, 1 \le i \le n\}$$

Consider the case that $(a_{ef}^i = 0)$. Since $F > 0$ and $(F + a_{ep}^f) > 0$ after Lemma 2.3.1, we have $\frac{2a_{ef}^i}{F + a_{ep}^i} = 0 < \frac{2F}{F + a_{ep}^f}$, which is contradictory to $\frac{2a_{ef}^i}{F + a_{ep}^i} > \frac{2F}{F + a_{ep}^f}$. Thus,

$$\{s_i \,|\, a_{ef}^i = 0 \text{ and } \frac{2a_{ef}^i}{F + a_{ep}^i} > \frac{2F}{F + a_{ep}^f}, 1 \le i \le n\} = \emptyset$$

Hence, we have

$$S_B^D = \{s_i \,|\, a_{ef}^i > 0 \text{ and } \frac{2a_{ef}^i}{F + a_{ep}^i} > \frac{2F}{F + a_{ep}^f}, 1 \le i \le n\} \qquad (A.23)$$

- Assume that $s_i \in S_B^D$. After (A.23), we have

$$a_{ef}^i > 0 \text{ and } \frac{2a_{ef}^i}{F + a_{ep}^i} > \frac{2F}{F + a_{ep}^f}$$

Since $a_{ef}^i > 0$, $F > 0$, $(F + a_{ep}^i) > 0$, and $(F + a_{ep}^f) > 0$ (after Lemma 2.3.1), we have $\frac{F + a_{ep}^i}{a_{ef}^i} < \frac{F + a_{ep}^f}{F}$ from $\frac{2a_{ef}^i}{F + a_{ep}^i} > \frac{2F}{F + a_{ep}^f}$. After rearranging the terms, $\frac{F + a_{ep}^i}{a_{ef}^i} < \frac{F + a_{ep}^f}{F}$ becomes $1 + \frac{a_{ep}^f}{F} - \frac{F}{a_{ef}^i} - \frac{a_{ep}^i}{a_{ef}^i} > 0$. It follows from (A.8) that $s_i \in X^2$. Therefore, $S_B^D \subseteq X^2$.

- Assume that $s_i \in X^2$. After (A.8), we have

$$a_{ef}^i > 0 \text{ and } 1 + \frac{a_{ep}^f}{F} - \frac{F}{a_{ef}^i} - \frac{a_{ep}^i}{a_{ef}^i} > 0$$

Obviously, $1+\frac{a_{ep}^f}{F}-\frac{F}{a_{ef}^i}-\frac{a_{ep}^i}{a_{ef}^i}>0$ can be rearranged as $\frac{F+a_{ep}^i}{a_{ef}^i}<\frac{F+a_{ep}^f}{F}$, which

implies $\frac{2a_{ef}^i}{F+a_{ep}^i}>\frac{2F}{F+a_{ep}^f}$ after $a_{ef}^i>0$, $F>0$, $(F+a_{ep}^i)>0$, and $(F+a_{ep}^f)>0$.

Then, we have $s_i \in S_B^D$ after (A.23). Therefore, $X^2 \subseteq S_B^D$.

In summary, we have proved that $S_B^D=X^2$.
Similarly, we can prove that $S_F^D=Y^2$.
Next, we are going to prove $S_A^D=Z^2$. S_A^D in (A.22) can be rewritten as follows.

$$2S_A^D=\{s_i|a_{ef}^i=0 \text{ and } \frac{2a_{ef}^i}{F+a_{ep}^i}<\frac{2F}{F+a_{ep}^f}, 1\leq i \leq n\}$$

$$\cup\{s_i|a_{ef}^i>0 \text{ and } \frac{2a_{ef}^i}{F+a_{ep}^i}<\frac{2F}{F+a_{ep}^f}, 1\leq i \leq n\}$$

Consider the case $(a_{ef}^i=0)$, which implies $\frac{2a_{ef}^i}{F+a_{ep}^i}=0<\frac{2F}{F+a_{ep}^f}$. Thus, $(a_{ef}^i=0$

and $\frac{2a_{ef}^i}{F+a_{ep}^i}<\frac{2F}{F+a_{ep}^f})$ is logically equivalent to $(a_{ef}^i=0)$. Therefore, S_A^D becomes

$$\{s_i|a_{ef}^i=0, 1\leq i \leq n\}\cup\{s_i|a_{ef}^i>0 \text{ and } \frac{2a_{ef}^i}{F+a_{ep}^i}<\frac{2F}{F+a_{ep}^f}, 1\leq i \leq n\}$$

Similar to the proof of $S_B^D=X^2$, we can prove

$$\{s_i|a_{ef}^i>0 \text{ and } \frac{2a_{ef}^i}{F+a_{ep}^i}<\frac{2F}{F+a_{ep}^f}, 1\leq i \leq n\}$$

$$=\{s_i|a_{ef}^i>0 \text{ and } 1+\frac{a_{ep}^f}{F}-\frac{F}{a_{ef}^i}-\frac{a_{ep}^i}{a_{ef}^i}<0, 1\leq i \leq n\}$$

Therefore, we have

$$S_A^D=\{s_i|(a_{ef}^i=0) \text{ or } (a_{ef}^i>0 \text{ and } 1+\frac{a_{ep}^f}{F}-\frac{F}{a_{ef}^i}-\frac{a_{ep}^i}{a_{ef}^i}<0), 1\leq i \leq n\}=Z^2$$

In conclusion, we have proved that $S_B^D=X^2$, $S_F^D=Y^2$, and $S_A^D=Z^2$.

(6) **Goodman**

As stated in Table 2.1, formula Goodman is defined as

$$R_G(s_i) = \frac{2a_{ef}^i - a_{nf}^i - a_{ep}^i}{2a_{ef}^i + a_{nf}^i + a_{ep}^i}$$

It follows from Lemmas 2.3.1 and 2.3.2 that $R_G(s_i) = \dfrac{3a_{ef}^i - F - a_{ep}^i}{a_{ef}^i + F + a_{ep}^i}$ and

$R_G(s_f) = \dfrac{2F - a_{ep}^f}{2F + a_{ep}^f}$. Then, after Definition 2.2.1, we have

$$S_B^G = \{s_i \mid \frac{3a_{ef}^i - F - a_{ep}^i}{a_{ef}^i + F + a_{ep}^i} > \frac{2F - a_{ep}^f}{2F + a_{ep}^f}, \ 1 \le i \le n\} \tag{A.24}$$

$$S_F^G = \{s_i \mid \frac{3a_{ef}^i - F - a_{ep}^i}{a_{ef}^i + F + a_{ep}^i} = \frac{2F - a_{ep}^f}{2F + a_{ep}^f}, \ 1 \le i \le n\} \tag{A.25}$$

$$S_A^G = \{s_i \mid \frac{3a_{ef}^i - F - a_{ep}^i}{a_{ef}^i + F + a_{ep}^i} < \frac{2F - a_{ep}^f}{2F + a_{ep}^f}, \ 1 \le i \le n\} \tag{A.26}$$

We are going to prove that S_B^G, S_F^G, and S_A^G are equal to the above sets X^2 in (A.8), Y^2 in (A.9), and Z^2 in (A.10), respectively.

First, we will prove $S_B^G = X^2$. For any s_i, we have either $(a_{ef}^i = 0)$ or $(a_{ef}^i > 0)$. Therefore, S_B^G defined in (A.24) can be rewritten as

$$S_B^G = \{s_i \mid a_{ef}^i = 0 \text{ and } \frac{3a_{ef}^i - F - a_{ep}^i}{a_{ef}^i + F + a_{ep}^i} > \frac{2F - a_{ep}^f}{2F + a_{ep}^f}, \ 1 \le i \le n\}$$

$$\cup \{s_i \mid a_{ef}^i > 0 \text{ and } \frac{3a_{ef}^i - F - a_{ep}^i}{a_{ef}^i + F + a_{ep}^i} > \frac{2F - a_{ep}^f}{2F + a_{ep}^f}, \ 1 \le i \le n\}$$

Consider the case that $(a_{ef}^i = 0)$. Since $F > 0$, we have $\dfrac{2F - a_{ep}^f}{2F + a_{ep}^f} > -1$. Thus, we have $\dfrac{3a_{ef}^i - F - a_{ep}^i}{a_{ef}^i + F + a_{ep}^i} = -1 < \dfrac{2F - a_{ep}^f}{2F + a_{ep}^f}$, which is contradictory to $\dfrac{3a_{ef}^i - F - a_{ep}^i}{a_{ef}^i + F + a_{ep}^i} > \dfrac{2F - a_{ep}^f}{2F + a_{ep}^f}$.

Thus,

$$\{s_i \mid a_{ef}^i = 0 \text{ and } \frac{3a_{ef}^i - F - a_{ep}^i}{a_{ef}^i + F + a_{ep}^i} > \frac{2F - a_{ep}^f}{2F + a_{ep}^f}, \ 1 \le i \le n\} = \emptyset$$

Hence, we have

$$S_B^G = \{s_i \mid a_{ef}^i > 0 \text{ and } \frac{3a_{ef}^i - F - a_{ep}^i}{a_{ef}^i + F + a_{ep}^i} > \frac{2F - a_{ep}^f}{2F + a_{ep}^f}, \ 1 \le i \le n\} \tag{A.27}$$

• Assume that $s_i \in S_B^G$. After (A.27), we have

$$a_{ef}^i > 0 \text{ and } \frac{3a_{ef}^i - F - a_{ep}^i}{a_{ef}^i + F + a_{ep}^i} > \frac{2F - a_{ep}^f}{2F + a_{ep}^f}$$

After rearranging the terms, $\dfrac{3a_{ef}^i-F-a_{ep}^i}{a_{ef}^i+F+a_{ep}^i}>\dfrac{2F-a_{ep}^f}{2F+a_{ep}^f}$ becomes

$$\frac{4Fa_{ef}^i+4a_{ep}^fa_{ef}^i-4Fa_{ep}^i-4F^2}{(a_{ef}^i+F+a_{ep}^i)(2F+a_{ep}^f)}>0$$

Since $a_{ef}^i>0$ and $F>0$, we have $Fa_{ef}^i>0$. Furthermore, after Lemma 2.3.1 we have $(a_{ef}^i+F+a_{ep}^i)(2F+a_{ep}^f)>0$; thus, $\dfrac{4Fa_{ef}^i+4a_{ep}^fa_{ef}^i-4Fa_{ep}^i-4F^2}{(a_{ef}^i+F+a_{ep}^i)(2F+a_{ep}^f)}>0$ implies $\dfrac{Fa_{ef}^i+a_{ep}^fa_{ef}^i-Fa_{ep}^i-F^2}{Fa_{ef}^i}>0$, which can be rearranged as $1+\dfrac{a_{ep}^f}{F}-\dfrac{F}{a_{ef}^i}-\dfrac{a_{ep}^i}{a_{ef}^i}>0$. Then, we have $s_i\in X^2$ after (A.8). Therefore, $S_B^G\subseteq X^2$.

- Assume that $s_i\in X^2$. After (A.8), we have

$$a_{ef}^i>0 \text{ and } 1+\frac{a_{ep}^f}{F}-\frac{F}{a_{ef}^i}-\frac{a_{ep}^i}{a_{ef}^i}>0$$

Obviously, $1+\dfrac{a_{ep}^f}{F}-\dfrac{F}{a_{ef}^i}-\dfrac{a_{ep}^i}{a_{ef}^i}>0$ can be rearranged as $\dfrac{Fa_{ef}^i+a_{ep}^fa_{ef}^i-Fa_{ep}^i-F^2}{Fa_{ef}^i}>0$. Since $a_{ef}^i>0$, we have $Fa_{ef}^i>0$ because $F>0$. Furthermore, after Lemma 2.3.1, we have

$$(a_{ef}^i+F+a_{ep}^i)(2F+a_{ep}^f)>0$$

Thus $\dfrac{Fa_{ef}^i+a_{ep}^fa_{ef}^i-Fa_{ep}^i-F^2}{Fa_{ef}^i}>0$ implies $\dfrac{4(Fa_{ef}^i+a_{ep}^fa_{ef}^i-Fa_{ep}^i-F^2)}{(a_{ef}^i+F+a_{ep}^i)(2F+a_{ep}^f)}>0$, which can be rearranged as $\dfrac{3a_{ef}^i-F-a_{ep}^i}{a_{ef}^i+F+a_{ep}^i}>\dfrac{2F-a_{ep}^f}{2F+a_{ep}^f}$. Then, we have $s_i\in S_B^G$ after (A.27). Therefore, $X^2\subseteq S_B^G$.

In summary, we have proved that $S_B^G=X^2$.
Similarly, we can prove that $S_F^G=Y^2$.
Next, we are going to prove $S_A^G=Z^2$. S_A^G in (A.26) can be rewritten as follows.

$$S_A^G=\{s_i\,|\,a_{ef}^i=0 \text{ and } \frac{3a_{ef}^i-F-a_{ep}^i}{a_{ef}^i+F+a_{ep}^i}<\frac{2F-a_{ep}^f}{2F+a_{ep}^f}, 1\leq i\leq n\}$$

$$\cup\{s_i\,|\,a_{ef}^i>0 \text{ and } \frac{3a_{ef}^i-F-a_{ep}^i}{a_{ef}^i+F+a_{ep}^i}<\frac{2F-a_{ep}^f}{2F+a_{ep}^f}, 1\leq i\leq n\}$$

Consider the case that $(a_{ef}^i{=}0)$. As shown in the above proof of $S_B^G{=}X^2$, $(a_{ef}^i{=}0)$ implies $\frac{3a_{ef}^i-F-a_{ep}^i}{a_{ef}^i+F+a_{ep}^i}<\frac{2F-a_{ep}^f}{2F+a_{ep}^f}$. Thus, $(a_{ef}^i{=}0$ and $\frac{3a_{ef}^i-F-a_{ep}^i}{a_{ef}^i+F+a_{ep}^i}<\frac{2F-a_{ep}^f}{2F+a_{ep}^f})$ is logically equivalent to $(a_{ef}^i{=}0)$. Therefore, S_A^G becomes

$$\{s_i|a_{ef}^i{=}0,\,1{\leq}i{\leq}n\}\cup\{s_i|a_{ef}^i{>}0 \text{ and } \frac{3a_{ef}^i-F-a_{ep}^i}{a_{ef}^i+F+a_{ep}^i}<\frac{2F-a_{ep}^f}{2F+a_{ep}^f},\,1{\leq}i{\leq}n\}$$

Similar to the proof of $S_B^G{=}X^2$, we can prove

$$\{s_i|a_{ef}^i{>}0 \text{ and } \frac{3a_{ef}^i-F-a_{ep}^i}{a_{ef}^i+F+a_{ep}^i}<\frac{2F-a_{ep}^f}{2F+a_{ep}^f},\,1{\leq}i{\leq}n\}$$

$$={\{s_i|a_{ef}^i{>}0 \text{ and } 1+\frac{a_{ep}^f}{F}-\frac{F}{a_{ef}^i}-\frac{a_{ep}^i}{a_{ef}^i}<0,\,1{\leq}i{\leq}n\}}$$

Therefore, we have

$$S_A^G=\{s_i|(a_{ef}^i{=}0) \text{ or } (a_{ef}^i{>}0 \text{ and } 1+\frac{a_{ep}^f}{F}-\frac{F}{a_{ef}^i}-\frac{a_{ep}^i}{a_{ef}^i}<0),\,1{\leq}i{\leq}n\}$$

$$=Z^2$$

In conclusion, we have proved that $S_B^G{=}X^2$, $S_F^G{=}Y^2$, and $S_A^G{=}Z^2$.

(7) **Tarantula**

As stated in Table 2.1, formula Tarantula is defined as follows.

$$R_T(s_i) = \frac{a_{ef}^i}{a_{ef}^i + a_{nf}^i} \left/ \left(\frac{a_{ef}^i}{a_{ef}^i + a_{nf}^i} + \frac{a_{ep}^i}{a_{ep}^i + a_{np}^i} \right) \right.$$

It follows from Lemmas 2.3.1 and 2.3.2 that $R_T(s_i){=}\frac{a_{ef}^i}{F}/(\frac{a_{ef}^i}{F} + \frac{a_{ep}^i}{P})$ and $R_T(s_f){=}1/(1 + \frac{a_{ep}^f}{P})$. Then, after Definition 2.2.1, we have

$$S_B^T = \{s_i|\frac{a_{ef}^i}{F}/(\frac{a_{ef}^i}{F}+\frac{a_{ep}^i}{P})>1/(1+\frac{a_{ep}^f}{P}),\,1{\leq}i{\leq}n\} \tag{A.28}$$

$$S_F^T = \{s_i|\frac{a_{ef}^i}{F}/(\frac{a_{ef}^i}{F}+\frac{a_{ep}^i}{P})=1/(1+\frac{a_{ep}^f}{P}),\,1{\leq}i{\leq}n\} \tag{A.29}$$

$$S_A^T = \{s_i|\frac{a_{ef}^i}{F}/(\frac{a_{ef}^i}{F}+\frac{a_{ep}^i}{P})<1/(1+\frac{a_{ep}^f}{P}),\,1{\leq}i{\leq}n\} \tag{A.30}$$

We are going to prove that S_B^T, S_F^T, and S_A^T are equal to the following sets X^3, Y^3, and Z^3, respectively.

$$X^3=\{s_i\,|\,a_{ef}^i>0 \text{ and } \frac{a_{ep}^f}{F}-\frac{a_{ep}^i}{a_{ef}^i}>0, 1\leq i\leq n\} \tag{A.31}$$

$$Y^3=\{s_i\,|\,a_{ef}^i>0 \text{ and } \frac{a_{ep}^f}{F}-\frac{a_{ep}^i}{a_{ef}^i}=0, 1\leq i\leq n\} \tag{A.32}$$

$$Z^3=\{s_i\,|\,(a_{ef}^i=0) \text{ or } (a_{ef}^i>0 \text{ and } \frac{a_{ep}^f}{F}-\frac{a_{ep}^i}{a_{ef}^i}<0), 1\leq i\leq n\} \tag{A.33}$$

First, we will prove $S_B^T=X^3$. For any s_i, we have either $(a_{ef}^i=0)$ or $(a_{ef}^i>0)$. Therefore, S_B^T defined in (A.28) can be rewritten as

$$S_B^T=\{s_i\,|\,a_{ef}^i=0 \text{ and } \frac{a_{ef}^i}{F}/(\frac{a_{ef}^i}{F}+\frac{a_{ep}^i}{P})>1/(1+\frac{a_{ep}^f}{P}), 1\leq i\leq n\}$$
$$\cup\{s_i\,|\,a_{ef}^i>0 \text{ and } \frac{a_{ef}^i}{F}/(\frac{a_{ef}^i}{F}+\frac{a_{ep}^i}{P})>1/(1+\frac{a_{ep}^f}{P}), 1\leq i\leq n\}$$

Consider the case that $(a_{ef}^i=0)$. Since $(1+\frac{a_{ep}^f}{P})>0$ after Lemma 2.3.1, we have $\frac{a_{ef}^i}{F}/(\frac{a_{ef}^i}{F}+\frac{a_{ep}^i}{P})=0<1/(1+\frac{a_{ep}^f}{P})$, which is contradictory to $\frac{a_{ef}^i}{F}/(\frac{a_{ef}^i}{F}+\frac{a_{ep}^i}{P})>1/(1+\frac{a_{ep}^f}{P})$. Thus,

$$\{s_i\,|\,a_{ef}^i=0 \text{ and } \frac{a_{ef}^i}{F}/(\frac{a_{ef}^i}{F}+\frac{a_{ep}^i}{P})>1/(1+\frac{a_{ep}^f}{P}), 1\leq i\leq n\}=\emptyset$$

Hence, we have

$$S_B^T=\{s_i\,|\,a_{ef}^i>0 \text{ and } \frac{a_{ef}^i}{F}/(\frac{a_{ef}^i}{F}+\frac{a_{ep}^i}{P})>1/(1+\frac{a_{ep}^f}{P}), 1\leq i\leq n\} \tag{A.34}$$

- Assume that $s_i\in S_B^T$. After (A.34), we have

$$a_{ef}^i>0 \text{ and } \frac{a_{ef}^i}{F}/(\frac{a_{ef}^i}{F}+\frac{a_{ep}^i}{P})>1/(1+\frac{a_{ep}^f}{P})$$

Since $a_{ep}^i>0$, we have $\frac{F}{a_{ef}^i}>0$ because $F>0$. Then,

$\frac{a_{ef}^i}{F}/(\frac{a_{ef}^i}{F}+\frac{a_{ep}^i}{P})>1/(1+\frac{a_{ep}^f}{P})$ implies $1/(1+\frac{a_{ep}^i}{P}\frac{F}{a_{ef}^i})>1/(1+\frac{a_{ep}^f}{P})$. Further-

more, it follows from $\frac{F}{a_{ef}^i}>0$ and Lemma 2.3.1 that $(1+\frac{a_{ep}^i}{P}\frac{F}{a_{ef}^i})>0$ and

$(1+\frac{a_{ep}^f}{P})>0$; then, we have $\frac{a_{ep}^i}{P}\frac{F}{a_{ef}^i}<\frac{a_{ep}^f}{P}$. Since $\frac{P}{F}>0$, after multiplying each

side by $\frac{P}{F}$ and rearranging the terms, we have $\frac{a_{ep}^f}{F}-\frac{a_{ep}^i}{a_{ef}^i}>0$. Then, we have

$s_i\in X^3$ after (A.31). Therefore, $S_B^T\subseteq X^3$.

- Assume that $s_i\in X^3$. After (A.31), we have

$$a_{ef}^i>0 \text{ and } \frac{a_{ep}^f}{F}-\frac{a_{ep}^i}{a_{ef}^i}>0$$

Since $\frac{F}{P}>0$, after rearranging the terms and multiplying each side by $\frac{F}{P}$,

$\frac{a_{ep}^f}{F}-\frac{a_{ep}^i}{a_{ef}^i}>0$ becomes $\frac{a_{ep}^i}{P}\frac{F}{a_{ef}^i}<\frac{a_{ep}^f}{P}$. Since $a_{ef}^i>0$, $F>0$, $\frac{a_{ep}^i}{P}>0$, and $\frac{a_{ep}^f}{P}>0$,

$\frac{a_{ep}^i}{P}\frac{F}{a_{ef}^i}<\frac{a_{ep}^f}{P}$ implies $\frac{a_{ef}^i}{F}/(\frac{a_{ef}^i}{F}+\frac{a_{ep}^i}{P})>1/(1+\frac{a_{ep}^f}{P})$. Then, we have $s_i\in S_B^T$

after (A.34). Therefore, $X^3\subseteq S_B^T$.

In summary, we have proved that $S_B^T=X^3$.
Similarly, we can prove that $S_F^T=Y^3$.
Next, we are going to prove $S_A^T=Z^3$. S_A^T in (A.30) can be rewritten as follows.

$$S_A^T=\{s_i\,|\,a_{ef}^i=0 \text{ and } \frac{a_{ef}^i}{F}/(\frac{a_{ef}^i}{F}+\frac{a_{ep}^i}{P})<1/(1+\frac{a_{ep}^f}{P}),\,1\leq i\leq n\}$$

$$\cup\{s_i\,|\,a_{ef}^i>0 \text{ and } \frac{a_{ef}^i}{F}/(\frac{a_{ef}^i}{F}+\frac{a_{ep}^i}{P})<1/(1+\frac{a_{ep}^f}{P}),\,1\leq i\leq n\}$$

Consider the case $(a_{ef}^i=0)$, which implies $\frac{a_{ef}^i}{F}/(\frac{a_{ef}^i}{F}+\frac{a_{ep}^i}{P})=0<1/(1+\frac{a_{ep}^f}{P})$.

Thus, $(a_{ef}^i=0$ and $\frac{a_{ef}^i}{F}/(\frac{a_{ef}^i}{F}+\frac{a_{ep}^i}{P})<1/(1+\frac{a_{ep}^f}{P}))$ is logically equivalent to

$(a_{ef}^i=0)$. Therefore, S_A^T becomes

$$\{s_i\,|\,a_{ef}^i=0,\,1\leq i\leq n\}\cup\{s_i\,|\,a_{ef}^i>0 \text{ and } \frac{a_{ef}^i}{F}/(\frac{a_{ef}^i}{F}+\frac{a_{ep}^i}{P})<1/(1+\frac{a_{ep}^f}{P}),\,1\leq i\leq n\}$$

Similar to the proof of $S_B^T = X^3$, we can prove

$$\{s_i | a_{ef}^i > 0 \text{ and } \frac{a_{ef}^i}{F} / (\frac{a_{ef}^i}{F} + \frac{a_{ep}^i}{P}) < 1/(1 + \frac{a_{ep}^f}{P}), 1 \leq i \leq n\}$$

$$= \{s_i | a_{ef}^i > 0 \text{ and } \frac{a_{ep}^f}{F} - \frac{a_{ep}^i}{a_{ef}^i} < 0, 1 \leq i \leq n\}$$

Therefore, we have

$$S_A^T = \{s_i | (a_{ef}^i = 0) \text{ or } (a_{ef}^i > 0 \text{ and } \frac{a_{ep}^f}{F} - \frac{a_{ep}^i}{a_{ef}^i} < 0), 1 \leq i \leq n\}$$

$$= Z^3$$

In conclusion, we have proved that $S_B^T = X^3$, $S_F^T = Y^3$, and $S_A^T = Z^3$.

(8) **q_e**

As stated in Table 2.1, formula q_e is defined as follows.

$$R_{QE}(s_i) = \frac{a_{ef}^i}{a_{ef}^i + a_{ep}^i}$$

It follows from Lemma 2.3.2 that $R_{QE}(s_f) = \frac{F}{F + a_{ep}^f}$. Then, after Definition 2.2.1, we have

$$S_B^{QE} = \{s_i | \frac{a_{ef}^i}{a_{ef}^i + a_{ep}^i} > \frac{F}{F + a_{ep}^f}, 1 \leq i \leq n\} \tag{A.35}$$

$$S_F^{QE} = \{s_i | \frac{a_{ef}^i}{a_{ef}^i + a_{ep}^i} = \frac{F}{F + a_{ep}^f}, 1 \leq i \leq n\} \tag{A.36}$$

$$S_A^{QE} = \{s_i | \frac{a_{ef}^i}{a_{ef}^i + a_{ep}^i} < \frac{F}{F + a_{ep}^f}, 1 \leq i \leq n\} \tag{A.37}$$

We are going to prove that S_B^{QE}, S_F^{QE}, and S_A^{QE} are equal to the above sets X^3 in (A.31), Y^3 in (A.32), and Z^3 in (A.33), respectively.

First, we will prove $S_B^{QE} = X^3$. For any s_i, we have either $(a_{ef}^i = 0)$ or $(a_{ef}^i > 0)$. Therefore, S_B^{QE} in (A.35) can be rewritten as

$$S_B^{QE} = \{s_i | a_{ef}^i = 0 \text{ and } \frac{a_{ef}^i}{a_{ef}^i + a_{ep}^i} > \frac{F}{F + a_{ep}^f}, 1 \leq i \leq n\}$$

$$\cup \{s_i | a_{ef}^i > 0 \text{ and } \frac{a_{ef}^i}{a_{ef}^i + a_{ep}^i} > \frac{F}{F + a_{ep}^f}, 1 \leq i \leq n\}$$

Consider the case that (a_{ef}^i=0). Since $F>0$ and $(F+a_{ep}^f)>0$ after Lemma 2.3.1, we have $\dfrac{a_{ef}^i}{a_{ef}^i+a_{ep}^i}=0<\dfrac{F}{F+a_{ep}^f}$, which is contradictory to $\dfrac{a_{ef}^i}{a_{ef}^i+a_{ep}^i}>\dfrac{F}{F+a_{ep}^f}$. Thus,

$$\{s_i|a_{ef}^i=0 \text{ and } \frac{a_{ef}^i}{a_{ef}^i+a_{ep}^i}>\frac{F}{F+a_{ep}^f}, 1\le i\le n\}=\emptyset$$

Hence, we have

$$S_B^{QE}=\{s_i|a_{ef}^i>0 \text{ and } \frac{a_{ef}^i}{a_{ef}^i+a_{ep}^i}>\frac{F}{F+a_{ep}^f}, 1\le i\le n\} \tag{A.38}$$

- Assume that $s_i\in S_B^{QE}$. After (A.38), we have

$$a_{ef}^i>0 \text{ and } \frac{a_{ef}^i}{a_{ef}^i+a_{ep}^i}>\frac{F}{F+a_{ep}^f}$$

Since $a_{ef}^i>0$, $F>0$, we have $1/(1+\frac{a_{ep}^i}{a_{ef}^i})>1/(1+\frac{a_{ep}^f}{F})$ from $\frac{a_{ef}^i}{a_{ef}^i+a_{ep}^i}>\frac{F}{F+a_{ep}^f}$. Furthermore, since $\frac{a_{ep}^i}{a_{ef}^i}>0$ and $\frac{a_{ep}^f}{F}>0$ after $a_{ef}^i>0$, $F>0$ and Lemma 2.3.1, $1/(1+\frac{a_{ep}^i}{a_{ef}^i})>1/(1+\frac{a_{ep}^f}{F})$ implies $\frac{a_{ep}^f}{F}-\frac{a_{ep}^i}{a_{ef}^i}>0$. Then, we have $s_i\in X^3$ after (A.31). Therefore, $S_B^{QE}\subseteq X^3$.

- Assume that $s_i\in X^3$. After (A.31), we have

$$a_{ef}^i>0 \text{ and } \frac{a_{ep}^f}{F}-\frac{a_{ep}^i}{a_{ef}^i}>0$$

Obviously, $\frac{a_{ep}^f}{F}-\frac{a_{ep}^i}{a_{ef}^i}>0$ can be rewritten as $\frac{a_{ep}^i}{a_{ef}^i}<\frac{a_{ep}^f}{F}$. Since $\frac{a_{ep}^i}{a_{ef}^i}>0$ and $\frac{a_{ep}^f}{F}>0$ after $a_{ef}^i>0$, $F>0$ and Lemma 2.3.1, $\frac{a_{ep}^i}{a_{ef}^i}<\frac{a_{ep}^f}{F}$ implies $1/(1+\frac{a_{ep}^i}{a_{ef}^i})>1/(1+\frac{a_{ep}^f}{F})$. Furthermore, we have $\frac{a_{ef}^i}{a_{ef}^i+a_{ep}^i}>\frac{F}{F+a_{ep}^f}$ because $a_{ef}^i>0$ and $F>0$. Then, we have $s_i\in S_B^{QE}$ after (A.38). Therefore, $X^3\subseteq S_B^{QE}$.

In summary, we have proved that $S_B^{QE}=X^3$.

Similarly, we can prove that $S_F^{QE}=Y^3$.

Next, we are going to prove $S_A^{QE}=Z^3$. S_A^{QE} in (A.37) can be rewritten as follows.

$$S_A^{QE}=\{s_i|a_{ef}^i=0 \text{ and } \frac{a_{ef}^i}{a_{ef}^i+a_{ep}^i}<\frac{F}{F+a_{ep}^f}, 1\le i\le n\}$$

$$\cup\{s_i|a_{ef}^i>0 \text{ and } \frac{a_{ef}^i}{a_{ef}^i+a_{ep}^i}<\frac{F}{F+a_{ep}^f}, 1\le i\le n\}$$

Consider the case ($a_{ef}^i=0$), which implies $\frac{a_{ef}^i}{a_{ef}^i+a_{ep}^i}=0<\frac{F}{F+a_{ep}^f}$. Thus, ($a_{ef}^i=0$ and $\frac{a_{ef}^i}{a_{ef}^i+a_{ep}^i}<\frac{F}{F+a_{ep}^f}$) is logically equivalent to ($a_{ef}^i=0$). Therefore, S_A^{QE} becomes

$$\{s_i|a_{ef}^i=0, 1\le i\le n\}\cup\{s_i|a_{ef}^i>0 \text{ and } \frac{a_{ef}^i}{a_{ef}^i+a_{ep}^i}<\frac{F}{F+a_{ep}^f}, 1\le i\le n\}$$

Similar to the proof of $S_B^{QE}=X^3$, $\{s_i|a_{ef}^i>0 \text{ and } \frac{a_{ef}^i}{a_{ef}^i+a_{ep}^i}<\frac{F}{F+a_{ep}^f}, 1\le i\le n\}$ can be proved to be equivalent to $\{s_i|a_{ef}^i>0 \text{ and } \frac{a_{ep}^f}{F}-\frac{a_{ep}^i}{a_{ef}^i}<0, 1\le i\le n\}$.

Therefore, we have

$$S_A^{QE}=\{s_i|(a_{ef}^i = 0) \text{ or } (a_{ef}^i>0 \text{ and } \frac{a_{ep}^f}{F}-\frac{a_{ep}^i}{a_{ef}^i}<0), 1\le i\le n\}$$

$$=Z^3$$

In conclusion, we have proved that $S_B^{QE}=X^3$, $S_F^{QE}=Y^3$, and $S_A^{QE}=Z^3$.

(9) **CBI Inc.**

As stated in Table 2.1, formula CBI Inc. is defined as follows.

$$R_C(s_i) = \frac{a_{ef}^i}{a_{ef}^i + a_{ep}^i} - \frac{a_{ef}^i + a_{nf}^i}{a_{ef}^i + a_{nf}^i + a_{ep}^i + a_{np}^i}$$

It follows from Lemmas 2.3.1 and 2.3.2 that $R_C(s_i) = \dfrac{a_{ef}^i}{a_{ef}^i + a_{ep}^i} - \dfrac{F}{F+P}$ and $R_C(s_f) = \dfrac{F}{F+a_{ep}^f} - \dfrac{F}{F+P}$. Then, after Definition 2.2.1, we have

$$S_B^C = \{ s_i \mid \frac{a_{ef}^i}{a_{ef}^i + a_{ep}^i} - \frac{F}{F+P} > \frac{F}{F+a_{ep}^f} - \frac{F}{F+P}, \ 1 \le i \le n \}$$

$$= \{ s_i \mid \frac{a_{ef}^i}{a_{ef}^i + a_{ep}^i} > \frac{F}{F+a_{ep}^f}, \ 1 \le i \le n \} \tag{A.39}$$

$$S_F^C = \{ s_i \mid \frac{a_{ef}^i}{a_{ef}^i + a_{ep}^i} - \frac{F}{F+P} = \frac{F}{F+a_{ep}^f} - \frac{F}{F+P}, \ 1 \le i \le n \}$$

$$= \{ s_i \mid \frac{a_{ef}^i}{a_{ef}^i + a_{ep}^i} = \frac{F}{F+a_{ep}^f}, \ 1 \le i \le n \} \tag{A.40}$$

$$S_A^C = \{ s_i \mid \frac{a_{ef}^i}{a_{ef}^i + a_{ep}^i} - \frac{F}{F+P} < \frac{F}{F+a_{ep}^f} - \frac{F}{F+P}, \ 1 \le i \le n \}$$

$$= \{ s_i \mid \frac{a_{ef}^i}{a_{ef}^i + a_{ep}^i} < \frac{F}{F+a_{ep}^f}, \ 1 \le i \le n \} \tag{A.41}$$

Obviously, the above sets defined in (A.39), (A.40), and (A.41) are the same as S_B^{QE} in (A.35), S_F^{QE} in (A.36), and S_A^{QE} in (A.37), respectively, and hence are equal to X^3 in (A.31), Y^3 in (A.32), and Z^3 in (A.33), respectively.

(10) **Wong2**

As stated in Table 2.1, formula Wong2 is defined as follows.

$$R_{W2}(s_i) = a_{ef}^i - a_{ep}^i$$

After Lemma 2.3.2 and Definition 2.2.1, by rearranging the terms, we have

$$S_B^{W2} = \{ s_i \mid (a_{ef}^i - F) + (a_{ep}^f - a_{ep}^i) > 0, \ 1 \le i \le n \} \tag{A.42}$$

$$S_F^{W2} = \{ s_i \mid (a_{ef}^i - F) + (a_{ep}^f - a_{ep}^i) = 0, \ 1 \le i \le n \} \tag{A.43}$$

$$S_A^{W2} = \{ s_i \mid (a_{ef}^i - F) + (a_{ep}^f - a_{ep}^i) < 0, \ 1 \le i \le n \} \tag{A.44}$$

(11) **Hamann**

As stated in Table 2.1, formula Hamann is defined as follows.

$$R_{HN}(s_i) = \frac{a_{ef}^i + a_{np}^i - a_{nf}^i - a_{ep}^i}{a_{ef}^i + a_{nf}^i + a_{ep}^i + a_{np}^i}$$

It follows from Lemmas 2.3.1 and 2.3.2 that $R_{HN}(s_i)=\frac{P-F+2a_{ef}^i-2a_{ep}^i}{F+P}$ and $R_{HN}(s_f)=\frac{P+F-2a_{ep}^f}{F+P}$. Then, after Definition 2.2.1, we have

$$S_B^{HN} = \{s_i | \frac{P-F+2a_{ef}^i-2a_{ep}^i}{F+P} > \frac{P+F-2a_{ep}^f}{F+P}, 1\leq i \leq n\} \tag{A.45}$$

$$S_F^{HN} = \{s_i | \frac{P-F+2a_{ef}^i-2a_{ep}^i}{F+P} = \frac{P+F-2a_{ep}^f}{F+P}, 1\leq i \leq n\} \tag{A.46}$$

$$S_A^{HN} = \{s_i | \frac{P-F+2a_{ef}^i-2a_{ep}^i}{F+P} < \frac{P+F-2a_{ep}^f}{F+P}, 1\leq i \leq n\} \tag{A.47}$$

We are going to prove that S_B^{HN}, S_F^{HN}, and S_A^{HN} are equal to the above sets S_B^{W2} in (A.42), S_F^{W2} in (A.43), and S_A^{W2} in (A.44), respectively.
First, we will prove $S_B^{HN}=S_B^{W2}$.

- Assume that $s_i \in S_B^{HN}$. After (A.45), we have

$$\frac{P-F+2a_{ef}^i-2a_{ep}^i}{F+P} > \frac{P+F-2a_{ep}^f}{F+P}$$

Since $F+P>0$, we have

$$P-F+2a_{ef}^i-2a_{ep}^i > P+F-2a_{ep}^f$$

Thus, $(a_{ef}^i-F)+(a_{ep}^f-a_{ep}^i)>0$, and hence $s_i \in S_B^{W2}$ after (A.42). Therefore, $S_B^{HN}\subseteq S_B^{W2}$.

- Assume that $s_i \in S_B^{W2}$. After (A.42), we have

$$(a_{ef}^i-F)+(a_{ep}^f-a_{ep}^i)>0$$

which implies $P-F+2a_{ef}^i-2a_{ep}^i > P+F-2a_{ep}^f$. Since $F+P>0$, we have

$$\frac{P-F+2a_{ef}^i-2a_{ep}^i}{F+P} > \frac{P+F-2a_{ep}^f}{F+P}$$

Then, we have $s_i \in S_B^{HN}$ after (A.45). Therefore, $S_B^{W2}\subseteq S_B^{HN}$.

In summary, we have proved that $S_B^{HN}=S_B^{W2}$.
Similarly, we can prove $S_F^{HN}=S_F^{W2}$ and $S_A^{HN}=S_A^{W2}$.

(12) **Simple Matching**

As stated in Table 2.1, formula Simple Matching is defined as follows.

$$R_{SM}(s_i) = \frac{a_{ef}^i + a_{np}^i}{a_{ef}^i + a_{nf}^i + a_{ep}^i + a_{np}^i}$$

It follows from Lemmas 2.3.1 and 2.3.2 that $R_{SM}(s_i) = \frac{P + a_{ef}^i - a_{ep}^i}{F+P}$ and $R_{SM}(s_f) = \frac{P + F - a_{ep}^f}{F+P}$. Then, after Definition 2.2.1, we have

$$S_B^{SM} = \{s_i \mid \frac{P + a_{ef}^i - a_{ep}^i}{F+P} > \frac{P + F - a_{ep}^f}{F+P}, 1 \le i \le n\} \qquad (A.48)$$

$$S_F^{SM} = \{s_i \mid \frac{P + a_{ef}^i - a_{ep}^i}{F+P} = \frac{P + F - a_{ep}^f}{F+P}, 1 \le i \le n\} \qquad (A.49)$$

$$S_A^{SM} = \{s_i \mid \frac{P + a_{ef}^i - a_{ep}^i}{F+P} < \frac{P + F - a_{ep}^f}{F+P}, 1 \le i \le n\} \qquad (A.50)$$

We are going to prove that S_B^{SM}, S_F^{SM}, and S_A^{SM} are equal to the above sets S_B^{W2} in (A.42), S_F^{W2} in (A.43), and S_A^{W2} in (A.44), respectively. First, we will prove $S_B^{SM} = S_B^{W2}$.

• Assume that $s_i \in S_B^{SM}$. After (A.48), we have

$$\frac{P + a_{ef}^i - a_{ep}^i}{F+P} > \frac{P + F - a_{ep}^f}{F+P}$$

Since $F + P > 0$, we have

$$P + a_{ef}^i - a_{ep}^i > P + F - a_{ep}^f$$

and

$$(a_{ef}^i - F) + (a_{ep}^f - a_{ep}^i) > 0$$

After (A.42), $s_i \in S_B^{W2}$. Therefore, $S_B^{SM} \subseteq S_B^{W2}$.

• Assume that $s_i \in S_B^{W2}$. After (A.42), we have

$$(a_{ef}^i - F) + (a_{ep}^f - a_{ep}^i) > 0$$

and hence

$$P + a_{ef}^i - a_{ep}^i > P + F - a_{ep}^f$$

Since $F+P>0$, we have

$$\frac{P+a_{ef}^i-a_{ep}^i}{F+P} > \frac{P+F-a_{ep}^f}{F+P}$$

Then, after (A.48), $s_i \in S_B^{SM}$. Therefore, $S_B^{W2} \subseteq S_B^{SM}$.

In summary, we have proved that $S_B^{SM}=S_B^{W2}$.
Similarly, we can prove $S_F^{SM}=S_F^{W2}$ and $S_A^{SM}=S_A^{W2}$.

(13) **Sokal**

As stated in Table 2.1, formula Sokal is defined as follows.

$$R_S(s_i) = \frac{2(a_{ef}^i + a_{np}^i)}{2(a_{ef}^i + a_{np}^i) + a_{nf}^i + a_{ep}^i}$$

It follows from Lemmas 2.3.1 and 2.3.2 that $R_S(s_i)=\frac{2P+2a_{ef}^i-2a_{ep}^i}{2P+F+a_{ef}^i-a_{ep}^i}$ and $R_S(s_f)=\frac{2P+2F-2a_{ep}^f}{2P+2F-a_{ep}^f}$. Then, after Definition 2.2.1, we have

$$S_B^S = \{s_i | \frac{2P+2a_{ef}^i-2a_{ep}^i}{2P+F+a_{ef}^i-a_{ep}^i} > \frac{2P+2F-2a_{ep}^f}{2P+2F-a_{ep}^f}, 1\leq i \leq n\} \qquad \text{(A.51)}$$

$$S_F^S = \{s_i | \frac{2P+2a_{ef}^i-2a_{ep}^i}{2P+F+a_{ef}^i-a_{ep}^i} = \frac{2P+2F-2a_{ep}^f}{2P+2F-a_{ep}^f}, 1\leq i \leq n\} \qquad \text{(A.52)}$$

$$S_A^S = \{s_i | \frac{2P+2a_{ef}^i-2a_{ep}^i}{2P+F+a_{ef}^i-a_{ep}^i} < \frac{2P+2F-2a_{ep}^f}{2P+2F-a_{ep}^f}, 1\leq i \leq n\} \qquad \text{(A.53)}$$

We are going to prove that S_B^S, S_F^S, and S_A^S are equal to the above sets S_B^{W2} in (A.42), S_F^{W2} in (A.43), and S_A^{W2} in (A.44), respectively.
First, we will prove $S_B^S=S_B^{W2}$.

• Assume that $s_i \in S_B^S$. After (A.51), we have

$$\frac{2P+2a_{ef}^i-2a_{ep}^i}{2P+F+a_{ef}^i-a_{ep}^i} > \frac{2P+2F-2a_{ep}^f}{2P+2F-a_{ep}^f}$$

Since $(2P+F+a_{ef}^i-a_{ep}^i)>0$ and $(2P+2F-a_{ep}^f)>0$ after Lemma 2.3.1, we have

$$(2P+2a_{ef}^i-2a_{ep}^i)(2P+2F-a_{ep}^f)>(2P+2F-2a_{ep}^f)(2P+F+a_{ef}^i-a_{ep}^i)$$

After simplification, we have

$$(F+P)(a_{ef}^i - F + a_{ep}^f - a_{ep}^i) > 0$$

Since $F+P>0$, we have

$$(a_{ef}^i - F) + (a_{ep}^f - a_{ep}^i) > 0$$

After (A.42), $s_i \in S_B^{W2}$. Therefore, $S_B^S \subseteq S_B^{W2}$.

- Assume that $s_i \in S_B^{W2}$. After (A.42), we have

$$(a_{ef}^i - F) + (a_{ep}^f - a_{ep}^i) > 0$$

which implies

$$2(F+P)(a_{ef}^i - F + a_{ep}^f - a_{ep}^i) > 0$$

because $F+P>0$.

It can be proved that

$$2(F+P)(a_{ef}^i - F + a_{ep}^f - a_{ep}^i)$$
$$= (2P + 2a_{ef}^i - 2a_{ep}^i)(2P + 2F - a_{ep}^f) - (2P + 2F - 2a_{ep}^f)(2P + F + a_{ef}^i - a_{ep}^i)$$

Thus, we have

$$(2P + 2a_{ef}^i - 2a_{ep}^i)(2P + 2F - a_{ep}^f) > (2P + 2F - 2a_{ep}^f)(2P + F + a_{ef}^i - a_{ep}^i)$$

It follows from Lemma 2.3.1 that $(2P + F + a_{ef}^i - a_{ep}^i) > 0$ and $(2P + 2F - a_{ep}^f) > 0$. Thus, we have

$$\frac{2P + 2a_{ef}^i - 2a_{ep}^i}{2P + F + a_{ef}^i - a_{ep}^i} > \frac{2P + 2F - 2a_{ep}^f}{2P + 2F - a_{ep}^f}$$

After (A.51), $s_i \in S_B^S$. Therefore, $S_B^{W2} \subseteq S_B^S$.

In summary, we have proved that $S_B^S = S_B^{W2}$.

Similarly, we can prove $S_F^S = S_F^{W2}$ and $S_A^S = S_A^{W2}$.

(14) Rogers & Tanimoto

As stated in Table 2.1, formula Rogers & Tanimoto is defined as follows.

$$R_{RT}(s_i) = \frac{a_{ef}^i + a_{np}^i}{a_{ef}^i + a_{np}^i + 2(a_{nf}^i + a_{ep}^i)}$$

It follows from Lemmas 2.3.1 and 2.3.2 that $R_{RT}(s_i)=\dfrac{P+a_{ef}^i-a_{ep}^i}{2F+P-a_{ef}^i+a_{ep}^i}$ and

$R_{RT}(s_f)=\dfrac{F+P-a_{ep}^f}{F+P+a_{ep}^f}$. Then, after Definition 2.2.1, we have

$$S_B^{RT} = \{s_i \mid \frac{P+a_{ef}^i-a_{ep}^i}{2F+P-a_{ef}^i+a_{ep}^i} > \frac{F+P-a_{ep}^f}{F+P+a_{ep}^f}, 1 \le i \le n\} \qquad (A.54)$$

$$S_F^{RT} = \{s_i \mid \frac{P+a_{ef}^i-a_{ep}^i}{2F+P-a_{ef}^i+a_{ep}^i} = \frac{F+P-a_{ep}^f}{F+P+a_{ep}^f}, 1 \le i \le n\} \qquad (A.55)$$

$$S_A^{RT} = \{s_i \mid \frac{P+a_{ef}^i-a_{ep}^i}{2F+P-a_{ef}^i+a_{ep}^i} < \frac{F+P-a_{ep}^f}{F+P+a_{ep}^f}, 1 \le i \le n\} \qquad (A.56)$$

We are going to prove that S_B^{RT}, S_F^{RT}, and S_A^{RT} are equal to the above sets S_B^{W2} in (A.42), S_F^{W2} in (A.43), and S_A^{W2} in (A.44), respectively.
First, we will prove $S_B^{RT}=S_B^{W2}$.

- Assume that $s_i \in S_B^{RT}$. After (A.54), we have

$$\frac{P+a_{ef}^i-a_{ep}^i}{2F+P-a_{ef}^i+a_{ep}^i} > \frac{F+P-a_{ep}^f}{F+P+a_{ep}^f}$$

Since $(2F+P-a_{ef}^i+a_{ep}^i)>0$ and $(F+P+a_{ep}^f)>0$ after Lemma 2.3.1, we have

$$(P+a_{ef}^i-a_{ep}^i)(F+P+a_{ep}^f)>(F+P-a_{ep}^f)(2F+P-a_{ef}^i+a_{ep}^i)$$

After simplification, we have

$$(F+P)(a_{ef}^i-F+a_{ep}^f-a_{ep}^i)>0$$

Since $F+P>0$, we have

$$(a_{ef}^i-F)+(a_{ep}^f-a_{ep}^i)>0$$

After (A.42), $s_i \in S_B^{W2}$. Therefore, $S_B^{RT} \subseteq S_B^{W2}$.
- Assume that $s_i \in S_B^{W2}$. After (A.42), we have

$$(a_{ef}^i-F)+(a_{ep}^f-a_{ep}^i)>0$$

which implies

$$(F+P)(a_{ef}^i - F + a_{ep}^f - a_{ep}^i) > 0$$

because $F+P > 0$. It can be proved that

$$(F+P)(a_{ef}^i - F + a_{ep}^f - a_{ep}^i)$$

$$= (P + a_{ef}^i - a_{ep}^i)(F + P + a_{ep}^f) - (F + P - a_{ep}^f)(2F + P - a_{ef}^i + a_{ep}^i)$$

Thus, we have

$$(P + a_{ef}^i - a_{ep}^i)(F + P + a_{ep}^f) > (F + P - a_{ep}^f)(2F + P - a_{ef}^i + a_{ep}^i)$$

Since $(2F + P - a_{ef}^i + a_{ep}^i) > 0$ and $(F + P + a_{ep}^f) > 0$ after Lemma 2.3.1, we have

$$\frac{P + a_{ef}^i - a_{ep}^i}{2F + P - a_{ef}^i + a_{ep}^i} > \frac{F + P - a_{ep}^f}{F + P + a_{ep}^f}$$

After (A.54), $s_i \in S_B^{RT}$. Thus $S_B^{W2} \subseteq S_B^{RT}$.

In summary, we have proved that $S_B^{RT} = S_B^{W2}$.
Similarly, we can prove $S_F^{RT} = S_F^{W2}$ and $S_A^{RT} = S_A^{W2}$.

(15) Hamming etc.

As stated in Table 2.1, Hamming etc. is defined as follows.

$$R_{HM}(s_i) = a_{ef}^i + a_{np}^i$$

After Lemmas 2.3.1 and 2.3.2 and Definition 2.2.1, we have

$$S_B^{HM} = \{s_i \,|\, a_{ef}^i + P - a_{ep}^i > F + P - a_{ep}^f, \, 1 \le i \le n\} \tag{A.57}$$

$$S_F^{HM} = \{s_i \,|\, a_{ef}^i + P - a_{ep}^i = F + P - a_{ep}^f, \, 1 \le i \le n\} \tag{A.58}$$

$$S_A^{HM} = \{s_i \,|\, a_{ef}^i + P - a_{ep}^i < F + P - a_{ep}^f, \, 1 \le i \le n\} \tag{A.59}$$

It is obvious that the above sets defined in (A.57), (A.58), and (A.59) are equal to S_B^{W2} in (A.42), S_F^{W2} in (A.43), and S_A^{W2} in (A.44), respectively.

(16) Euclid

As stated in Table 2.1, formula Euclid is defined as follows.

$$R_E(s_i) = \sqrt{a_{ef}^i + a_{np}^i}$$

After Lemmas 2.3.1 and 2.3.2 and Definition 2.2.1, we have

$$S_B^E = \{s_i \mid \sqrt{a_{ef}^i + P - a_{ep}^i} > \sqrt{F + P - a_{ep}^f}, 1 \le i \le n\} \tag{A.60}$$

$$S_F^E = \{s_i \mid \sqrt{a_{ef}^i + P - a_{ep}^i} = \sqrt{F + P - a_{ep}^f}, 1 \le i \le n\} \tag{A.61}$$

$$S_A^E = \{s_i \mid \sqrt{a_{ef}^i + P - a_{ep}^i} < \sqrt{F + P - a_{ep}^f}, 1 \le i \le n\} \tag{A.62}$$

Since $a_{ef}^i + P - a_{ep}^i \ge 0$ and $F + P - a_{ep}^f > 0$ after Lemma 2.3.1, obviously,

$$\sqrt{a_{ef}^i + P - a_{ep}^i} \,\Theta\, \sqrt{F + P - a_{ep}^f}$$

if and only if

$$(a_{ef}^i + P - a_{ep}^i) \,\Theta\, (F + P - a_{ep}^f)$$

where "Θ" is "<," "=," or ">." As a consequence, sets defined in (A.60), (A.61), and (A.62) are equal to sets in (A.57), (A.58), and (A.59), respectively. Therefore, S_B^E, S_F^E, and S_A^E are equal to S_B^{W2}, S_F^{W2}, and S_A^{W2}, respectively.

(17) **Wong1**

As stated in Table 2.1, formula Wong1 is defined as follows.

$$R_{W1}(s_i) = a_{ef}^i$$

It follows from Lemma 2.3.2 that $R_{W1}(s_f) = F$. Then, after Definition 2.2.1, we have

$$S_B^{W1} = \{s_i \mid a_{ef}^i > F, 1 \le i \le n\} \tag{A.63}$$

$$S_F^{W1} = \{s_i \mid a_{ef}^i = F, 1 \le i \le n\} \tag{A.64}$$

$$S_A^{W1} = \{s_i \mid a_{ef}^i < F, 1 \le i \le n\} \tag{A.65}$$

Since $a_{ef}^i \le F$ after Lemma 2.3.1, we have $S_B^{W1} = \emptyset$.

(18) **Russell & Rao**

As stated in Table 2.1, formula Russell & Rao is defined as follows.

$$R_{RR}(s_i) = \frac{a_{ef}^i}{a_{ef}^i + a_{nf}^i + a_{ep}^i + a_{np}^i}$$

It follows from Lemmas 2.3.1 and 2.3.2 that $R_{RR}(s_i)=\frac{a_{ef}^i}{F+P}$ and $R_{RR}(s_f)=\frac{F}{F+P}$. Then, after Definition 2.2.1, we have

$$S_B^{RR} = \{s_i \mid \frac{a_{ef}^i}{F+P} > \frac{F}{F+P}, 1 \le i \le n\} \tag{A.66}$$

$$S_F^{RR} = \{s_i \mid \frac{a_{ef}^i}{F+P} = \frac{F}{F+P}, 1 \le i \le n\} \tag{A.67}$$

$$S_A^{RR} = \{s_i \mid \frac{a_{ef}^i}{F+P} < \frac{F}{F+P}, 1 \le i \le n\} \tag{A.68}$$

Since $F+P>0$, obviously, $(\frac{a_{ef}^i}{F+P} \Theta \frac{F}{F+P})$ if and only if $(a_{ef}^i \Theta F)$, where "Θ" is $<$, $=$, or $>$. As a consequence, sets defined in (A.66), (A.67), and (A.68) are equal to sets defined in (A.63), (A.64), and (A.65), respectively.

(19) **Binary**

As stated in Table 2.1, formula Binary is defined as follows.

$$R_B(s_i) = \begin{cases} 0 \text{ if } a_{ef}^i < F \\ 1 \text{ if } a_{ef}^i = F \end{cases}$$

It follows from Lemma 2.3.2 that $R_B(s_f)=1$. Then, after Definition 2.2.1, we have

$$S_B^B=\{s_i \mid (a_{ef}^i < F \text{ and } 0>1) \text{ or } (a_{ef}^i=F \text{ and } 1>1), 1 \le i \le n\} \tag{A.69}$$

$$S_F^B=\{s_i \mid (a_{ef}^i < F \text{ and } 0=1) \text{ or } (a_{ef}^i=F \text{ and } 1=1), 1 \le i \le n\} \tag{A.70}$$

$$S_A^B=\{s_i \mid (a_{ef}^i < F \text{ and } 0<1) \text{ or } (a_{ef}^i=F \text{ and } 1<1), 1 \le i \le n\} \tag{A.71}$$

We are going to prove that S_B^B, S_F^B, and S_A^B are equal to sets S_B^{W1} in (A.63), S_F^{W1} in (A.64), and S_A^{W1} in (A.65), respectively.

Firstly, we will prove $S_B^B=S_B^{W1}$. It is obvious that neither $(0>1)$ nor $(1>1)$ is possible. Thus, $S_B^B=\emptyset=S_B^{W1}$.

Secondly, we will prove $S_F^B=S_F^{W1}$. S_F^B defined in (A.70) can be rewritten as

$$S_F^B=\{s_i \mid a_{ef}^i < F \text{ and } 0=1, 1 \le i \le n\}$$

$$\cup\{s_i \mid a_{ef}^i=F \text{ and } 1=1, 1 \le i \le n\}$$

Obviously, $(0=1)$ is false and $(a_{ef}^i=F \text{ and } 1=1)$ is logically equivalent to $(a_{ef}^i=F)$. Thus, S_F^B becomes $\{s_i \mid a_{ef}^i=F, 1 \le i \le n\}=S_F^{W1}$.

Similarly, we can prove that $S_A^B=\{s_i \mid a_{ef}^i < F, 1 \le i \le n\}=S_A^{W1}$.

In conclusion, S_B^B in (A.69), S_F^B in (A.70), and S_A^B in (A.71) are equal to sets defined in (A.63), (A.64), and (A.65), respectively.

(20) **Scott**

As stated in Table 2.1, formula Scott is defined as follows.

$$R_{SC}(s_i) = \frac{4a_{ef}^i a_{np}^i - 4a_{nf}^i a_{ep}^i - (a_{nf}^i - a_{ep}^i)^2}{(2a_{ef}^i + a_{nf}^i + a_{ep}^i)(2a_{np}^i + a_{nf}^i + a_{ep}^i)}$$

From Definition 2.2.1 and Lemmas 2.3.1 and 2.3.2, after simplification, we have

$$S_B^{SC} = \{s_i \mid \frac{-F^2 + 4a_{ef}^i P + 2Fa_{ef}^i - 2Fa_{ep}^i - (a_{ep}^i + a_{ef}^i)^2}{(F + 2P - a_{ep}^i - a_{ef}^i)(F + a_{ef}^i + a_{ep}^i)}$$

$$> \frac{4PF - 4Fa_{ep}^f - (a_{ep}^f)^2}{(2F + a_{ep}^f)(2P - a_{ep}^f)}, 1 \le i \le n\} \tag{A.72}$$

$$S_F^{SC} = \{s_i \mid \frac{-F^2 + 4a_{ef}^i P + 2Fa_{ef}^i - 2Fa_{ep}^i - (a_{ep}^i + a_{ef}^i)^2}{(F + 2P - a_{ep}^i - a_{ef}^i)(F + a_{ef}^i + a_{ep}^i)}$$

$$= \frac{4PF - 4Fa_{ep}^f - (a_{ep}^f)^2}{(2F + a_{ep}^f)(2P - a_{ep}^f)}, 1 \le i \le n\} \tag{A.73}$$

$$S_A^{SC} = \{s_i \mid \frac{-F^2 + 4a_{ef}^i P + 2Fa_{ef}^i - 2Fa_{ep}^i - (a_{ep}^i + a_{ef}^i)^2}{(F + 2P - a_{ep}^i - a_{ef}^i)(F + a_{ef}^i + a_{ep}^i)}$$

$$< \frac{4PF - 4Fa_{ep}^f - (a_{ep}^f)^2}{(2F + a_{ep}^f)(2P - a_{ep}^f)}, 1 \le i \le n\} \tag{A.74}$$

(21) **Rogot1**

As stated in Table 2.1, formula Rogot1 is defined as follows.

$$R_{RO}(s_i) = \frac{1}{2}\left(\frac{a_{ef}^i}{2a_{ef}^i + a_{nf}^i + a_{ep}^i} + \frac{a_{np}^i}{2a_{np}^i + a_{nf}^i + a_{ep}^i}\right)$$

It follows from Lemmas 2.3.1 and 2.3.2 that

$$R_{RO}(s_f) = \frac{1}{2}\left(\frac{F}{2F + a_{ep}^f} + \frac{P - a_{ep}^f}{2P - a_{ep}^f}\right)$$

and

$$R_{RO}(s_i) = \frac{1}{2}\left(\frac{a_{ef}^i}{2a_{ef}^i + F - a_{ef}^i + a_{ep}^i} + \frac{P - a_{ep}^i}{2(P - a_{ep}^i) + F - a_{ef}^i + a_{ep}^i}\right)$$

Then, after Definition 2.2.1, we have

$$S_B^{RO} = \{s_i \mid \frac{1}{2}\left(\frac{a_{ef}^i}{2a_{ef}^i + F - a_{ef}^i + a_{ep}^i} + \frac{P - a_{ep}^i}{2(P - a_{ep}^i) + F - a_{ef}^i + a_{ep}^i}\right)$$
$$> \frac{1}{2}\left(\frac{F}{2F + a_{ep}^f} + \frac{P - a_{ep}^f}{2P - a_{ep}^f}\right), 1 \le i \le n\} \tag{A.75}$$

$$S_F^{RO} = \{s_i \mid \frac{1}{2}\left(\frac{a_{ef}^i}{2a_{ef}^i + F - a_{ef}^i + a_{ep}^i} + \frac{P - a_{ep}^i}{2(P - a_{ep}^i) + F - a_{ef}^i + a_{ep}^i}\right)$$
$$= \frac{1}{2}\left(\frac{F}{2F + a_{ep}^f} + \frac{P - a_{ep}^f}{2P - a_{ep}^f}\right), 1 \le i \le n\} \tag{A.76}$$

$$S_A^{RO} = \{s_i \mid \frac{1}{2}\left(\frac{a_{ef}^i}{2a_{ef}^i + F - a_{ef}^i + a_{ep}^i} + \frac{P - a_{ep}^i}{2(P - a_{ep}^i) + F - a_{ef}^i + a_{ep}^i}\right)$$
$$< \frac{1}{2}\left(\frac{F}{2F + a_{ep}^f} + \frac{P - a_{ep}^f}{2P - a_{ep}^f}\right), 1 \le i \le n\} \tag{A.77}$$

We are going to prove that the sets S_B^{RO}, S_F^{RO}, and S_A^{RO} are equal to S_B^{SC} in (A.72), S_F^{SC} in (A.73), and S_A^{SC} in (A.74), respectively.
First, we will prove $S_B^{RO} = S_B^{SC}$.

- Assume that $s_i \in S_B^{RO}$. After (A.75), we have

$$\frac{1}{2}\left(\frac{a_{ef}^i}{2a_{ef}^i + F - a_{ef}^i + a_{ep}^i} + \frac{P - a_{ep}^i}{2(P - a_{ep}^i) + F - a_{ef}^i + a_{ep}^i}\right)$$
$$> \frac{1}{2}\left(\frac{F}{2F + a_{ep}^f} + \frac{P - a_{ep}^f}{2P - a_{ep}^f}\right)$$

which implies

$$\frac{a_{ef}^i}{2a_{ef}^i + F - a_{ef}^i + a_{ep}^i} + \frac{P - a_{ep}^i}{2(P - a_{ep}^i) + F - a_{ef}^i + a_{ep}^i} - 1$$
$$> \frac{F}{2F + a_{ep}^f} + \frac{P - a_{ep}^f}{2P - a_{ep}^f} - 1$$

After rearranging the terms, we have

$$\frac{-F^2+4a_{ef}^iP+2Fa_{ef}^i-2Fa_{ep}^i-(a_{ep}^i+a_{ef}^i)^2}{(F+2P-a_{ep}^i-a_{ef}^i)(F+a_{ef}^i+a_{ep}^i)}$$
$$>\frac{4PF-4Fa_{ep}^f-(a_{ep}^f)^2}{(2F+a_{ep}^f)(2P-a_{ep}^f)}$$

Thus, $s_i \in S_B^{SC}$ after (A.72). Therefore, $S_B^{RO} \subseteq S_B^{SC}$.

• Assume that $s_i \in S_B^{SC}$. After (A.72), we have

$$\frac{-F^2+4a_{ef}^iP+2Fa_{ef}^i-2Fa_{ep}^i-(a_{ep}^i+a_{ef}^i)^2}{(F+2P-a_{ep}^i-a_{ef}^i)(F+a_{ef}^i+a_{ep}^i)}$$
$$>\frac{4PF-4Fa_{ep}^f-(a_{ep}^f)^2}{(2F+a_{ep}^f)(2P-a_{ep}^f)}$$

which implies

$$\frac{1}{2}\left(\frac{-F^2+4a_{ef}^iP+2Fa_{ef}^i-2Fa_{ep}^i-(a_{ep}^i+a_{ef}^i)^2}{(F+2P-a_{ep}^i-a_{ef}^i)(F+a_{ef}^i+a_{ep}^i)}+1\right)$$
$$>\frac{1}{2}\left(\frac{4PF-4Fa_{ep}^f-(a_{ep}^f)^2}{(2F+a_{ep}^f)(2P-a_{ep}^f)}+1\right)$$

After rearranging the terms, we have

$$\frac{1}{2}\left(\frac{a_{ef}^i}{2a_{ef}^i+F-a_{ef}^i+a_{ep}^i}+\frac{P-a_{ep}^i}{2(P-a_{ep}^i)+F-a_{ef}^i+a_{ep}^i}\right)$$
$$>\frac{1}{2}\left(\frac{F}{2F+a_{ep}^f}+\frac{P-a_{ep}^f}{2P-a_{ep}^f}\right)$$

It follows from (A.75) that $s_i \in S_B^{RO}$. Therefore, $S_B^{SC} \subseteq S_B^{RO}$.

In summary, we have proved that $S_B^{RO}=S_B^{SC}$.

Similarly, we can prove $S_F^{RO}=S_F^{SC}$ and $S_A^{RO}=S_A^{SC}$.

(22) **Kulczynski2**

As stated in Table 2.1, formula Kulczynski2 is defined as follows.

$$R_{K2}(s_i) = \frac{1}{2}(\frac{a_{ef}^i}{a_{ef}^i + a_{nf}^i} + \frac{a_{ef}^i}{a_{ef}^i + a_{ep}^i})$$

It follows from Lemmas 2.3.1 and 2.3.2 that $R_{K2}(s_i)=\frac{1}{2}(\frac{a_{ef}^i}{F}+\frac{a_{ef}^i}{a_{ef}^i+a_{ep}^i})$ and $R_{K2}(s_f)=\frac{1}{2}(1+\frac{F}{F+a_{ep}^f})$. Then, after Definition 2.2.1, we have

$$S_B^{K2}=\{s_i\,|\,\frac{1}{2}(\frac{a_{ef}^i}{F}+\frac{a_{ef}^i}{a_{ef}^i+a_{ep}^i})>\frac{1}{2}(1+\frac{F}{F+a_{ep}^f}),\,1\le i\le n\} \qquad (A.78)$$

$$S_F^{K2}=\{s_i\,|\,\frac{1}{2}(\frac{a_{ef}^i}{F}+\frac{a_{ef}^i}{a_{ef}^i+a_{ep}^i})=\frac{1}{2}(1+\frac{F}{F+a_{ep}^f}),\,1\le i\le n\} \qquad (A.79)$$

$$S_A^{K2}=\{s_i\,|\,\frac{1}{2}(\frac{a_{ef}^i}{F}+\frac{a_{ef}^i}{a_{ef}^i+a_{ep}^i})<\frac{1}{2}(1+\frac{F}{F+a_{ep}^f}),\,1\le i\le n\} \qquad (A.80)$$

We are going to prove that the above sets S_B^{K2}, S_F^{K2}, and S_A^{K2} are equal to the following sets X^{K2}, Y^{K2}, and Z^{K2}, respectively.

$$X^{K2}=\{s_i\,|\,a_{ef}^i>0 \text{ and } \frac{a_{ef}^i F+a_{ef}^i a_{ep}^f-F^2}{F^2+(F+a_{ep}^f)(F-a_{ef}^i)}-\frac{a_{ep}^i}{a_{ef}^i}>0,$$

$$1\le i\le n\} \qquad (A.81)$$

$$Y^{K2}=\{s_i\,|\,a_{ef}^i>0 \text{ and } \frac{a_{ef}^i F+a_{ef}^i a_{ep}^f-F^2}{F^2+(F+a_{ep}^f)(F-a_{ef}^i)}-\frac{a_{ep}^i}{a_{ef}^i}=0,$$

$$1\le i\le n\} \qquad (A.82)$$

$$Z^{K2}=\{s_i\,|\,(a_{ef}^i=0) \text{ or } (a_{ef}^i>0 \text{ and } \frac{a_{ef}^i F+a_{ef}^i a_{ep}^f-F^2}{F^2+(F+a_{ep}^f)(F-a_{ef}^i)}-\frac{a_{ep}^i}{a_{ef}^i}<0),$$

$$1\le i\le n\} \qquad (A.83)$$

First, we will prove $S_B^{K2}=X^{K2}$. For any s_i, we have either $(a_{ef}^i=0)$ or $(a_{ef}^i>0)$. Therefore, S_B^{K2} defined in (A.78) can be rewritten as

$$S_B^{K2}=\{s_i\,|\,a_{ef}^i=0 \text{ and } \frac{1}{2}(\frac{a_{ef}^i}{F}+\frac{a_{ef}^i}{a_{ef}^i+a_{ep}^i})>\frac{1}{2}(1+\frac{F}{F+a_{ep}^f}),\,1\le i\le n\}$$

$$\cup\{s_i\,|\,a_{ef}^i>0 \text{ and } \frac{1}{2}(\frac{a_{ef}^i}{F}+\frac{a_{ef}^i}{a_{ef}^i+a_{ep}^i})>\frac{1}{2}(1+\frac{F}{F+a_{ep}^f}),\,1\le i\le n\}$$

Consider the case that (a_{ef}^i=0). Since $F>0$ and $F+a_{ep}^f>0$ after Lemma 2.3.1,

we have $\frac{1}{2}(\frac{a_{ef}^i}{F}+\frac{a_{ef}^i}{a_{ef}^i+a_{ep}^i})=0<\frac{1}{2}(1+\frac{F}{F+a_{ep}^f})$, which is contradictory to

$\frac{1}{2}(\frac{a_{ef}^i}{F}+\frac{a_{ef}^i}{a_{ef}^i+a_{ep}^i})>\frac{1}{2}(1+\frac{F}{F+a_{ep}^f})$. Thus,

$$\{s_i|a_{ef}^i=0 \text{ and } \frac{1}{2}\frac{a_{ef}^i}{F}+\frac{a_{ef}^i}{a_{ef}^i+a_{ep}^i})>\frac{1}{2}(1+\frac{F}{F+a_{ep}^f}), 1\leq i\leq n\}=\emptyset$$

Hence, we have

$$S_B^{K2}=\{s_i|a_{ef}^i>0 \text{ and } \frac{1}{2}\frac{a_{ef}^i}{F}+\frac{a_{ef}^i}{a_{ef}^i+a_{ep}^i})>\frac{1}{2}(1+\frac{F}{F+a_{ep}^f}), 1\leq i\leq n\} \quad (A.84)$$

- Assume that $s_i\in S_B^{K2}$. After (A.84), we have

$$a_{ef}^i>0 \text{ and } \frac{1}{2}(\frac{a_{ef}^i}{F}+\frac{a_{ef}^i}{a_{ef}^i+a_{ep}^i})>\frac{1}{2}(1+\frac{F}{F+a_{ep}^f})$$

By simplification and rearrangement of the terms,

$$\frac{1}{2}(\frac{a_{ef}^i}{F}+\frac{a_{ef}^i}{a_{ef}^i+a_{ep}^i})>\frac{1}{2}(1+\frac{F}{F+a_{ep}^f})$$

becomes

$$\frac{a_{ef}^i}{a_{ef}^i+a_{ep}^i}>\frac{F(2F+a_{ep}^f)-a_{ef}^i(F+a_{ep}^f)}{F(F+a_{ep}^f)}$$

It follows from $F>0$ and Lemma 2.3.1 that $a_{ef}^i+a_{ep}^i>0$, $F(F+a_{ep}^f)>0$, and $F(2F+a_{ep}^f)-a_{ef}^i(F+a_{ep}^f)>0$. Since $a_{ef}^i>0$,

$$\frac{a_{ef}^i}{a_{ef}^i+a_{ep}^i}>\frac{F(2F+a_{ep}^f)-a_{ef}^i(F+a_{ep}^f)}{F(F+a_{ep}^f)}$$

implies

$$\frac{a_{ef}^iF+a_{ef}^ia_{ep}^f-F^2}{F^2+(F+a_{ep}^f)(F-a_{ef}^i)}-\frac{a_{ep}^i}{a_{ef}^i}>0$$

After (A.81), $s_i\in X^{K2}$. Therefore, $S_B^{K2}\subseteq X^{K2}$.

- Assume that $s_i \in X^{K2}$. After (A.81), we have

$$a_{ef}^i > 0 \text{ and } \frac{a_{ef}^i F + a_{ef}^i a_{ep}^f - F^2}{F^2 + (F + a_{ep}^f)(F - a_{ef}^i)} - \frac{a_{ep}^i}{a_{ef}^i} > 0$$

Then,

$$\frac{a_{ef}^i F + a_{ef}^i a_{ep}^f - F^2}{F^2 + (F + a_{ep}^f)(F - a_{ef}^i)} - \frac{a_{ep}^i}{a_{ef}^i} > 0$$

can be rewritten as

$$\frac{a_{ep}^i}{a_{ef}^i} < \frac{F(F + a_{ep}^f)}{F(2F + a_{ep}^f) - a_{ef}^i(F + a_{ep}^f)} - 1$$

Since $a_{ef}^i > 0$, $a_{ef}^i + a_{ep}^i > 0$, $F(F + a_{ep}^f) > 0$, and $F(2F + a_{ep}^f) - a_{ef}^i(F + a_{ep}^f) > 0$ after Lemma 2.3.1,

$$\frac{a_{ep}^i}{a_{ef}^i} < \frac{F(F + a_{ep}^f)}{F(2F + a_{ep}^f) - a_{ef}^i(F + a_{ep}^f)} - 1$$

implies

$$\frac{1}{2}\left(\frac{a_{ef}^i}{F} + \frac{a_{ef}^i}{a_{ef}^i + a_{ep}^i}\right) > \frac{1}{2}\left(1 + \frac{F}{F + a_{ep}^f}\right)$$

Then, we have $s_i \in S_B^{K2}$ after (A.84). Therefore, $X^{K2} \subseteq S_B^{K2}$.

In summary, we have proved that $S_B^{K2} = X^{K2}$.
Similarly, we can prove that $S_F^{K2} = Y^{K2}$.
Next, we are going to prove $S_A^{K2} = Z^{K2}$. S_A^{K2} in (A.80) can be rewritten as follows.

$$S_A^{K2} = \{s_i | a_{ef}^i = 0 \text{ and } \frac{1}{2}\left(\frac{a_{ef}^i}{F} + \frac{a_{ef}^i}{a_{ef}^i + a_{ep}^i}\right) < \frac{1}{2}\left(1 + \frac{F}{F + a_{ep}^f}\right), 1 \le i \le n\}$$

$$\cup \{s_i | a_{ef}^i > 0 \text{ and } \frac{1}{2}\left(\frac{a_{ef}^i}{F} + \frac{a_{ef}^i}{a_{ef}^i + a_{ep}^i}\right) < \frac{1}{2}\left(1 + \frac{F}{F + a_{ep}^f}\right), 1 \le i \le n\}$$

Consider the case ($a_{ef}^i = 0$), which implies

$$\frac{1}{2}(\frac{a_{ef}^i}{F} + \frac{a_{ef}^i}{a_{ef}^i + a_{ep}^i}) = 0 < \frac{1}{2}(1 + \frac{F}{F + a_{ep}^f})$$

Thus,

$$a_{ef}^i = 0 \text{ and } \frac{1}{2}(\frac{a_{ef}^i}{F} + \frac{a_{ef}^i}{a_{ef}^i + a_{ep}^i}) < \frac{1}{2}(1 + \frac{F}{F + a_{ep}^f})$$

is logically equivalent to ($a_{ef}^i = 0$). Therefore, S_A^{K2} becomes

$$\{s_i | a_{ef}^i = 0, 1 \leq i \leq n\}$$

$$\cup \{s_i | a_{ef}^i > 0 \text{ and } \frac{1}{2}(\frac{a_{ef}^i}{F} + \frac{a_{ef}^i}{a_{ef}^i + a_{ep}^i}) < \frac{1}{2}(1 + \frac{F}{F + a_{ep}^f}), 1 \leq i \leq n\}$$

Similar to the proof of $S_B^{K2} = X^{K2}$, we can prove

$$\{s_i | a_{ef}^i > 0 \text{ and } \frac{1}{2}(\frac{a_{ef}^i}{F} + \frac{a_{ef}^i}{a_{ef}^i + a_{ep}^i}) < \frac{1}{2}(1 + \frac{F}{F + a_{ep}^f}), 1 \leq i \leq n\}$$

$$= \{s_i | a_{ef}^i > 0 \text{ and } \frac{a_{ef}^i F + a_{ef}^i a_{ep}^f - F^2}{F^2 + (F + a_{ep}^f)(F - a_{ef}^i)} - \frac{a_{ep}^i}{a_{ef}^i} < 0, 1 \leq i \leq n\}$$

Therefore, we have

$$S_A^{K2} = \{s_i | (a_{ef}^i = 0) \text{ or } (a_{ef}^i > 0 \text{ and } \frac{a_{ef}^i F + a_{ef}^i a_{ep}^f - F^2}{F^2 + (F + a_{ep}^f)(F - a_{ef}^i)} - \frac{a_{ep}^i}{a_{ef}^i} < 0), 1 \leq i \leq n\}$$

$$= Z^{K2}$$

In conclusion, we have proved that $S_B^{K2} = X^{K2}$, $S_F^{K2} = Y^{K2}$, and $S_A^{K2} = Z^{K2}$.

(23) **M2**

As stated in Table 2.1, formula M2 is defined as follows.

$$R_{M2}(s_i) = \frac{a_{ef}^i}{a_{ef}^i + a_{np}^i + 2(a_{nf}^i + a_{ep}^i)}$$

It follows from Lemmas 2.3.1 and 2.3.2 that $R_{M2}(s_i) = \dfrac{a_{ef}^i}{2F+P-a_{ef}^i+a_{ep}^i}$ and

$R_{M2}(s_f) = \dfrac{F}{F+P+a_{ep}^f}$. Then, after Definition 2.2.1, we have

$$S_B^{M2} = \{s_i \mid \frac{a_{ef}^i}{2F+P-a_{ef}^i+a_{ep}^i} > \frac{F}{F+P+a_{ep}^f}, 1 \leq i \leq n\} \tag{A.85}$$

$$S_F^{M2} = \{s_i \mid \frac{a_{ef}^i}{2F+P-a_{ef}^i+a_{ep}^i} = \frac{F}{F+P+a_{ep}^f}, 1 \leq i \leq n\} \tag{A.86}$$

$$S_A^{M2} = \{s_i \mid \frac{a_{ef}^i}{2F+P-a_{ef}^i+a_{ep}^i} < \frac{F}{F+P+a_{ep}^f}, 1 \leq i \leq n\} \tag{A.87}$$

We are going to prove that the above sets S_B^{M2}, S_F^{M2}, and S_A^{M2} are equal to the following sets X^{M2}, Y^{M2}, and Z^{M2}, respectively.

$$X^{M2} = \{s_i \mid a_{ef}^i > 0 \text{ and } \frac{P+a_{ep}^f}{F} - \frac{2F+P}{a_{ef}^i} + 2 - \frac{a_{ep}^i}{a_{ef}^i} > 0, 1 \leq i \leq n\} \tag{A.88}$$

$$Y^{M2} = \{s_i \mid a_{ef}^i > 0 \text{ and } \frac{P+a_{ep}^f}{F} - \frac{2F+P}{a_{ef}^i} + 2 - \frac{a_{ep}^i}{a_{ef}^i} = 0, 1 \leq i \leq n\} \tag{A.89}$$

$$Z^{M2} = \{s_i \mid (a_{ef}^i = 0) \text{ or } (a_{ef}^i > 0 \text{ and } \frac{P+a_{ep}^f}{F} - \frac{2F+P}{a_{ef}^i} + 2 - \frac{a_{ep}^i}{a_{ef}^i} < 0), 1 \leq i \leq n\} \tag{A.90}$$

First, we will prove $S_B^{M2} = X^{M2}$. For any s_i, we have either $(a_{ef}^i = 0)$ or $(a_{ef}^i > 0)$. Therefore, S_B^{M2} defined in (A.85) can be rewritten as

$$S_B^{M2} = \{s_i \mid a_{ef}^i = 0 \text{ and } \frac{a_{ef}^i}{2F+P-a_{ef}^i+a_{ep}^i} > \frac{F}{F+P+a_{ep}^f}, 1 \leq i \leq n\}$$

$$\cup \{s_i \mid a_{ef}^i > 0 \text{ and } \frac{a_{ef}^i}{2F+P-a_{ef}^i+a_{ep}^i} > \frac{F}{F+P+a_{ep}^f}, 1 \leq i \leq n\}$$

Consider the case that $(a_{ef}^i = 0)$. Since $F > 0$ and $F+P+a_{ep}^f > 0$ after Lemma 2.3.1, we have $\dfrac{a_{ef}^i}{2F+P-a_{ef}^i+a_{ep}^i} = 0 < \dfrac{F}{F+P+a_{ep}^f}$, which is contradictory to

$$\frac{a_{ef}^i}{2F+P-a_{ef}^i+a_{ep}^i} > \frac{F}{F+P+a_{ep}^f}$$

Thus,

$$\{s_i \,|\, a_{ef}^i = 0 \text{ and } \frac{a_{ef}^i}{2F+P-a_{ef}^i+a_{ep}^i} > \frac{F}{F+P+a_{ep}^f}, \, 1 \le i \le n\} = \emptyset$$

Then, we have

$$S_B^{M2} = \{s_i \,|\, a_{ef}^i > 0 \text{ and } \frac{a_{ef}^i}{2F+P-a_{ef}^i+a_{ep}^i} > \frac{F}{F+P+a_{ep}^f}, \, 1 \le i \le n\} \qquad (A.91)$$

- Assume that $s_i \in S_B^{M2}$. After (A.91), we have

$$a_{ef}^i > 0 \text{ and } \frac{a_{ef}^i}{2F+P-a_{ef}^i+a_{ep}^i} > \frac{F}{F+P+a_{ep}^f}$$

Since $a_{ef}^i > 0$, $F > 0$, $(2F+P-a_{ef}^i+a_{ep}^i) > 0$, and $(F+P+a_{ep}^f) > 0$ (after Lemma 2.3.1), we have

$$\frac{2F+P-a_{ef}^i+a_{ep}^i}{a_{ef}^i} < \frac{F+P+a_{ep}^f}{F}$$

After rearranging the terms, we have

$$\frac{P+a_{ep}^f}{F} - \frac{2F+P}{a_{ef}^i} + 2 - \frac{a_{ep}^i}{a_{ef}^i} > 0$$

After (A.88), $s_i \in X^{M2}$. Therefore, $S_B^{M2} \subseteq X^{M2}$.
- Assume that $s_i \in X^{M2}$. After (A.88), we have

$$a_{ef}^i > 0 \text{ and } \frac{P+a_{ep}^f}{F} - \frac{2F+P}{a_{ef}^i} + 2 - \frac{a_{ep}^i}{a_{ef}^i} > 0$$

It is easy to know that

$$\frac{P+a_{ep}^f}{F} - \frac{2F+P}{a_{ef}^i} + 2 - \frac{a_{ep}^i}{a_{ef}^i} > 0$$

can be rewritten as

$$\frac{2F+P-a_{ef}^i+a_{ep}^i}{a_{ef}^i} < \frac{F+P+a_{ep}^f}{F}$$

Since $a_{ef}^i>0$, $F>0$, $(2F+P-a_{ef}^i+a_{ep}^i)>0$, and $(F+P+a_{ep}^f)>0$, we have

$$\frac{a_{ef}^i}{2F+P-a_{ef}^i+a_{ep}^i} > \frac{F}{F+P+a_{ep}^f}$$

Then, we have $s_i \in S_B^{M2}$ after (A.91). Therefore, $X^{M2} \subseteq S_B^{M2}$.

In summary, we have proved that $S_B^{M2}=X^{M2}$.
Similarly, we can prove that $S_F^{M2}=Y^{M2}$.
Next, we are going to prove $S_A^{M2}=Z^{M2}$. S_A^{M2} in (A.87) can be rewritten as follows.

$$S_A^{M2}=\{s_i \,|\, a_{ef}^i=0 \text{ and } \frac{a_{ef}^i}{2F+P-a_{ef}^i+a_{ep}^i} < \frac{F}{F+P+a_{ep}^f}, 1 \le i \le n\}$$

$$\cup\{s_i \,|\, a_{ef}^i>0 \text{ and } \frac{a_{ef}^i}{2F+P-a_{ef}^i+a_{ep}^i} < \frac{F}{F+P+a_{ep}^f}, 1 \le i \le n\}$$

Consider the case $(a_{ef}^i=0)$, which implies

$$\frac{a_{ef}^i}{2F+P-a_{ef}^i+a_{ep}^i} =0< \frac{F}{F+P+a_{ep}^f}$$

Thus,

$$(a_{ef}^i=0 \text{ and } \frac{a_{ef}^i}{2F+P-a_{ef}^i+a_{ep}^i} < \frac{F}{F+P+a_{ep}^f})$$

is logically equivalent to $(a_{ef}^i=0)$.
Therefore, S_A^{M2} becomes

$$\{s_i \,|\, a_{ef}^i=0, 1 \le i \le n\}$$

$$\cup\{s_i \,|\, a_{ef}^i>0 \text{ and } \frac{a_{ef}^i}{2F+P-a_{ef}^i+a_{ep}^i} < \frac{F}{F+P+a_{ep}^f}, 1 \le i \le n\}$$

Similar to the proof of $S_B^{M2}=X^{M2}$, we can prove

$$\{s_i\,|\,a_{ef}^i>0 \text{ and } \frac{a_{ef}^i}{2F+P-a_{ef}^i+a_{ep}^i}<\frac{F}{F+P+a_{ep}^f},\,1\leq i\leq n\}$$

$$=\{s_i\,|\,a_{ef}^i>0 \text{ and } \frac{P+a_{ep}^f}{F}-\frac{2F+P}{a_{ef}^i}+2-\frac{a_{ep}^i}{a_{ef}^i}<0,\,1\leq i\leq n\}$$

Therefore, we have

$$S_A^{M2}=\{s_i\,|\,(a_{ef}^i=0) \text{ or } (a_{ef}^i>0 \text{ and } \frac{P+a_{ep}^f}{F}-\frac{2F+P}{a_{ef}^i}+2-\frac{a_{ep}^i}{a_{ef}^i}<0),\,1\leq i\leq n\}$$

$$=Z^{M2}$$

In conclusion, we have proved that $S_B^{M2}=X^{M2}$, $S_F^{M2}=Y^{M2}$, and $S_A^{M2}=Z^{M2}$.

(24) **Ochiai**

As stated in Table 2.1, formula Ochiai is defined as follows.

$$R_O(s_i)=\frac{a_{ef}^i}{\sqrt{(a_{ef}^i+a_{nf}^i)(a_{ef}^i+a_{ep}^i)}}$$

It follows from Lemmas 2.3.1 and 2.3.2 that $R_O(s_i)=\dfrac{a_{ef}^i}{\sqrt{F(a_{ef}^i+a_{ep}^i)}}$ and $R_O(s_f)=\dfrac{F}{\sqrt{F(F+a_{ep}^f)}}$. Then, after Definition 2.2.1, we have

$$S_B^O=\{s_i\,|\,\frac{a_{ef}^i}{\sqrt{F(a_{ef}^i+a_{ep}^i)}}>\frac{F}{\sqrt{F(F+a_{ep}^f)}},\,1\leq i\leq n\} \tag{A.92}$$

$$S_F^O=\{s_i\,|\,\frac{a_{ef}^i}{\sqrt{F(a_{ef}^i+a_{ep}^i)}}=\frac{F}{\sqrt{F(F+a_{ep}^f)}},\,1\leq i\leq n\} \tag{A.93}$$

$$S_A^O=\{s_i\,|\,\frac{a_{ef}^i}{\sqrt{F(a_{ef}^i+a_{ep}^i)}}<\frac{F}{\sqrt{F(F+a_{ep}^f)}},\,1\leq i\leq n\} \tag{A.94}$$

We are going to prove that the above sets S_B^O, S_F^O, and S_A^O are equal to the following sets X^O, Y^O, and Z^O, respectively.

$$X^O = \{s_i \,|\, a_{ef}^i > 0 \text{ and } (1 + \frac{a_{ep}^f}{F})\frac{a_{ef}^i}{F} - 1 - \frac{a_{ep}^i}{a_{ef}^i} > 0,\, 1 \le i \le n\} \tag{A.95}$$

$$Y^O = \{s_i \,|\, a_{ef}^i > 0 \text{ and } (1 + \frac{a_{ep}^f}{F})\frac{a_{ef}^i}{F} - 1 - \frac{a_{ep}^i}{a_{ef}^i} = 0,\, 1 \le i \le n\} \tag{A.96}$$

$$Z^O = \{s_i \,|\, (a_{ef}^i = 0) \text{ or } (a_{ef}^i > 0 \text{ and } (1 + \frac{a_{ep}^f}{F})\frac{a_{ef}^i}{F} - 1 - \frac{a_{ep}^i}{a_{ef}^i} < 0),\, 1 \le i \le n\} \tag{A.97}$$

First, we will prove $S_B^O = X^O$. For any s_i, we have either $(a_{ef}^i = 0)$ or $(a_{ef}^i > 0)$. Therefore, S_B^O defined in (A.92) can be rewritten as

$$S_B^O = \{s_i \,|\, a_{ef}^i = 0 \text{ and } \frac{a_{ef}^i}{\sqrt{F(a_{ef}^i + a_{ep}^i)}} > \frac{F}{\sqrt{F(F + a_{ep}^f)}},\, 1 \le i \le n\}$$

$$\cup \{s_i \,|\, a_{ef}^i > 0 \text{ and } \frac{a_{ef}^i}{\sqrt{F(a_{ef}^i + a_{ep}^i)}} > \frac{F}{\sqrt{F(F + a_{ep}^f)}},\, 1 \le i \le n\}$$

Consider the case that $(a_{ef}^i = 0)$. Since $F > 0$ and $F + a_{ep}^f > 0$ after Lemma 2.3.1, we have

$$\frac{a_{ef}^i}{\sqrt{F(a_{ef}^i + a_{ep}^i)}} = 0 < \frac{F}{\sqrt{F(F + a_{ep}^f)}}$$

which is contradictory to

$$\frac{a_{ef}^i}{\sqrt{F(a_{ef}^i + a_{ep}^i)}} > \frac{F}{\sqrt{F(F + a_{ep}^f)}}$$

Thus,

$$\{s_i \,|\, a_{ef}^i = 0 \text{ and } \frac{a_{ef}^i}{\sqrt{F(a_{ef}^i + a_{ep}^i)}} > \frac{F}{\sqrt{F(F + a_{ep}^f)}},\, 1 \le i \le n\} = \emptyset$$

Then, we have

$$S_B^O = \{s_i \mid a_{ef}^i > 0 \text{ and } \frac{a_{ef}^i}{\sqrt{F(a_{ef}^i + a_{ep}^i)}} > \frac{F}{\sqrt{F(F + a_{ep}^f)}}, 1 \le i \le n\} \qquad (A.98)$$

- Assume that $s_i \in S_B^O$. After (A.98), we have

$$a_{ef}^i > 0 \text{ and } \frac{a_{ef}^i}{\sqrt{F(a_{ef}^i + a_{ep}^i)}} > \frac{F}{\sqrt{F(F + a_{ep}^f)}}$$

Since $a_{ef}^i > 0$ and $F > 0$, we have

$$\sqrt{\frac{F(a_{ef}^i + a_{ep}^i)}{(a_{ef}^i)^2}} < \sqrt{\frac{F(F + a_{ep}^f)}{F^2}}$$

because

$$\frac{a_{ef}^i}{\sqrt{F(a_{ef}^i + a_{ep}^i)}} > \frac{F}{\sqrt{F(F + a_{ep}^f)}}$$

Then, we have

$$\frac{F(a_{ef}^i + a_{ep}^i)}{(a_{ef}^i)^2} < \frac{F(F + a_{ep}^f)}{F^2}$$

After rearranging the terms, we have

$$(1 + \frac{a_{ep}^f}{F}) - \frac{F}{a_{ef}^i}(1 + \frac{a_{ep}^i}{a_{ef}^i}) > 0$$

which implies

$$(1 + \frac{a_{ep}^f}{F})\frac{a_{ef}^i}{F} - 1 - \frac{a_{ep}^i}{a_{ef}^i} > 0$$

because $\frac{a_{ef}^i}{F} > 0$. Then, we have $s_i \in X^O$ after (A.95). Therefore, $S_B^O \subseteq X^O$.

- Assume that $s_i \in X^O$. After (A.95), we have

$$a_{ef}^i > 0 \text{ and } (1 + \frac{a_{ep}^f}{F}) \frac{a_{ef}^i}{F} - 1 - \frac{a_{ep}^i}{a_{ef}^i} > 0$$

Since $a_{ef}^i > 0$ and $F > 0$, through multiplying $\frac{F}{a_{ef}^i}$ by $(1 + \frac{a_{ep}^f}{F}) \frac{a_{ef}^i}{F} - 1 - \frac{a_{ep}^i}{a_{ef}^i} > 0$, we have

$$(1 + \frac{a_{ep}^f}{F}) - \frac{F}{a_{ef}^i}(1 + \frac{a_{ep}^i}{a_{ef}^i}) > 0$$

After rearranging the terms, we have

$$\frac{F(a_{ef}^i + a_{ep}^i)}{(a_{ef}^i)^2} < \frac{F(F + a_{ep}^f)}{F^2}$$

Since $a_{ef}^i > 0$, $F > 0$, $F + a_{ep}^f > 0$, and $a_{ef}^i + a_{ep}^i > 0$ (after Lemma 2.3.1),

$$\frac{F(a_{ef}^i + a_{ep}^i)}{(a_{ef}^i)^2} < \frac{F(F + a_{ep}^f)}{F^2}$$

implies

$$\frac{a_{ef}^i}{\sqrt{F(a_{ef}^i + a_{ep}^i)}} > \frac{F}{\sqrt{F(F + a_{ep}^f)}}$$

Then, we have $s_i \in S_B^O$ after (A.98). Therefore, $X^O \subseteq S_B^O$.

In summary, we have proved that $S_B^O = X^O$.
Similarly, we can prove that $S_F^O = Y^O$.
Next, we are going to prove $S_A^O = Z^O$. S_A^O defined in (A.94) can be rewritten as follows.

$$S_A^O = \{s_i | a_{ef}^i = 0 \text{ and } \frac{a_{ef}^i}{\sqrt{F(a_{ef}^i + a_{ep}^i)}} < \frac{F}{\sqrt{F(F + a_{ep}^f)}}, 1 \leq i \leq n\}$$

$$\cup \{s_i | a_{ef}^i > 0 \text{ and } \frac{a_{ef}^i}{\sqrt{F(a_{ef}^i + a_{ep}^i)}} < \frac{F}{\sqrt{F(F + a_{ep}^f)}}, 1 \leq i \leq n\}$$

Consider the case $(a_{ef}^i=0)$, which implies

$$\frac{a_{ef}^i}{\sqrt{F(a_{ef}^i+a_{ep}^i)}}=0<\frac{F}{\sqrt{F(F+a_{ep}^f)}}$$

Thus,

$$(a_{ef}^i=0 \text{ and } \frac{a_{ef}^i}{\sqrt{F(a_{ef}^i+a_{ep}^i)}}<\frac{F}{\sqrt{F(F+a_{ep}^f)}})$$

is logically equivalent to $(a_{ef}^i=0)$. Therefore, S_A^O becomes

$$\{s_i\,|\,a_{ef}^i=0,\ 1\le i\le n\}$$

$$\cup\{s_i\,|\,a_{ef}^i>0 \text{ and } \frac{a_{ef}^i}{\sqrt{F(a_{ef}^i+a_{ep}^i)}}<\frac{F}{\sqrt{F(F+a_{ep}^f)}},\ 1\le i\le n\}$$

Similar to the proof of $S_B^O=X^O$, we can prove

$$\{s_i\,|\,a_{ef}^i>0 \text{ and } \frac{a_{ef}^i}{\sqrt{F(a_{ef}^i+a_{ep}^i)}}<\frac{F}{\sqrt{F(F+a_{ep}^f)}},\ 1\le i\le n\}$$

$$=\{s_i\,|\,a_{ef}^i>0 \text{ and } (1+\frac{a_{ep}^f}{F})\frac{a_{ef}^i}{F}-1-\frac{a_{ep}^i}{a_{ef}^i}<0,\ 1\le i\le n\}$$

Therefore, we have

$$S_A^O=\{s_i\,|\,(a_{ef}^i=0) \text{ or } (a_{ef}^i>0 \text{ and } (1+\frac{a_{ep}^f}{F})\frac{a_{ef}^i}{F}-1-\frac{a_{ep}^i}{a_{ef}^i}<0),\ 1\le i\le n\}$$

$$=Z^O$$

In conclusion, we have proved that $S_B^O=X^O$, $S_F^O=Y^O$, and $S_A^O=Z^O$.

(25) **AMPLE2**

As stated in Table 2.1, formula AMPLE2 is defined as follows.

$$R_A(s_i)=\frac{a_{ef}^i}{a_{ef}^i+a_{nf}^i}-\frac{a_{ep}^i}{a_{ep}^i+a_{np}^i}$$

It follows from Lemmas 2.3.1 and 2.3.2 that $R_A(s_i) = \frac{a_{ef}^i}{F} - \frac{a_{ep}^i}{P}$ and $R_A(s_f) = 1 - \frac{a_{ep}^f}{P}$. Then, after Definition 2.2.1, we have

$$S_B^A = \{s_i \mid \frac{a_{ef}^i}{F} - \frac{a_{ep}^i}{P} > 1 - \frac{a_{ep}^f}{P}, 1 \le i \le n\} \tag{A.99}$$

$$S_F^A = \{s_i \mid \frac{a_{ef}^i}{F} - \frac{a_{ep}^i}{P} = 1 - \frac{a_{ep}^f}{P}, 1 \le i \le n\} \tag{A.100}$$

$$S_A^A = \{s_i \mid \frac{a_{ef}^i}{F} - \frac{a_{ep}^i}{P} < 1 - \frac{a_{ep}^f}{P}, 1 \le i \le n\} \tag{A.101}$$

We are going to prove that the above sets S_B^A, S_F^A, and S_A^A are equal to the following sets X^A, Y^A, and Z^A, respectively.

$$X^A = \{s_i \mid a_{ef}^i > 0 \text{ and } \frac{Pa_{ef}^i - PF + Fa_{ep}^f}{Fa_{ef}^i} - \frac{a_{ep}^i}{a_{ef}^i} > 0, 1 \le i \le n\} \tag{A.102}$$

$$Y^A = \{s_i \mid a_{ef}^i > 0 \text{ and } \frac{Pa_{ef}^i - PF + Fa_{ep}^f}{Fa_{ef}^i} - \frac{a_{ep}^i}{a_{ef}^i} = 0, 1 \le i \le n\} \tag{A.103}$$

$$Z^A = \{s_i \mid (a_{ef}^i = 0) \text{ or } (a_{ef}^i > 0 \text{ and } \frac{Pa_{ef}^i - PF + Fa_{ep}^f}{Fa_{ef}^i} - \frac{a_{ep}^i}{a_{ef}^i} < 0), 1 \le i \le n\} \tag{A.104}$$

First, we will prove $S_B^A = X^A$. For any s_i, we have either $(a_{ef}^i = 0)$ or $(a_{ef}^i > 0)$. Therefore, S_B^A defined in (A.99) can be rewritten as

$$S_B^A = \{s_i \mid a_{ef}^i = 0 \text{ and } \frac{a_{ef}^i}{F} - \frac{a_{ep}^i}{P} > 1 - \frac{a_{ep}^f}{P}, 1 \le i \le n\}$$

$$\cup \{s_i \mid a_{ef}^i > 0 \text{ and } \frac{a_{ef}^i}{F} - \frac{a_{ep}^i}{P} > 1 - \frac{a_{ep}^f}{P}, 1 \le i \le n\}$$

Consider the case $(a_{ef}^i = 0)$, which implies $a_{ep}^i > 0$ because $a_{ef}^i + a_{ep}^i > 0$ after Lemma 2.3.1. Then, we have

$$\frac{a_{ef}^i}{F} - \frac{a_{ep}^i}{P} = -\frac{a_{ep}^i}{P} < 0$$

Besides, since $a_{ep}^f \leq P$, we have $1 - \frac{a_{ep}^f}{P} \geq 0$. As a consequence, $\frac{a_{ef}^i}{F} - \frac{a_{ep}^i}{P} < 1 - \frac{a_{ep}^f}{P}$, which is contradictory to $\frac{a_{ef}^i}{F} - \frac{a_{ep}^i}{P} > 1 - \frac{a_{ep}^f}{P}$. Thus,

$$\{s_i | a_{ef}^i = 0 \text{ and } \frac{a_{ef}^i}{F} - \frac{a_{ep}^i}{P} > 1 - \frac{a_{ep}^f}{P}, 1 \leq i \leq n\} = \emptyset$$

Hence, we have

$$S_B^A = \{s_i | a_{ef}^i > 0 \text{ and } \frac{a_{ef}^i}{F} - \frac{a_{ep}^i}{P} > 1 - \frac{a_{ep}^f}{P}, 1 \leq i \leq n\} \qquad (A.105)$$

- Assume that $s_i \in S_B^A$. After (A.105), we have

$$a_{ef}^i > 0 \text{ and } \frac{a_{ef}^i}{F} - \frac{a_{ep}^i}{P} > 1 - \frac{a_{ep}^f}{P}$$

Since $a_{ef}^i > 0$ and $P > 0$, after $\frac{a_{ef}^i}{F} - \frac{a_{ep}^i}{P} > 1 - \frac{a_{ep}^f}{P}$, we have

$$\frac{P}{a_{ef}^i} \left(\frac{a_{ef}^i}{F} - \frac{a_{ep}^i}{P} \right) > \frac{P}{a_{ef}^i} \left(1 - \frac{a_{ep}^f}{P} \right)$$

After simplification, we have

$$\frac{P a_{ef}^i - PF + F a_{ep}^f}{F a_{ef}^i} - \frac{a_{ep}^i}{a_{ef}^i} > 0$$

After (A.102), $s_i \in X^A$. Therefore, $S_B^A \subseteq X^A$.
- Assume that $s_i \in X^A$. After (A.102), we have

$$a_{ef}^i > 0 \text{ and } \frac{P a_{ef}^i - PF + F a_{ep}^f}{F a_{ef}^i} - \frac{a_{ep}^i}{a_{ef}^i} > 0$$

Then,

$$\frac{P a_{ef}^i - PF + F a_{ep}^f}{F a_{ef}^i} - \frac{a_{ep}^i}{a_{ef}^i} > 0$$

can be rearranged as

$$\frac{P}{F} - \frac{a_{ep}^i}{a_{ef}^i} > \frac{P}{a_{ef}^i} - \frac{a_{ep}^f}{a_{ef}^i}$$

Since $a_{ef}^i > 0$ and $P > 0$, we have

$$\frac{a_{ef}^i}{P} \left(\frac{P}{F} - \frac{a_{ep}^i}{a_{ef}^i} \right) > \frac{a_{ef}^i}{P} \left(\frac{P}{a_{ef}^i} - \frac{a_{ep}^f}{a_{ef}^i} \right)$$

After simplification, we have

$$\frac{a_{ef}^i}{F} - \frac{a_{ep}^i}{P} > 1 - \frac{a_{ep}^f}{P}$$

After (A.105), $s_i \in S_B^A$. Therefore, $X^A \subseteq S_B^A$.

In summary, we have proved that $S_B^A = X^A$.
Similarly, we can prove that $S_F^A = Y^A$.
Next, we are going to prove $S_A^A = Z^A$. S_A^A in (A.101) can be rewritten as follows.

$$S_A^A = \{ s_i | a_{ef}^i = 0 \text{ and } \frac{a_{ef}^i}{F} - \frac{a_{ep}^i}{P} < 1 - \frac{a_{ep}^f}{P}, 1 \leq i \leq n \}$$

$$\cup \{ s_i | a_{ef}^i > 0 \text{ and } \frac{a_{ef}^i}{F} - \frac{a_{ep}^i}{P} < 1 - \frac{a_{ep}^f}{P}, 1 \leq i \leq n \}$$

Consider the case that $(a_{ef}^i = 0)$. As shown in the above proof of $S_B^A = X^A$, $(a_{ef}^i = 0)$ implies $\frac{a_{ef}^i}{F} - \frac{a_{ep}^i}{P} < 1 - \frac{a_{ep}^f}{P}$. Thus,

$$\left(a_{ef}^i = 0 \text{ and } \frac{a_{ef}^i}{F} - \frac{a_{ep}^i}{P} < 1 - \frac{a_{ep}^f}{P} \right)$$

is logically equivalent to $(a_{ef}^i = 0)$. Therefore, S_A^A becomes

$$\{ s_i | a_{ef}^i = 0, 1 \leq i \leq n \}$$

$$\cup \{ s_i | a_{ef}^i > 0 \text{ and } \frac{a_{ef}^i}{F} - \frac{a_{ep}^i}{P} < 1 - \frac{a_{ep}^f}{P}, 1 \leq i \leq n \}$$

Similar to the proof of $S_B^A = X^A$, we can prove

$$\{s_i \,|\, a_{ef}^i > 0 \text{ and } \frac{a_{ef}^i}{F} - \frac{a_{ep}^i}{P} < 1 - \frac{a_{ep}^f}{P}, 1 \leq i \leq n\}$$

$$= \{s_i \,|\, a_{ef}^i > 0 \text{ and } \frac{P a_{ef}^i - PF + F a_{ep}^f}{F a_{ef}^i} - \frac{a_{ep}^i}{a_{ef}^i} < 0, 1 \leq i \leq n\}$$

Therefore, we have

$$S_A^A = \{s_i \,|\, (a_{ef}^i = 0) \text{ or } (a_{ef}^i > 0 \text{ and } \frac{P a_{ef}^i - PF + F a_{ep}^f}{F a_{ef}^i} - \frac{a_{ep}^i}{a_{ef}^i} < 0), 1 \leq i \leq n\}$$

$$= Z^A$$

In conclusion, we have proved that $S_B^A = X^A$, $S_F^A = Y^A$, and $S_A^A = Z^A$.

(26) **Wong3**

As stated in Table 2.1, formula Wong3 is defined as $R_{W3}(s_i) = a_{ef}^i - h$, where

$$h = \begin{cases} a_{ep}^i & \text{if } a_{ep}^i \leq 2 \\ 2 + 0.1(a_{ep}^i - 2) & \text{if } 2 < a_{ep}^i \leq 10 \\ 2.8 + 0.001(a_{ep}^i - 10) & \text{if } a_{ep}^i > 10 \end{cases}$$

(a) Assume that $a_{ep}^f \leq 2$. Then, $R_{W3}(s_f) = F - a_{ep}^f$. After Definition 2.2.1 and rearranging the terms, we have

$$S_B^{W3} = \{s_i \,|\, a_{ep}^i \leq 2 \text{ and } (a_{ef}^i - F) + (a_{ep}^f - a_{ep}^i) > 0, 1 \leq i \leq n\}$$

$$\cup \{s_i \,|\, 2 < a_{ep}^i \leq 10 \text{ and } (a_{ef}^i - F) + (a_{ep}^f - 0.1 a_{ep}^i) - 1.8 > 0, 1 \leq i \leq n\}$$

$$\cup \{s_i \,|\, a_{ep}^i > 10 \text{ and } (a_{ef}^i - F) + (a_{ep}^f - 0.001 a_{ep}^i) - 2.79 > 0, 1 \leq i \leq n\}$$

$$\text{(A.106)}$$

$$S_F^{W3} = \{s_i \,|\, a_{ep}^i \leq 2 \text{ and } (a_{ef}^i - F) + (a_{ep}^f - a_{ep}^i) = 0, 1 \leq i \leq n\}$$

$$\cup \{s_i \,|\, 2 < a_{ep}^i \leq 10 \text{ and } (a_{ef}^i - F) + (a_{ep}^f - 0.1 a_{ep}^i) - 1.8 = 0, 1 \leq i \leq n\}$$

$$\cup \{s_i \,|\, a_{ep}^i > 10 \text{ and } (a_{ef}^i - F) + (a_{ep}^f - 0.001 a_{ep}^i) - 2.79 = 0, 1 \leq i \leq n\}$$

$$\text{(A.107)}$$

$$S_A^{W3}=\{s_i\,|\,a_{ep}^i\leq 2 \text{ and } (a_{ef}^i-F)+(a_{ep}^f-a_{ep}^i)<0,\ 1\leq i\leq n\}$$

$$\cup\{s_i\,|\,2<a_{ep}^i\leq 10 \text{ and } (a_{ef}^i-F)+(a_{ep}^f-0.1a_{ep}^i)-1.8<0,\ 1\leq i\leq n\}$$

$$\cup\{s_i\,|\,a_{ep}^i>10 \text{ and } (a_{ef}^i-F)+(a_{ep}^f-0.001a_{ep}^i)-2.79<0,\ 1\leq i\leq n\}$$

$$(A.108)$$

We are going to prove that the above sets in (A.106), (A.107), and (A.108) are equal to the following sets, X_1^{W3}, Y_1^{W3}, and Z_1^{W3}, respectively.

$$X_1^{W3}=\{s_i\,|\,a_{ep}^i\leq 2 \text{ and } (a_{ef}^i-F)+(a_{ep}^f-a_{ep}^i)>0,\ 1\leq i\leq n\} \qquad (A.109)$$

$$Y_1^{W3}=\{s_i\,|\,a_{ep}^i\leq 2 \text{ and } (a_{ef}^i-F)+(a_{ep}^f-a_{ep}^i)=0,\ 1\leq i\leq n\} \qquad (A.110)$$

$$Z_1^{W3}=\{s_i\,|\,(a_{ep}^i>2) \text{ or } (a_{ep}^i\leq 2 \text{ and } (a_{ef}^i-F)+(a_{ep}^f-a_{ep}^i)<0),\ 1\leq i\leq n\}$$

$$(A.111)$$

First, we will prove that S_B^{W3} defined in (A.106) is equal to X_1^{W3} in (A.109).

- Consider the case that $(2<a_{ep}^i\leq 10)$. Since $a_{ep}^f\leq 2<a_{ep}^i\leq 10$, we have

$$(a_{ep}^f-0.1a_{ep}^i)-1.8<0$$

And since $a_{ef}^i-F\leq 0$ after Lemma 2.3.1, we have

$$(a_{ef}^i-F)+(a_{ep}^f-0.1a_{ep}^i)-1.8<0$$

which is contradictory to

$$(a_{ef}^i-F)+(a_{ep}^f-0.1a_{ep}^i)-1.8>0$$

Thus,

$$\{s_i\,|\,2<a_{ep}^i\leq 10 \text{ and } (a_{ef}^i-F)+(a_{ep}^f-0.1a_{ep}^i)-1.8>0,\ 1\leq i\leq n\}=\emptyset$$

- Consider the case that $(a_{ep}^i>10)$. We have $(a_{ep}^f-0.001a_{ep}^i)-2.79<0$ after $a_{ep}^f\leq 2$ and $a_{ep}^i>10$. Since $a_{ef}^i-F\leq 0$, we have

$$(a_{ef}^i-F)+(a_{ep}^f-0.001a_{ep}^i)-2.79<0$$

which is contradictory to

$$(a_{ef}^i - F) + (a_{ep}^f - 0.001a_{ep}^i) - 2.79 > 0$$

Thus,

$$\{s_i \,|\, a_{ep}^i > 10 \text{ and } (a_{ef}^i - F) + (a_{ep}^f - 0.001a_{ep}^i) - 2.79 > 0, \, 1 \le i \le n\} = \emptyset$$

As a consequence, S_B^{W3} in (A.106) becomes

$$S_B^{W3} = \{s_i \,|\, a_{ep}^i \le 2 \text{ and } (a_{ef}^i - F) + (a_{ep}^f - a_{ep}^i) > 0, \, 1 \le i \le n\}$$
$$= X_1^{W3}$$

Similarly, we can prove that S_F^{W3} defined in (A.107) is equal to Y_1^{W3} in (A.110).

Next, we are going to prove that S_A^{W3} defined in (A.108) is equal to Z_1^{W3} in (A.111). As shown in the above proof of $S_B^{W3} = X_1^{W3}$, $(2 < a_{ep}^i \le 10)$ implies

$$(a_{ef}^i - F) + (a_{ep}^f - 0.1a_{ep}^i) - 1.8 < 0$$

and $(a_{ep}^i > 10)$ implies

$$(a_{ef}^i - F) + (a_{ep}^f - 0.001a_{ep}^i) - 2.79 < 0$$

Thus,

$$(2 < a_{ep}^i \le 10 \text{ and } (a_{ef}^i - F) + (a_{ep}^f - 0.1a_{ep}^i) - 1.8 < 0)$$

is logically equivalent to $(2 < a_{ep}^i \le 10)$, and

$$(a_{ep}^i > 10 \text{ and } (a_{ef}^i - F) + (a_{ep}^f - 0.001a_{ep}^i) - 2.79 < 0)$$

is logically equivalent to $(a_{ep}^i > 10)$. Therefore, S_A^{W3} in (A.108) becomes

$$\{s_i \,|\, (a_{ep}^i > 2) \text{ or } (a_{ep}^i \le 2 \text{ and } (a_{ef}^i - F) + (a_{ep}^f - a_{ep}^i) < 0), \, 1 \le i \le n\} = Z_1^{W3}$$

(b) Assume that $2 < a_{ep}^f \le 10$. Then,

$$R_{W3}(s_f) = F - 2 - 0.1(a_{ep}^f - 2) = F - 0.1a_{ep}^f - 1.8$$

After Definition 2.2.1 and rearranging the terms, we have

$$S_B^{W3}=\{s_i\,|\,a_{ep}^i\leq2 \text{ and } (a_{ef}^i-F)+(0.1a_{ep}^f-a_{ep}^i)+1.8>0,\,1\leq i\leq n\}$$

$$\cup\{s_i\,|\,2<a_{ep}^i\leq10 \text{ and } (a_{ef}^i-F)+(0.1a_{ep}^f-0.1a_{ep}^i)>0,\,1\leq i\leq n\}$$

$$\cup\{s_i\,|\,a_{ep}^i>10 \text{ and } (a_{ef}^i-F)+(0.1a_{ep}^f-0.001a_{ep}^i)-0.99>0,\,1\leq i\leq n\}$$
$$(A.112)$$

$$S_F^{W3}=\{s_i\,|\,a_{ep}^i\leq2 \text{ and } (a_{ef}^i-F)+(0.1a_{ep}^f-a_{ep}^i)+1.8=0,\,1\leq i\leq n\}$$

$$\cup\{s_i\,|\,2<a_{ep}^i\leq10 \text{ and } (a_{ef}^i-F)+(0.1a_{ep}^f-0.1a_{ep}^i)=0,\,1\leq i\leq n\}$$

$$\cup\{s_i\,|\,a_{ep}^i>10 \text{ and } (a_{ef}^i-F)+(0.1a_{ep}^f-0.001a_{ep}^i)-0.99=0,\,1\leq i\leq n\}$$
$$(A.113)$$

$$S_A^{W3}=\{s_i\,|\,a_{ep}^i\leq2 \text{ and } (a_{ef}^i-F)+(0.1a_{ep}^f-a_{ep}^i)+1.8<0,\,1\leq i\leq n\}$$

$$\cup\{s_i\,|\,2<a_{ep}^i\leq10 \text{ and } (a_{ef}^i-F)+(0.1a_{ep}^f-0.1a_{ep}^i)<0,\,1\leq i\leq n\}$$

$$\cup\{s_i\,|\,a_{ep}^i>10 \text{ and } (a_{ef}^i-F)+(0.1a_{ep}^f-0.001a_{ep}^i)-0.99<0,\,1\leq i\leq n\}$$
$$(A.114)$$

We are going to prove that the above sets defined in (A.112), (A.113), and (A.114) are equal to the following sets X_2^{W3}, Y_2^{W3}, and Z_2^{W3}, respectively.

$$X_2^{W3}=\{s_i\,|\,(a_{ep}^i\leq2 \text{ and } (a_{ef}^i-F)+(0.1a_{ep}^f-a_{ep}^i)+1.8>0)$$

$$\text{or } (2<a_{ep}^i\leq10 \text{ and } (a_{ef}^i-F)+(0.1a_{ep}^f-0.1a_{ep}^i)>0),\,1\leq i\leq n\}$$
$$(A.115)$$

$$Y_2^{W3}=\{s_i\,|\,2<a_{ep}^i\leq10 \text{ and } (a_{ef}^i-F)+(0.1a_{ep}^f-0.1a_{ep}^i)=0,\,1\leq i\leq n\}$$
$$(A.116)$$

$$Z_2^{W3}=\{s_i\,|\,(a_{ep}^i\leq2 \text{ and } (a_{ef}^i-F)+(0.1a_{ep}^f-a_{ep}^i)+1.8<0)$$

$$\text{or } (2<a_{ep}^i\leq10 \text{ and } (a_{ef}^i-F)+(0.1a_{ep}^f-0.1a_{ep}^i)<0)$$

$$\text{or } (a_{ep}^i>10),\,1\leq i\leq n\}$$
$$(A.117)$$

Firstly, we will prove that S_B^{W3} defined in (A.112) is equal to X_2^{W3} in (A.115). Consider the case that $a_{ep}^i>10$. Thus, we have $2<a_{ep}^f\leq10<a_{ep}^i$, which implies

$$(0.1a_{ep}^f-0.001a_{ep}^i)-0.99<0$$

And since $a_{ef}^i - F \leq 0$ after Lemma 2.3.1, we have

$$(a_{ef}^i - F) + (0.1a_{ep}^f - 0.001a_{ep}^i) - 0.99 < 0$$

which is contradictory to

$$(a_{ef}^i - F) + (0.1a_{ep}^f - 0.001a_{ep}^i) - 0.99 > 0$$

Thus,

$$\{s_i | a_{ep}^i > 10 \text{ and } (a_{ef}^i - F) + (0.1a_{ep}^f - 0.001a_{ep}^i) - 0.99 > 0, 1 \leq i \leq n\} = \emptyset$$

Then, S_B^{W3} in (A.112) becomes

$$S_B^{W3} = \{s_i | (a_{ep}^i \leq 2 \text{ and } (a_{ef}^i - F) + (0.1a_{ep}^f - a_{ep}^i) + 1.8 > 0)$$

$$\text{or } (2 < a_{ep}^i \leq 10 \text{ and } (a_{ef}^i - F) + (0.1a_{ep}^f - 0.1a_{ep}^i) > 0), 1 \leq i \leq n\}$$

$$= X_2^{W3}$$

Secondly, we will prove that S_F^{W3} defined in (A.113) is equal to Y_2^{W3} in (A.116).

- Consider the case that $a_{ep}^i > 10$. Thus, we have $2 < a_{ep}^f \leq 10 < a_{ep}^i$, which implies $(0.1a_{ep}^f - 0.001a_{ep}^i) - 0.99 < 0$. Since $a_{ef}^i - F \leq 0$ after Lemma 2.3.1, we have

$$(a_{ef}^i - F) + (0.1a_{ep}^f - 0.001a_{ep}^i) - 0.99 < 0$$

which is contradictory to

$$(a_{ef}^i - F) + (0.1a_{ep}^f - 0.001a_{ep}^i) - 0.99 = 0$$

Thus,

$$\{s_i | a_{ep}^i > 10 \text{ and } (a_{ef}^i - F) + (0.1a_{ep}^f - 0.001a_{ep}^i) - 0.99 = 0, 1 \leq i \leq n\} = \emptyset$$

- Consider the case that $a_{ep}^i \leq 2$. Thus, we have $a_{ep}^i \leq 2 < a_{ep}^f \leq 10$. Then, $0.1a_{ep}^f$ will be within the range of $(0.2, 1]$. Therefore, $(0.1a_{ep}^f + 1.8)$ cannot be integer. As a consequence,

$$(a_{ef}^i - F) + (0.1a_{ep}^f - a_{ep}^i) + 1.8 = (a_{ef}^i - F - a_{ep}^i) + (0.1a_{ep}^f + 1.8) \neq 0$$

because a_{ef}^i, F and a_{ep}^i are all integers. Thus,

$$\{s_i \mid a_{ep}^i \le 2 \text{ and } (a_{ef}^i - F) + (0.1a_{ep}^f - a_{ep}^i) + 1.8 = 0, \ 1 \le i \le n\} = \emptyset$$

Therefore, S_F^{W3} in (A.113) becomes

$$S_F^{W3} = \{s_i \mid 2 < a_{ep}^i \le 10 \text{ and } (a_{ef}^i - F) + (0.1a_{ep}^f - 0.1a_{ep}^i) = 0, \ 1 \le i \le n\}$$
$$= Y_2^{W3}$$

Next, we are going to prove that S_A^{W3} defined in (A.114) is equal to Z_2^{W3} in (A.117). As shown in the above proof of $S_B^{W3} = X_2^{W3}$, $(a_{ep}^i > 10)$ implies

$$(a_{ef}^i - F) + (0.1a_{ep}^f - 0.001a_{ep}^i) - 0.99 < 0$$

Thus,

$$(a_{ep}^i > 10 \text{ and } (a_{ef}^i - F) + (0.1a_{ep}^f - 0.001a_{ep}^i) - 0.99 < 0)$$

is logically equivalent to $(a_{ep}^i > 10)$. Therefore, S_A^{W3} in (A.114) becomes

$$S_A^{W3} = \{s_i \mid (a_{ep}^i \le 2 \text{ and } (a_{ef}^i - F) + (0.1a_{ep}^f - a_{ep}^i) + 1.8 < 0)$$
$$\text{or } (2 < a_{ep}^i \le 10 \text{ and } (a_{ef}^i - F) + (0.1a_{ep}^f - 0.1a_{ep}^i) < 0)$$
$$\text{or } (a_{ep}^i > 10), \ 1 \le i \le n\}$$
$$= Z_2^{W3}$$

(c) Assume that $a_{ep}^f > 10$. Then,

$$R_{W3}(s_f) = F - 2.8 - 0.001(a_{ep}^f - 10) = F - 0.001a_{ep}^f - 2.79$$

After Definition 2.2.1, we have

$$S_B^{W3} = \{s_i \mid a_{ep}^i \le 2 \text{ and } a_{ef}^i - a_{ep}^i > F - 0.001a_{ep}^f - 2.79, \ 1 \le i \le n\}$$
$$\cup \{s_i \mid 2 < a_{ep}^i \le 10 \text{ and } a_{ef}^i - 2 - 0.1(a_{ep}^i - 2) > F - 0.001a_{ep}^f - 2.79, \ 1 \le i \le n\}$$
$$\cup \{s_i \mid a_{ep}^i > 10 \text{ and } a_{ef}^i - 2.8 - 0.001(a_{ep}^i - 10) > F - 0.001a_{ep}^f - 2.79, \ 1 \le i \le n\}$$

$$\text{(A.118)}$$

$$S_F^{W3}=\{s_i\,|\,a_{ep}^i\leq2 \text{ and } a_{ef}^i-a_{ep}^i=F-0.001a_{ep}^f-2.79,\ 1\leq i\leq n\}$$

$$\cup\{s_i\,|\,2<a_{ep}^i\leq10 \text{ and } a_{ef}^i-2-0.1(a_{ep}^i-2)=F-0.001a_{ep}^f-2.79,\ 1\leq i\leq n\}$$

$$\cup\{s_i\,|\,a_{ep}^i>10 \text{ and } a_{ef}^i-2.8-0.001(a_{ep}^i-10)=F-0.001a_{ep}^f-2.79,\ 1\leq i\leq n\}$$

$$(A.119)$$

$$S_A^{W3}=\{s_i\,|\,a_{ep}^i\leq2 \text{ and } a_{ef}^i-a_{ep}^i<F-0.001a_{ep}^f-2.79,\ 1\leq i\leq n\}$$

$$\cup\{s_i\,|\,2<a_{ep}^i\leq10 \text{ and } a_{ef}^i-2-0.1(a_{ep}^i-2)<F-0.001a_{ep}^f-2.79,\ 1\leq i\leq n\}$$

$$\cup\{s_i\,|\,a_{ep}^i>10 \text{ and } a_{ef}^i-2.8-0.001(a_{ep}^i-10)<F-0.001a_{ep}^f-2.79,\ 1\leq i\leq n\}$$

$$(A.120)$$

It is obvious that through rearranging the terms and merging the subsets, the above sets defined in (A.118), (A.119), and (A.120) are equal to the following sets, X_3^{W3}, Y_3^{W3}, and Z_3^{W3}, respectively.

$$X_3^{W3}=\{s_i\,|\,(a_{ep}^i\leq2 \text{ and } (a_{ef}^i-F)+(0.001a_{ep}^f-a_{ep}^i)+2.79>0)$$

$$\text{or } (2<a_{ep}^i\leq10 \text{ and } (a_{ef}^i-F)+(0.001a_{ep}^f-0.1a_{ep}^i)+0.99>0)$$

$$\text{or } (a_{ep}^i>10 \text{ and } (a_{ef}^i-F)+(0.001a_{ep}^f-0.001a_{ep}^i)>0),\ 1\leq i\leq n\}$$

$$(A.121)$$

$$Y_3^{W3}=\{s_i\,|\,(a_{ep}^i\leq2 \text{ and } (a_{ef}^i-F)+(0.001a_{ep}^f-a_{ep}^i)+2.79=0)$$

$$\text{or } (2<a_{ep}^i\leq10 \text{ and } (a_{ef}^i-F)+(0.001a_{ep}^f-0.1a_{ep}^i)+0.99=0)$$

$$\text{or } (a_{ep}^i>10 \text{ and } (a_{ef}^i-F)+(0.001a_{ep}^f-0.001a_{ep}^i)=0),\ 1\leq i\leq n\}$$

$$(A.122)$$

$$Z_3^{W3}=\{s_i\,|\,(a_{ep}^i\leq2 \text{ and } (a_{ef}^i-F)+(0.001a_{ep}^f-a_{ep}^i)+2.79<0)$$

$$\text{or } (2<a_{ep}^i\leq10 \text{ and } (a_{ef}^i-F)+(0.001a_{ep}^f-0.1a_{ep}^i)+0.99<0)$$

$$\text{or } (a_{ep}^i>10 \text{ and } (a_{ef}^i-F)+(0.001a_{ep}^f-0.001a_{ep}^i)<0),\ 1\leq i\leq n\}$$

$$(A.123)$$

(27) Arithmetic Mean

As stated in Table 2.1, formula Arithmetic Mean is defined as follows.

$$R_{AM}(s_i)=\frac{2a_{ef}^i a_{np}^i-2a_{nf}^i a_{ep}^i}{(a_{ef}^i+a_{ep}^i)(a_{np}^i+a_{nf}^i)+(a_{ef}^i+a_{nf}^i)(a_{ep}^i+a_{np}^i)}$$

From Definition 2.2.1 and Lemmas 2.3.1 and 2.3.2, after simplification, we have

$$S_B^{AM} = \{s_i \mid \frac{a_{ef}^i P - a_{ep}^i F}{(a_{ef}^i + a_{ep}^i)(P + F - a_{ef}^i - a_{ep}^i) + PF} > \frac{PF - F a_{ep}^f}{(F + a_{ep}^f)(P - a_{ep}^f) + PF},$$

$$1 \leq i \leq n\} \tag{A.124}$$

$$S_F^{AM} = \{s_i \mid \frac{a_{ef}^i P - a_{ep}^i F}{(a_{ef}^i + a_{ep}^i)(P + F - a_{ef}^i - a_{ep}^i) + PF} = \frac{PF - F a_{ep}^f}{(F + a_{ep}^f)(P - a_{ep}^f) + PF},$$

$$1 \leq i \leq n\} \tag{A.125}$$

$$S_A^{AM} = \{s_i \mid \frac{a_{ef}^i P - a_{ep}^i F}{(a_{ef}^i + a_{ep}^i)(P + F - a_{ef}^i - a_{ep}^i) + PF} < \frac{PF - F a_{ep}^f}{(F + a_{ep}^f)(P - a_{ep}^f) + PF},$$

$$1 \leq i \leq n\} \tag{A.126}$$

(28) Cohen

As stated in Table 2.1, formula Cohen is defined as follows.

$$R_{CO}(s_i) = \frac{2a_{ef}a_{np} - 2a_{nf}a_{ep}}{(a_{ef} + a_{ep})(a_{np} + a_{ep}) + (a_{ef} + a_{nf})(a_{nf} + a_{np})}$$

From Definition 2.2.1 and Lemmas 2.3.1 and 2.3.2, after simplification, we have

$$S_B^{CO} = \{s_i \mid \frac{a_{ef}^i P - a_{ep}^i F}{P(a_{ef}^i + a_{ep}^i) + F(P + F - a_{ef}^i - a_{ep}^i)} > \frac{PF - F a_{ep}^f}{P(F + a_{ep}^f) + F(P - a_{ep}^f)},$$

$$1 \leq i \leq n\} \tag{A.127}$$

$$S_F^{CO} = \{s_i \mid \frac{a_{ef}^i P - a_{ep}^i F}{P(a_{ef}^i + a_{ep}^i) + F(P + F - a_{ef}^i - a_{ep}^i)} = \frac{PF - F a_{ep}^f}{P(F + a_{ep}^f) + F(P - a_{ep}^f)},$$

$$1 \leq i \leq n\} \tag{A.128}$$

$$S_A^{CO} = \{s_i \mid \frac{a_{ef}^i P - a_{ep}^i F}{P(a_{ef}^i + a_{ep}^i) + F(P + F - a_{ef}^i - a_{ep}^i)} < \frac{PF - F a_{ep}^f}{P(F + a_{ep}^f) + F(P - a_{ep}^f)},$$

$$1 \leq i \leq n\} \tag{A.129}$$

(29) Fleiss

As stated in Table 2.1, formula Fleiss is defined as follows.

$$R_F(s_i) = \frac{4a_{ef}a_{np} - 4a_{nf}a_{ep} - (a_{nf} - a_{ep})^2}{(2a_{ef} + a_{nf} + a_{ep}) + (2a_{np} + a_{nf} + a_{ep})}$$

From Definition 2.2.1 and Lemmas 2.3.1 and 2.3.2, after simplification, we have

$$S_B^F = \{s_i \mid \frac{-F^2 + 4a_{ef}^i P + 2F a_{ef}^i - 2F a_{ep}^i - (a_{ep}^i + a_{ef}^i)^2}{2P + 2F}$$

$$> \frac{4PF - 4F a_{ep}^f - (a_{ep}^f)^2}{2P + 2F}, \, 1 \leq i \leq n\}$$

$$S_F^F = \{s_i \mid \frac{-F^2 + 4a_{ef}^i P + 2F a_{ef}^i - 2F a_{ep}^i - (a_{ep}^i + a_{ef}^i)^2}{2P + 2F}$$

$$= \frac{4PF - 4F a_{ep}^f - (a_{ep}^f)^2}{2P + 2F}, \, 1 \leq i \leq n\}$$

$$S_A^F = \{s_i \mid \frac{-F^2 + 4a_{ef}^i P + 2F a_{ef}^i - 2F a_{ep}^i - (a_{ep}^i + a_{ef}^i)^2}{2P + 2F}$$

$$< \frac{4PF - 4F a_{ep}^f - (a_{ep}^f)^2}{2P + 2F}, \, 1 \leq i \leq n\}$$

Since $2P + 2F > 0$, obviously, S_B^F, S_F^F, and S_A^F are equal to the following sets, X^F, Y^F, and Z^F, respectively.

$$X^F = \{s_i \mid -F^2 + 4a_{ef}^i P + 2F a_{ef}^i - 2F a_{ep}^i - (a_{ep}^i + a_{ef}^i)^2$$

$$> 4PF - 4F a_{ep}^f - (a_{ep}^f)^2, \, 1 \leq i \leq n\} \tag{A.130}$$

$$Y^F = \{s_i \mid -F^2 + 4a_{ef}^i P + 2F a_{ef}^i - 2F a_{ep}^i - (a_{ep}^i + a_{ef}^i)^2$$

$$= 4PF - 4F a_{ep}^f - (a_{ep}^f)^2, \, 1 \leq i \leq n\} \tag{A.131}$$

$$Z^F = \{s_i \mid -F^2 + 4a_{ef}^i P + 2F a_{ef}^i - 2F a_{ep}^i - (a_{ep}^i + a_{ef}^i)^2$$

$$< 4PF - 4F a_{ep}^f - (a_{ep}^f)^2, \, 1 \leq i \leq n\} \tag{A.132}$$

Appendix B
Theoretical Comparison Among All Formulas

In Chap. 3, we have illustrated the proofs for all equivalent relations and one non-equivalent relation (i.e., "ER2 → ER3"). In this appendix, we will provide the detailed proofs for the comparison among different formulas in the remained non-equivalent relations.

Proposition B.1 *ER2 → ER4.*

Proof In order to prove ER2 → ER4, it is sufficient to prove Jaccard → Wong2. As proved in Appendix A, S_B^J and S_A^J are equal to the sets defined in (A.8) and (A.10), respectively, and S_B^{W2} and S_A^{W2} are equal to the sets defined in (A.42) and (A.44), respectively, as follows.

$$S_B^{W2} = \{s_i \,|\, (a_{ef}^i - F) + (a_{ep}^f - a_{ep}^i) > 0, 1 \leq i \leq n\}$$

$$S_A^{W2} = \{s_i \,|\, (a_{ef}^i - F) + (a_{ep}^f - a_{ep}^i) < 0, 1 \leq i \leq n\}$$

After rearranging the terms in $1 + \frac{a_{ep}^f}{F} - \frac{F}{a_{ef}^i} - \frac{a_{ep}^i}{a_{ef}^i}$ from (A.8) and (A.10), we have

$$1 + \frac{a_{ep}^f}{F} - \frac{F}{a_{ef}^i} - \frac{a_{ep}^i}{a_{ef}^i} = \left(1 + \frac{a_{ep}^f}{a_{ef}^i} - \frac{F}{a_{ef}^i} - \frac{a_{ep}^i}{a_{ef}^i}\right) + a_{ep}^f \left(\frac{1}{F} - \frac{1}{a_{ef}^i}\right)$$

Since $a_{ep}^f(\frac{1}{F} - \frac{1}{a_{ef}^i}) \leq 0$ after Lemma 2.3.1, we have

$$1 + \frac{a_{ep}^f}{F} - \frac{F}{a_{ef}^i} - \frac{a_{ep}^i}{a_{ef}^i} \leq 1 + \frac{a_{ep}^f}{a_{ef}^i} - \frac{F}{a_{ef}^i} - \frac{a_{ep}^i}{a_{ef}^i} \tag{B.1}$$

Now, we are going to prove $S_B^J \subseteq S_B^{W2}$ and $S_A^{W2} \subseteq S_A^J$.

X. Xie, B. Xu, *Essential Spectrum-based Fault Localization*,
https://doi.org/10.1007/978-981-33-6179-9

Firstly, we will prove $S_B^J \subseteq S_B^{W2}$. Assume $s_i \in S_B^J$. Then, after (A.8) we have

$$a_{ef}^i > 0 \text{ and } 1 + \frac{a_{ep}^f}{F} - \frac{F}{a_{ef}^i} - \frac{a_{ep}^i}{a_{ef}^i} > 0$$

As a consequence, from (B.1) we have

$$1 + \frac{a_{ep}^f}{a_{ef}^i} - \frac{F}{a_{ef}^i} - \frac{a_{ep}^i}{a_{ef}^i} > 0$$

Furthermore, since $a_{ef}^i > 0$ and

$$1 + \frac{a_{ep}^f}{a_{ef}^i} - \frac{F}{a_{ef}^i} - \frac{a_{ep}^i}{a_{ef}^i} = \frac{(a_{ef}^i - F) + (a_{ep}^f - a_{ep}^i)}{a_{ef}^i}$$

we have

$$(a_{ef}^i - F) + (a_{ep}^f - a_{ep}^i) > 0$$

After (A.42), $s_i \in S_B^{W2}$. Therefore, $S_B^J \subseteq S_B^{W2}$.

Secondly, we will prove $S_A^{W2} \subseteq S_A^J$. Assume $s_i \in S_A^{W2}$.

Then, we have $(a_{ef}^i - F) + (a_{ep}^f - a_{ep}^i) < 0$ after (A.44). Let us consider the following situations:

- Suppose $a_{ef}^i = 0$. Immediately after (A.10), $s_i \in S_A^J$.
- Suppose $a_{ef}^i > 0$. Since

$$\frac{(a_{ef}^i - F) + (a_{ep}^f - a_{ep}^i)}{a_{ef}^i} = 1 + \frac{a_{ep}^f}{a_{ef}^i} - \frac{F}{a_{ef}^i} - \frac{a_{ep}^i}{a_{ef}^i}$$

we have $1 + \frac{a_{ep}^f}{a_{ef}^i} - \frac{F}{a_{ef}^i} - \frac{a_{ep}^i}{a_{ef}^i} < 0$. As a consequence, we have $1 + \frac{a_{ep}^f}{F} - \frac{F}{a_{ef}^i} - \frac{a_{ep}^i}{a_{ef}^i} < 0$ after (B.1). Thus, $s_i \in S_A^J$ after (A.10).

In summary, we have proved that $S_A^{W2} \subseteq S_A^J$.

In conclusion, we have $S_B^J \subseteq S_B^{W2}$ and $S_A^{W2} \subseteq S_A^J$. Immediately after Theorem 2.2.2, Jaccard $\rightarrow$ Wong2. Since Jaccard belongs to ER2 and Wong2 belongs to ER4, we have ER2 $\rightarrow$ ER4.   □

Proposition B.2 *Ochiai $\rightarrow$ ER2.*

Proof In order to prove Ochiai $\rightarrow$ ER2, it is sufficient to prove Ochiai $\rightarrow$ Jaccard. As proved in Appendix A, S_B^J and S_A^J are equal to the sets defined in (A.8) and

(A.10), respectively, and S_B^O and S_A^O are equal to the sets defined in (A.95) and (A.97), respectively, as follows.

$$S_B^O = \{s_i \mid a_{ef}^i > 0 \text{ and } (1 + \frac{a_{ep}^f}{F}) \frac{a_{ef}^i}{F} - 1 - \frac{a_{ep}^i}{a_{ef}^i} > 0, 1 \leq i \leq n\}$$

$$S_A^O = \{s_i \mid (a_{ef}^i = 0) \text{ or } (a_{ef}^i > 0 \text{ and } (1 + \frac{a_{ep}^f}{F}) \frac{a_{ef}^i}{F} - 1 - \frac{a_{ep}^i}{a_{ef}^i} < 0), 1 \leq i \leq n\}$$

Let f_J and f_O denote the following expressions.

$$f_J(s_i) = 1 + \frac{a_{ep}^f}{F} - \frac{F}{a_{ef}^i} = \frac{a_{ef}^i F + a_{ef}^i a_{ep}^f - F^2}{F a_{ef}^i} \tag{B.2}$$

$$f_O(s_i) = (1 + \frac{a_{ep}^f}{F}) \frac{a_{ef}^i}{F} - 1 = \frac{a_{ef}^i F + a_{ef}^i a_{ep}^f - F^2}{F^2} \tag{B.3}$$

Now, we are going to prove $S_B^O \subseteq S_B^J$ and $S_A^J \subseteq S_A^O$.

First, we will prove that $S_B^O \subseteq S_B^J$. Assume $s_i \in S_B^O$. Then, after (A.95) we have

$$a_{ef}^i > 0 \text{ and } f_O(s_i) - \frac{a_{ep}^i}{a_{ef}^i} > 0$$

Since $a_{ep}^i \geq 0$, we have $\frac{a_{ep}^i}{a_{ef}^i} \geq 0$. Therefore, $f_O(s_i) > 0$. Then from Equation (B.3), we have $(a_{ef}^i F + a_{ef}^i a_{ep}^f - F^2) > 0$ because $F^2 > 0$. It follows from Lemma 2.3.1 that $F^2 \geq F a_{ef}^i$. Then, from Equations (B.3) and (B.2), we have $f_J(s_i) \geq f_O(s_i)$. As a consequence, we have

$$f_J(s_i) - \frac{a_{ep}^i}{a_{ef}^i} \geq f_O(s_i) - \frac{a_{ep}^i}{a_{ef}^i} > 0$$

It follows from (A.8) that $s_i \in S_B^J$. Thus, $S_B^O \subseteq S_B^J$.

Next, we will prove $S_A^J \subseteq S_A^O$. Assume $s_i \in S_A^J$. Then, we have either $(a_{ef}^i = 0)$ or $(a_{ef}^i > 0 \text{ and } f_J(s_i) - \frac{a_{ep}^i}{a_{ef}^i} < 0)$ after (A.10).

• Consider the case that $(a_{ef}^i = 0)$. Immediately, we have $s_i \in S_A^O$ after (A.97).

- Consider the case that $(a_{ef}^i > 0$ and $f_J(s_i) - \frac{a_{ep}^i}{a_{ef}^i} < 0)$. Assume further that $f_J(s_i)$ < 0. Since $Fa_{ef}^i > 0$, we have $(a_{ef}^i F + a_{ef}^i a_{ep}^f - F^2) < 0$ from Equation (B.2). Then, $f_O(s_i) < 0$ from Equation (B.3) because $F^2 > 0$. As a consequence,

$$f_O(s_i) - \frac{a_{ep}^i}{a_{ef}^i} < 0$$

Hence, $s_i \in S_A^O$ after (A.97). Next consider the sub-case that $f_J(s_i) = 0$. Then,

$$(a_{ef}^i F + a_{ef}^i a_{ep}^f - F^2) = 0$$

Thus we have $f_O(s_i) = f_J(s_i) = 0$ from Equation (B.3). Furthermore, since $f_J(s_i) - \frac{a_{ep}^i}{a_{ef}^i} < 0$ and $f_J(s_i) = 0$, we have $\frac{a_{ep}^i}{a_{ef}^i} > 0$. As a consequence, $f_O(s_i) - \frac{a_{ep}^i}{a_{ef}^i} < 0$. Hence, $s_i \in S_A^O$ after (A.97). Finally, consider the sub-case that $f_J(s_i) > 0$. Since $Fa_{ef}^i > 0$, we have

$$(a_{ef}^i F + a_{ef}^i a_{ep}^f - F^2) > 0$$

It follows from Lemma 2.3.1 that $F^2 \geq Fa_{ef}^i$. Then, from Equations (B.3) and (B.2), we have $f_J(s_i) \geq f_O(s_i)$. As a consequence, we have $f_O(s_i) - \frac{a_{ep}^i}{a_{ef}^i} \leq f_J(s_i) - \frac{a_{ep}^i}{a_{ef}^i} < 0$. Thus, $s_i \in S_A^O$ after (A.97).

In summary, we have proved that $S_A^J \subseteq S_A^O$.

In conclusion, we have $S_B^O \subseteq S_B^J$ and $S_A^J \subseteq S_A^O$. Immediately after Theorem 2.2.2, Ochiai $\rightarrow$ Jaccard. Since Jaccard belongs to ER2, we have Ochiai $\rightarrow$ ER2. $\square$

Proposition B.3 *Kulczynski2 $\rightarrow$ Ochiai.*

Proof As proved in Appendix A, S_B^O and S_A^O are equal to the sets defined in (A.95) and (A.97), respectively, and S_B^{K2} and S_A^{K2} are equal to the sets defined in (A.81) and (A.83), respectively, as follows.

$$S_B^{K2} = \{s_i \,|\, a_{ef}^i > 0 \text{ and } \frac{a_{ef}^i F + a_{ef}^i a_{ep}^f - F^2}{F^2 + (F + a_{ep}^f)(F - a_{ef}^i)} - \frac{a_{ep}^i}{a_{ef}^i} > 0, 1 \leq i \leq n\}$$

$$S_A^{K2} = \{s_i \,|\, (a_{ef}^i = 0) \text{ or } (a_{ef}^i > 0 \text{ and } \frac{a_{ef}^i F + a_{ef}^i a_{ep}^f - F^2}{F^2 + (F + a_{ep}^f)(F - a_{ef}^i)} - \frac{a_{ep}^i}{a_{ef}^i} < 0), 1 \leq i \leq n\}$$

Let f_{K2} denote the following expression.

$$f_{K2}(s_i) = \frac{a_{ef}^i F + a_{ef}^i a_{ep}^f - F^2}{F^2 + (F + a_{ep}^f)(F - a_{ef}^i)} \tag{B.4}$$

Now, we are going to prove $S_B^{K2} \subseteq S_B^O$ and $S_A^O \subseteq S_A^{K2}$.
Firstly, we will prove $S_B^{K2} \subseteq S_B^O$. Assume $s_i \in S_B^{K2}$. Then, after (A.81) we have

$$a_{ef}^i > 0 \text{ and } f_{K2}(s_i) - \frac{a_{ep}^i}{a_{ef}^i} > 0$$

Since $a_{ep}^i \geq 0$, we have $\frac{a_{ep}^i}{a_{ef}^i} \geq 0$. Therefore, $f_{K2}(s_i) > 0$. Then, from Equation (B.4), we have

$$(a_{ef}^i F + a_{ef}^i a_{ep}^f - F^2) > 0$$

because after Lemma 2.3.1, we have

$$(F^2 + (F + a_{ep}^f)(F - a_{ef}^i)) > 0$$

It also follows from Lemma 2.3.1 that

$$F^2 + (F + a_{ep}^f)(F - a_{ef}^i) \geq F^2 > 0$$

Thus from Equations (B.4) and (B.3), we have $f_O(s_i) \geq f_{K2}(s_i)$. As a consequence, we have

$$f_O(s_i) - \frac{a_{ep}^i}{a_{ef}^i} \geq f_{K2}(s_i) - \frac{a_{ep}^i}{a_{ef}^i} > 0$$

It follows from (A.95) that $s_i \in S_B^O$. Thus, $S_B^{K2} \subseteq S_B^O$.

Next, we will prove $S_A^O \subseteq S_A^{K2}$. Assume $s_i \in S_A^O$. Then, we have either $(a_{ef}^i = 0)$ or $(a_{ef}^i > 0$ and $f_O(s_i) - \frac{a_{ep}^i}{a_{ef}^i} < 0)$ after (A.97).

- Consider the case that $(a_{ef}^i = 0)$. It follows immediately from (A.83) that $s_i \in S_A^{K2}$.
- Consider the case that $(a_{ef}^i > 0$ and $f_O(s_i) - \frac{a_{ep}^i}{a_{ef}^i} < 0)$. Assume further that $f_O(s_i)$ < 0. Since $F^2 > 0$, from Equation (B.3) we have

$$(a_{ef}^i F + a_{ef}^i a_{ep}^f - F^2) < 0$$

Then, $f_{K2}(s_i)<0$ from Equation (B.4) because

$$(F^2+(F+a^f_{ep})(F-a^i_{ef}))>0$$

As a consequence,

$$f_{K2}(s_i)-\frac{a^i_{ep}}{a^i_{ef}}<0$$

Hence, $s_i\in S^{K2}_A$ after (A.83). Next consider the sub-case that $f_O(s_i)=0$. Then,

$$(a^i_{ef}F+a^i_{ef}a^f_{ep}-F^2)=0$$

Thus we have $f_{K2}(s_i)=f_O(s_i)=0$ from Equation (B.4). Furthermore, since $f_O(s_i)-\frac{a^i_{ep}}{a^i_{ef}}<0$ and $f_O(s_i)=0$, we have $\frac{a^i_{ep}}{a^i_{ef}}>0$. As a consequence,

$$f_{K2}(s_i)-\frac{a^i_{ep}}{a^i_{ef}}<0$$

Thus, $s_i\in S^{K2}_A$ after (A.83). Finally, consider the sub-case that $f_O(s_i)>0$. Since $F^2>0$, we have

$$(a^i_{ef}F+a^i_{ef}a^f_{ep}-F^2)>0$$

It follows from Lemma 2.3.1 that

$$F^2+(F+a^f_{ep})(F-a^i_{ef})\geq F^2>0$$

Thus, from Equations (B.4) and (B.3), we have $f_O(s_i)\geq f_{K2}(s_i)$. As a consequence, we have

$$f_{K2}(s_i)-\frac{a^i_{ep}}{a^i_{ef}}\leq f_O(s_i)-\frac{a^i_{ep}}{a^i_{ef}}<0$$

Thus, we have $s_i\in S^{K2}_A$ after (A.83).

In summary, we have proved that $S^O_A\subseteq S^{K2}_A$.

In conclusion, we have $S^{K2}_B\subseteq S^O_B$ and $S^O_A\subseteq S^{K2}_A$. Immediately after Theorem 2.2.2, Kulczynski2 $\rightarrow$ Ochiai.   □

Following from Propositions 3.2.7 to B.3, we have Kulczynski2 $\rightarrow$ Ochiai $\rightarrow$ ER2 $\rightarrow$ ER3 and ER2 $\rightarrow$ ER4.

Proposition B.4 *M2* $\to$ *AMPLE2*.

Proof As proved in Appendix A, S_B^{M2} and S_A^{M2} are equal to the sets defined in (A.88) and (A.90), respectively, as follows.

$$S_B^{M2}=\{s_i\,|\,a_{ef}^i>0 \text{ and } \frac{P+a_{ep}^f}{F}-\frac{2F+P}{a_{ef}^i}+2-\frac{a_{ep}^i}{a_{ef}^i}>0,\, 1\leq i\leq n\}$$

$$S_A^{M2}=\{s_i\,|\,(a_{ef}^i=0) \text{ or } (a_{ef}^i>0 \text{ and } \frac{P+a_{ep}^f}{F}-\frac{2F+P}{a_{ef}^i}+2-\frac{a_{ep}^i}{a_{ef}^i}<0),\, 1\leq i\leq n\}$$

And S_B^A and S_A^A are equal to the sets defined in (A.102) and (A.104), respectively, as follows.

$$S_B^A=\{s_i\,|\,a_{ef}^i>0 \text{ and } \frac{Pa_{ef}^i-PF+Fa_{ep}^f}{Fa_{ef}^i}-\frac{a_{ep}^i}{a_{ef}^i}>0,\, 1\leq i\leq n\}$$

$$S_A^A=\{s_i\,|\,(a_{ef}^i=0) \text{ or } (a_{ef}^i>0 \text{ and } \frac{Pa_{ef}^i-PF+Fa_{ep}^f}{Fa_{ef}^i}-\frac{a_{ep}^i}{a_{ef}^i}<0),\, 1\leq i\leq n\}$$

If $a_{ef}^i>0$, the expression $\frac{P+a_{ep}^f}{F}-\frac{2F+P}{a_{ef}^i}+2-\frac{a_{ep}^i}{a_{ef}^i}$ from (A.88) and (A.90) can be rewritten as follows.

$$\frac{P+a_{ep}^f}{F}-\frac{2F+P}{a_{ef}^i}+2-\frac{a_{ep}^i}{a_{ef}^i}$$

$$=\left(\frac{P}{F}-\frac{P}{a_{ef}^i}+\frac{a_{ep}^f}{a_{ef}^i}-\frac{a_{ep}^i}{a_{ef}^i}\right)+\left(\frac{a_{ep}^f}{F}-\frac{2F}{a_{ef}^i}-\frac{a_{ep}^f}{a_{ef}^i}+2\right)$$

$$=\left(\frac{Pa_{ef}^i-PF+Fa_{ep}^f}{Fa_{ef}^i}-\frac{a_{ep}^i}{a_{ef}^i}\right)+\frac{(a_{ep}^f+2F)(a_{ef}^i-F)}{Fa_{ef}^i}$$

Then, we have

$$\frac{P+a_{ep}^f}{F}-\frac{2F+P}{a_{ef}^i}+2-\frac{a_{ep}^i}{a_{ef}^i}\leq\frac{Pa_{ef}^i-PF+Fa_{ep}^f}{Fa_{ef}^i}-\frac{a_{ep}^i}{a_{ef}^i} \tag{B.5}$$

because $\frac{(a_{ep}^f+2F)(a_{ef}^i-F)}{Fa_{ef}^i}\leq 0$ after Lemma 2.3.1.

Now, we are going to prove $S_B^{M2}\subseteq S_B^A$ and $S_A^A\subseteq S_A^{M2}$.

Firstly, we will prove $S_B^{M2} \subseteq S_B^A$. Assume $s_i \in S_B^{M2}$. Then, after (A.88) we have

$$a_{ef}^i > 0 \quad \text{and} \quad \frac{P + a_{ep}^f}{F} - \frac{2F + P}{a_{ef}^i} + 2 - \frac{a_{ep}^i}{a_{ef}^i} > 0$$

As a consequence, from (B.5) we have

$$\frac{P a_{ef}^i - PF + F a_{ep}^f}{F a_{ef}^i} - \frac{a_{ep}^i}{a_{ef}^i} > 0$$

Thus, $s_i \in S_B^A$ after (A.102). Therefore, $S_B^{M2} \subseteq S_B^A$.

Secondly, we will prove $S_A^A \subseteq S_A^{M2}$. Assume $s_i \in S_A^A$. Then, we have either $(a_{ef}^i = 0)$ or $(a_{ef}^i > 0$ and $\frac{P a_{ef}^i - PF + F a_{ep}^f}{F a_{ef}^i} - \frac{a_{ep}^i}{a_{ef}^i} < 0)$ after (A.104).

- Consider the case that $(a_{ef}^i = 0)$. Immediately after (A.90), $s_i \in S_A^{M2}$.

- Consider the case that $(a_{ef}^i > 0$ and $\frac{P a_{ef}^i - PF + F a_{ep}^f}{F a_{ef}^i} - \frac{a_{ep}^i}{a_{ef}^i} < 0)$. Then, we have

$\frac{P + a_{ep}^f}{F} - \frac{2F + P}{a_{ef}^i} + 2 - \frac{a_{ep}^i}{a_{ef}^i} < 0$ after (B.5). Thus, $s_i \in S_A^{M2}$ after (A.90).

In summary, we have proved that $S_A^A \subseteq S_A^{M2}$.

In conclusion, we have $S_B^{M2} \subseteq S_B^A$ and $S_A^A \subseteq S_A^{M2}$. Immediately after Theorem 2.2.2, M2 → AMPLE2.   □

Proposition B.5 *ER1* → *M2*.

Proof In order to prove ER1 → M2, it is sufficient to prove Op1 → M2. As proved in Appendix A, S_B^{Op1} and S_A^{Op1} are equal to the sets defined in (2.1) and (2.3), respectively, and S_B^{M2} and S_A^{M2} are equal to the sets defined in (A.88) and (A.90), respectively.

We are going to prove $S_B^{Op1} \subseteq S_B^{M2}$ and $S_A^{M2} \subseteq S_A^{Op1}$.

Firstly, we will prove $S_B^{Op1} \subseteq S_B^{M2}$. Assume $s_i \in S_B^{Op1}$. Then we have $a_{ef}^i = F > 0$ and $(a_{ep}^f - a_{ep}^i) > 0$ after (2.1). As a consequence, we have

$$\frac{P + a_{ep}^f}{F} - \frac{2F + P}{a_{ef}^i} + 2 - \frac{a_{ep}^i}{a_{ef}^i} = \frac{P + a_{ep}^f - 2F - P + 2F - a_{ep}^i}{F} = \frac{a_{ep}^f - a_{ep}^i}{F} > 0$$

Therefore, $s_i \in S_B^{M2}$ after (A.88). Thus, $S_B^{Op1} \subseteq S_B^{M2}$.

Secondly, we are going to prove $S_A^{M2} \subseteq S_A^{Op1}$. Suppose $s_i \in S_A^{M2}$. Then we have either $(a_{ef}^i = 0)$ or $(a_{ef}^i > 0$ and $\frac{P + a_{ep}^f}{F} - \frac{2F + P}{a_{ef}^i} + 2 - \frac{a_{ep}^i}{a_{ef}^i} < 0)$ after (A.90).

- Consider the case that $(a^i_{ef}=0)$. Obviously, $a^i_{ef}<F$. Immediately after (2.3), $s_i \in S^{Op1}_A$.

- Consider the case that $(a^i_{ef}>0$ and $\frac{P+a^f_{ep}}{F}-\frac{2F+P}{a^i_{ef}}+2-\frac{a^i_{ep}}{a^i_{ef}}<0)$. Assume further that $0<a^i_{ef}<F$. After (2.3), we have $s_i \in S^{Op1}_A$. Next, consider the sub-case that $a^i_{ef}=F$. Then, we have

$$\frac{P+a^f_{ep}}{F}-\frac{2F+P}{a^i_{ef}}+2-\frac{a^i_{ep}}{a^i_{ef}}=\frac{a^f_{ep}-a^i_{ep}}{F}$$

Since $\frac{P+a^f_{ep}}{F}-\frac{2F+P}{a^i_{ef}}+2-\frac{a^i_{ep}}{a^i_{ef}}<0$ and $F>0$, we have $(a^f_{ep}-a^i_{ep})<0$. Thus, $s_i \in S^{Op1}_A$ after (2.3).

In summary, we have proved that $S^{M2}_A \subseteq S^{Op1}_A$.

In conclusion, we have $S^{Op1}_B \subseteq S^{M2}_B$ and $S^{M2}_A \subseteq S^{Op1}_A$. Immediately after Theorem 2.2.2, Op1 $\rightarrow$ M2. And after Proposition 3.2.1, ER1 $\rightarrow$ M2.   □

Proposition B.6 *ER1 $\rightarrow$ ER6.*

Proof In order to prove ER1 $\rightarrow$ ER6, it is sufficient to prove Op1 $\rightarrow$ Scott. As proved in Appendix A, S^{Op1}_B and S^{Op1}_A are equal to the sets defined in (2.1) and (2.3), respectively, and S^{SC}_B and S^{SC}_A are equal to the sets defined in (A.72) and (A.74), respectively, as follows.

$$S^{SC}_B=\{s_i \mid \frac{-F^2+4a^i_{ef}P+2Fa^i_{ef}-2Fa^i_{ep}-(a^i_{ep}+a^i_{ef})^2}{(F+2P-a^i_{ep}-a^i_{ef})(F+a^i_{ef}+a^i_{ep})} > \frac{4PF-4Fa^f_{ep}-(a^f_{ep})^2}{(2F+a^f_{ep})(2P-a^f_{ep})}, 1\leq i \leq n\}$$

$$S^{SC}_A=\{s_i \mid \frac{-F^2+4a^i_{ef}P+2Fa^i_{ef}-2Fa^i_{ep}-(a^i_{ep}+a^i_{ef})^2}{(F+2P-a^i_{ep}-a^i_{ef})(F+a^i_{ef}+a^i_{ep})} < \frac{4PF-4Fa^f_{ep}-(a^f_{ep})^2}{(2F+a^f_{ep})(2P-a^f_{ep})}, 1\leq i \leq n\}$$

If $a^i_{ef}=F$, we have

$$\frac{-F^2+4a^i_{ef}P+2Fa^i_{ef}-2Fa^i_{ep}-(a^i_{ep}+a^i_{ef})^2}{(F+2P-a^i_{ep}-a^i_{ef})(F+a^i_{ef}+a^i_{ep})}-\frac{4PF-4Fa^f_{ep}-(a^f_{ep})^2}{(2F+a^f_{ep})(2P-a^f_{ep})}$$

$$=\frac{4PF-4Fa^i_{ep}-(a^i_{ep})^2}{(2F+a^i_{ep})(2P-a^i_{ep})}-\frac{4PF-4Fa^f_{ep}-(a^f_{ep})^2}{(2F+a^f_{ep})(2P-a^f_{ep})}$$

$$=\frac{(8PF^2+8P^2F+2Pa^f_{ep}a^i_{ep}+2Fa^f_{ep}a^i_{ep})(a^f_{ep}-a^i_{ep})}{(2F+a^i_{ep})(2P-a^i_{ep})(2F+a^f_{ep})(2P-a^f_{ep})} \tag{B.6}$$

Now, we are going to prove $S^{Op1}_B \subseteq S^{SC}_B$ and $S^{SC}_A \subseteq S^{Op1}_A$.

Firstly, we will prove $S_B^{Op1} \subseteq S_B^{SC}$. Assume $s_i \in S_B^{Op1}$. Then, $a_{ef}^i = F$ and $(a_{ep}^f - a_{ep}^i) > 0$ after (2.1). It follows from Lemma 2.3.1 that

$$(8PF^2 + 8P^2F + 2Pa_{ep}^f a_{ep}^i + 2Fa_{ep}^f a_{ep}^i) > 0$$

and

$$(2F + a_{ep}^i)(2P - a_{ep}^i)(2F + a_{ep}^f)(2P - a_{ep}^f) > 0$$

Then we have

$$\frac{(8PF^2 + 8P^2F + 2Pa_{ep}^f a_{ep}^i + 2Fa_{ep}^f a_{ep}^i)(a_{ep}^f - a_{ep}^i)}{(2F + a_{ep}^i)(2P - a_{ep}^i)(2F + a_{ep}^f)(2P - a_{ep}^f)} > 0$$

because $(a_{ep}^f - a_{ep}^i) > 0$. From Equation (B.6), we have

$$\frac{-F^2 + 4a_{ef}^i P + 2Fa_{ef}^i - 2Fa_{ep}^i - (a_{ep}^i + a_{ef}^i)^2}{(F + 2P - a_{ep}^i - a_{ef}^i)(F + a_{ef}^i + a_{ep}^i)} > \frac{4PF - 4Fa_{ep}^f - (a_{ep}^f)^2}{(2F + a_{ep}^f)(2P - a_{ep}^f)}$$

Therefore, $s_i \in S_B^{SC}$ after (A.72). Thus, $S_B^{Op1} \subseteq S_B^{SC}$.

Secondly, we are going to prove $S_A^{SC} \subseteq S_A^{Op1}$. Suppose $s_i \in S_A^{SC}$. Then after (A.74) we have

$$\frac{-F^2 + 4a_{ef}^i P + 2Fa_{ef}^i - 2Fa_{ep}^i - (a_{ep}^i + a_{ef}^i)^2}{(F + 2P - a_{ep}^i - a_{ef}^i)(F + a_{ef}^i + a_{ep}^i)} < \frac{4PF - 4Fa_{ep}^f - (a_{ep}^f)^2}{(2F + a_{ep}^f)(2P - a_{ep}^f)}$$

- Suppose $(a_{ef}^i < F)$. Immediately after (2.3), $s_i \in S_A^{Op1}$.
- Suppose $(a_{ef}^i = F)$. It follows from

$$\frac{-F^2 + 4a_{ef}^i P + 2Fa_{ef}^i - 2Fa_{ep}^i - (a_{ep}^i + a_{ef}^i)^2}{(F + 2P - a_{ep}^i - a_{ef}^i)(F + a_{ef}^i + a_{ep}^i)} < \frac{4PF - 4Fa_{ep}^f - (a_{ep}^f)^2}{(2F + a_{ep}^f)(2P - a_{ep}^f)}$$

and Equation (B.6) that

$$\frac{(8PF^2 + 8P^2F + 2Pa_{ep}^f a_{ep}^i + 2Fa_{ep}^f a_{ep}^i)(a_{ep}^f - a_{ep}^i)}{(2F + a_{ep}^i)(2P - a_{ep}^i)(2F + a_{ep}^f)(2P - a_{ep}^f)} < 0$$

which implies $(a_{ep}^f - a_{ep}^i) < 0$, because $(8PF^2 + 8P^2F + 2Pa_{ep}^f a_{ep}^i + 2Fa_{ep}^f a_{ep}^i) > 0$ and $(2F + a_{ep}^i)(2P - a_{ep}^i)(2F + a_{ep}^f)(2P - a_{ep}^f) > 0$ after Lemma 2.3.1. Thus, $s_i \in S_A^{Op1}$ after (2.3).

In summary, we have proved that $S_A^{SC} \subseteq S_A^{Op1}$.

In conclusion, we have $S_B^{Op1} \subseteq S_B^{SC}$ and $S_A^{SC} \subseteq S_A^{Op1}$. Immediately after Theorem 2.2.2, Op1 $\rightarrow$ Scott. Since Op1 belongs to ER1 and Scott belongs to ER6, we have ER1 $\rightarrow$ ER6. $\qquad \square$

Proposition B.7 *ER1 $\rightarrow$ Wong3.*

Proof In order to prove ER1 $\rightarrow$ Wong3, it is sufficient to prove Op1 $\rightarrow$ Wong3. As proved in Appendix A, S_B^{Op1} and S_A^{Op1} are equal to the sets defined in (2.1) and (2.3), respectively; and for Wong3, the definitions of S_B^{W3} and S_A^{W3} vary in three situations: $a_{ep}^f \leq 2$, $2 < a_{ep}^f \leq 10$, and $a_{ep}^f > 10$. Under each of these situations, we are going to prove that $S_B^{Op1} \subseteq S_B^{W3}$ and $S_A^{W3} \subseteq S_A^{Op1}$.

1. **Case 1:** Assume $a_{ep}^f \leq 2$.
   As proved in Appendix A, S_B^{W3} and S_A^{W3} are equal to the sets defined in (A.109) and (A.111), respectively, as follows.

$$S_B^{W3} = \{s_i \mid a_{ep}^i \leq 2 \text{ and } (a_{ef}^i - F) + (a_{ep}^f - a_{ep}^i) > 0, 1 \leq i \leq n\}$$

$$S_A^{W3} = \{s_i \mid (a_{ep}^i > 2) \text{ or } (a_{ep}^i \leq 2 \text{ and } (a_{ef}^i - F) + (a_{ep}^f - a_{ep}^i) < 0), 1 \leq i \leq n\}$$

Firstly, we will prove $S_B^{Op1} \subseteq S_B^{W3}$. Assume $s_i \in S_B^{Op1}$. Then, $(a_{ef}^i = F)$ and $(a_{ep}^f - a_{ep}^i) > 0$ after (2.1). As a consequence,

$$(a_{ef}^i - F) + (a_{ep}^f - a_{ep}^i) = (a_{ep}^f - a_{ep}^i) > 0$$

Furthermore, since $a_{ep}^f \leq 2$, we have $a_{ep}^i < a_{ep}^f \leq 2$. Then, $s_i \in S_B^{W3}$ after (A.109). Thus, $S_B^{Op1} \subseteq S_B^{W3}$.

Secondly, we are going to prove $S_A^{W3} \subseteq S_A^{Op1}$. Assume $s_i \in S_A^{W3}$. Then we have either $a_{ep}^i > 2$ or $(a_{ep}^i \leq 2$ and $(a_{ef}^i - F) + (a_{ep}^f - a_{ep}^i) < 0)$ after (A.111).

- Consider the case that $a_{ep}^i > 2$. Assume further that $a_{ef}^i < F$. Immediately, we have $s_i \in S_A^{Op1}$ after (2.3). Then consider the sub-case that $a_{ef}^i = F$. Since $a_{ep}^i > 2$ and $a_{ep}^f \leq 2$, we have $(a_{ep}^f - a_{ep}^i) < 0$. Thus after (2.3), $s_i \in S_A^{Op1}$.

- Consider the case that $(a_{ep}^i \leq 2$ and $(a_{ef}^i - F) + (a_{ep}^f - a_{ep}^i) < 0)$. Assume further that $a_{ef}^i < F$. Then, $s_i \in S_A^{Op1}$ after (2.3). Now consider the sub-case that $a_{ef}^i = F$. We have

$$(a_{ef}^i - F) + (a_{ep}^f - a_{ep}^i) = (a_{ep}^f - a_{ep}^i)$$

Since $(a_{ef}^i - F) + (a_{ep}^f - a_{ep}^i) < 0$, then $(a_{ep}^f - a_{ep}^i) < 0$. After (2.3), $s_i \in S_A^{Op1}$.

In summary, we have proved that $S_A^{W3} \subseteq S_A^{Op1}$.

2. **Case 2:** Assume $2 < a_{ep}^f \leq 10$.
As proved in Appendix A, S_B^{W3} and S_A^{W3} are equal to the sets defined in (A.115) and (A.117), respectively, as follows.

$$S_B^{W3} = \{s_i | (a_{ep}^i \leq 2 \text{ and } (a_{ef}^i - F) + (0.1a_{ep}^f - a_{ep}^i) + 1.8 > 0)$$

$$\text{or } (2 < a_{ep}^i \leq 10 \text{ and } (a_{ef}^i - F) + (0.1a_{ep}^f - 0.1a_{ep}^i) > 0), 1 \leq i \leq n\}$$

$$S_A^{W3} = \{s_i | (a_{ep}^i \leq 2 \text{ and } (a_{ef}^i - F) + (0.1a_{ep}^f - a_{ep}^i) + 1.8 < 0)$$

$$\text{or } (2 < a_{ep}^i \leq 10 \text{ and } (a_{ef}^i - F) + (0.1a_{ep}^f - 0.1a_{ep}^i) < 0)$$

$$\text{or } (a_{ep}^i > 10), 1 \leq i \leq n\}$$

Firstly, we will prove $S_B^{Op1} \subseteq S_B^{W3}$. Assume $s_i \in S_B^{Op1}$. Then, $a_{ef}^i = F$ and $(a_{ep}^f - a_{ep}^i) > 0$ after (2.1). Since $2 < a_{ep}^f \leq 10$, we have $a_{ep}^i < 10$. Consider the following two cases:

- Suppose $a_{ep}^i \leq 2$. Since $a_{ef}^i = F$, we have

$$(a_{ef}^i - F) + (0.1a_{ep}^f - a_{ep}^i) + 1.8 = 0.1(a_{ep}^f - a_{ep}^i) + (1.8 - 0.9a_{ep}^i) > 0$$

because after $a_{ep}^i \leq 2$ we have

$$(a_{ep}^f - a_{ep}^i) > 0 \text{ and } (1.8 - 0.9a_{ep}^i) > 0$$

After (A.115), $s_i \in S_B^{W3}$.
- Suppose $2 < a_{ep}^i < 10$. Since $a_{ef}^i = F$, we have

$$(a_{ef}^i - F) + 0.1(a_{ep}^f - a_{ep}^i) = 0.1(a_{ep}^f - a_{ep}^i) > 0$$

because $(a_{ep}^f - a_{ep}^i) > 0$. Thus, $s_i \in S_B^{W3}$ after (A.115).

In summary, we have proved that $S_B^{Op1} \subseteq S_B^{W3}$.

Secondly, we are going to prove $S_A^{W3} \subseteq S_A^{Op1}$. Assume $s_i \in S_A^{W3}$. Then, we have either $(a_{ep}^i > 10)$, $(2 < a_{ep}^i \le 10$ and $(a_{ef}^i - F) + 0.1(a_{ep}^f - a_{ep}^i) < 0)$, or $(a_{ep}^i \le 2$ and $(a_{ef}^i - F) + (0.1a_{ep}^f - a_{ep}^i) + 1.8 < 0)$.

- Consider the case that $a_{ep}^i > 10$. Assume further $a_{ef}^i < F$. Immediately after (2.3), we have $s_i \in S_A^{Op1}$. Then consider the sub-case that $a_{ef}^i = F$. Since $2 < a_{ep}^f \le 10$ and $a_{ep}^i > 10$, we have $(a_{ep}^f - a_{ep}^i) < 0$. After (2.3), $s_i \in S_A^{Op1}$.

- Consider the case that $(2 < a_{ep}^i \le 10$ and $(a_{ef}^i - F) + 0.1(a_{ep}^f - a_{ep}^i) < 0)$. Assume further that $a_{ef}^i < F$. Then, we have $s_i \in S_A^{Op1}$ after (2.3). Now consider the sub-case that $a_{ef}^i = F$. Then, we have

$$(a_{ef}^i - F) + 0.1(a_{ep}^f - a_{ep}^i) = 0.1(a_{ep}^f - a_{ep}^i)$$

Since $(a_{ef}^i - F) + 0.1(a_{ep}^f - a_{ep}^i) < 0$, then $(a_{ep}^f - a_{ep}^i) < 0$. After (2.3), $s_i \in S_A^{Op1}$.

- Consider the case that $(a_{ep}^i \le 2$ and $(a_{ef}^i - F) + (0.1a_{ep}^f - a_{ep}^i) + 1.8 < 0)$. Assume further that $a_{ef}^i = F$. Then, we have

$$(a_{ef}^i - F) + (0.1a_{ep}^f - a_{ep}^i) + 1.8 = 0.1a_{ep}^f - a_{ep}^i + 1.8 < 0$$

However, it follows from $2 < a_{ep}^f \le 10$ and $a_{ep}^i \le 2$ that $0.1a_{ep}^f - a_{ep}^i + 1.8 > 0$, which is contradictory to $0.1a_{ep}^f - a_{ep}^i + 1.8 < 0$. Therefore, it is impossible to have $a_{ef}^i = F$, and all statements in this case have $a_{ef}^i < F$. Then, we have $s_i \in S_A^{Op1}$ after (2.3).

In summary, we have proved that $S_A^{W3} \subseteq S_A^{Op1}$.

3. **Case 3:** Assume $a_{ep}^f > 10$.

As proved in Appendix A, S_B^{W3} and S_A^{W3} are equal to the sets defined in (A.121) and (A.123), respectively, as follows.

$$S_B^{W3} = \{s_i \,|\, (a_{ep}^i \le 2 \text{ and } (a_{ef}^i - F) + (0.001a_{ep}^f - a_{ep}^i) + 2.79 > 0)$$

$$\text{or } (2 < a_{ep}^i \le 10 \text{ and } (a_{ef}^i - F) + (0.001a_{ep}^f - 0.1a_{ep}^i) + 0.99 > 0)$$

$$\text{or } (a_{ep}^i > 10 \text{ and } (a_{ef}^i - F) + (0.001a_{ep}^f - 0.001a_{ep}^i) > 0), \, 1 \le i \le n\}$$

$$S_A^{W3} = \{s_i \,|\, (a_{ep}^i \le 2 \text{ and } (a_{ef}^i - F) + (0.001a_{ep}^f - a_{ep}^i) + 2.79 < 0)$$

$$\text{or } (2 < a_{ep}^i \le 10 \text{ and } (a_{ef}^i - F) + (0.001a_{ep}^f - 0.1a_{ep}^i) + 0.99 < 0)$$

$$\text{or } (a_{ep}^i > 10 \text{ and } (a_{ef}^i - F) + (0.001a_{ep}^f - 0.001a_{ep}^i) < 0), \, 1 \le i \le n\}$$

Firstly, we will prove $S_B^{Op1} \subseteq S_B^{W3}$. Assume $s_i \in S_B^{Op1}$. Then, we have $a_{ef}^i = F$ and $(a_{ep}^f - a_{ep}^i) > 0$ after (2.1). Since $a_{ep}^f > 10$, a_{ep}^i can be any value within $[0, P]$. Now, let us consider the following cases:

- Suppose $a_{ep}^i \leq 2$. Since $a_{ef}^i = F$, we have

$$(a_{ef}^i - F) + (0.001a_{ep}^f - a_{ep}^i) + 2.79 = 0.001(a_{ep}^f - a_{ep}^i) + (2.79 - 0.999a_{ep}^i) > 0$$

because $(a_{ep}^f - a_{ep}^i) > 0$ and $(2.79 - 0.999a_{ep}^i) > 0$ after $a_{ep}^i \leq 2$. After (A.121), $s_i \in S_B^{W3}$.
- Suppose $2 < a_{ep}^i \leq 10$. Since $a_{ef}^i = F$, we have

$$(a_{ef}^i - F) + (0.001a_{ep}^f - 0.1a_{ep}^i) + 0.99 = 0.001(a_{ep}^f - a_{ep}^i) + (0.99 - 0.099a_{ep}^i) > 0$$

because $(a_{ep}^f - a_{ep}^i) > 0$ and $(0.99 - 0.099a_{ep}^i) \geq 0$ after $2 < a_{ep}^i \leq 10$. After (A.121), $s_i \in S_B^{W3}$.
- Suppose $a_{ep}^i > 10$. Since $a_{ef}^i = F$, we have

$$(a_{ef}^i - F) + 0.001(a_{ep}^f - a_{ep}^i) = 0.001(a_{ep}^f - a_{ep}^i) > 0$$

because $(a_{ep}^f - a_{ep}^i) > 0$. Thus, $s_i \in S_B^{W3}$ after (A.121).

In summary, we have proved that $S_B^{Op1} \subseteq S_B^{W3}$.
Secondly, we will prove $S_A^{W3} \subseteq S_A^{Op1}$. Assume $s_i \in S_A^{W3}$. Then we have either $(a_{ep}^i \leq 2$ and

$$(a_{ef}^i - F) + (0.001a_{ep}^f - a_{ep}^i) + 2.79 < 0)$$

or

$$2 < a_{ep}^i \leq 10 \text{ and } (a_{ef}^i - F) + (0.001a_{ep}^f - 0.1a_{ep}^i) + 0.99 < 0)$$

or

$$(a_{ep}^i > 10 \text{ and } (a_{ef}^i - F) + 0.001(a_{ep}^f - a_{ep}^i) < 0)$$

- Consider the case that $a_{ep}^i \leq 2$ and $(a_{ef}^i - F) + (0.001a_{ep}^f - a_{ep}^i) + 2.79 < 0$. Assume further $a_{ef}^i = F$. Then, we have

$$(a_{ef}^i - F) + (0.001a_{ep}^f - a_{ep}^i) + 2.79 = 0.001a_{ep}^f - a_{ep}^i + 2.79 < 0$$

However, it follows from $a_{ep}^f > 10$ and $a_{ep}^i \le 2$ that $0.001a_{ep}^f - a_{ep}^i + 2.79 > 0.8$, which is contradictory to $0.001a_{ep}^f - a_{ep}^i + 2.79 < 0$. Therefore, it is impossible to have $a_{ef}^i = F$, and all statements in this case have $a_{ef}^i < F$. Then, we have $s_i \in S_A^{Op1}$ after (2.3).

- Consider the case that $(2 < a_{ep}^i \le 10$ and $(a_{ef}^i - F) + (0.001a_{ep}^f - 0.1a_{ep}^i) + 0.99 < 0)$. Assume further $a_{ef}^i = F$. Then, we have

$$(a_{ef}^i - F) + (0.001a_{ep}^f - 0.1a_{ep}^i) + 0.99 = 0.001a_{ep}^f - 0.1a_{ep}^i + 0.99 < 0$$

However, it follows from $a_{ep}^f > 10$ and $2 < a_{ep}^i \le 10$ that

$$0.001a_{ep}^f - 0.1a_{ep}^i + 0.99 > 0$$

which is contradictory to

$$0.001a_{ep}^f - 0.1a_{ep}^i + 0.99 < 0$$

Therefore, it is impossible to have $a_{ef}^i = F$, and all statements in this case have $a_{ef}^i < F$. Then, we have $s_i \in S_A^{Op1}$ after (2.3).

- Consider the case that $(a_{ep}^i > 10$ and $(a_{ef}^i - F) + 0.001(a_{ep}^f - a_{ep}^i) < 0)$. Assume further $a_{ef}^i < F$. Then, $s_i \in S_A^{Op1}$ after (2.3). Now consider the sub-case that $a_{ef}^i = F$. Then, we have

$$(a_{ef}^i - F) + 0.001(a_{ep}^f - a_{ep}^i) = 0.001(a_{ep}^f - a_{ep}^i)$$

Since $(a_{ef}^i - F) + 0.001(a_{ep}^f - a_{ep}^i) < 0$, then $(a_{ep}^f - a_{ep}^i) < 0$. Therefore, $s_i \in S_A^{Op1}$ after (2.3).

In summary, we have proved that $S_A^{W3} \subseteq S_A^{Op1}$.

In conclusion, for any value of a_{ep}^f, we have $S_B^{Op1} \subseteq S_B^{W3}$ and $S_A^{W3} \subseteq S_A^{Op1}$. It follows from Theorem 2.2.2 that Op1 $\to$ Wong3. Therefore, ER1 $\to$ Wong3, since Op1 belongs to ER1.   □

Proposition B.8 *ER1 $\to$ Arithmetic Mean.*

Proof In order to prove ER1 $\to$ Arithmetic Mean, it is sufficient to prove Op1 $\to$ Arithmetic Mean. As proved in Appendix A, S_B^{Op1} and S_A^{Op1} are equal to the sets defined in (2.1) and (2.3), respectively, and S_B^{AM} and S_A^{AM} are equal to the sets defined in (A.124) and (A.126), respectively, as follows.

$$S_B^{AM}=\{s_i\,|\,\frac{a_{ef}^i P-a_{ep}^i F}{(a_{ef}^i+a_{ep}^i)(P+F-a_{ef}^i-a_{ep}^i)+PF}>\frac{PF-Fa_{ep}^f}{(F+a_{ep}^f)(P-a_{ep}^f)+PF},\,1\le i\le n\}$$

$$S_A^{AM}=\{s_i\,|\,\frac{a_{ef}^i P-a_{ep}^i F}{(a_{ef}^i+a_{ep}^i)(P+F-a_{ef}^i-a_{ep}^i)+PF}<\frac{PF-Fa_{ep}^f}{(F+a_{ep}^f)(P-a_{ep}^f)+PF},\,1\le i\le n\}$$

If $a_{ef}^i=F$, we have

$$\frac{a_{ef}^i P-a_{ep}^i F}{(a_{ef}^i+a_{ep}^i)(P+F-a_{ef}^i-a_{ep}^i)+PF}-\frac{PF-Fa_{ep}^f}{(F+a_{ep}^f)(P-a_{ep}^f)+PF}$$

$$=\frac{PF-Fa_{ep}^i}{(F+a_{ep}^i)(P-a_{ep}^i)+PF}-\frac{PF-Fa_{ep}^f}{(F+a_{ep}^f)(P-a_{ep}^f)+PF}$$

$$=\frac{F[(P-a_{ep}^i)(P-a_{ep}^f)+PF](a_{ep}^f-a_{ep}^i)}{[(F+a_{ep}^i)(P-a_{ep}^i)+PF][(F+a_{ep}^f)(P-a_{ep}^f)+PF]} \tag{B.7}$$

Now, we are going to prove $S_B^{Op1}\subseteq S_B^{AM}$ and $S_A^{AM}\subseteq S_A^{Op1}$.

Firstly, we will prove $S_B^{Op1}\subseteq S_B^{AM}$. Assume $s_i\in S_B^{Op1}$. Then, $a_{ef}^i=F$ and $(a_{ep}^f-a_{ep}^i)>0$ after (2.1). It follows from Lemma 2.3.1 that $F[(P-a_{ep}^i)(P-a_{ep}^f)+PF]>0$, $(F+a_{ep}^i)(P-a_{ep}^i)+PF>0$, and $(F+a_{ep}^f)(P-a_{ep}^f)+PF>0$; then we have

$$\frac{F[(P-a_{ep}^i)(P-a_{ep}^f)+PF](a_{ep}^f-a_{ep}^i)}{[(F+a_{ep}^i)(P-a_{ep}^i)+PF][(F+a_{ep}^f)(P-a_{ep}^f)+PF]}>0$$

because $(a_{ep}^f-a_{ep}^i)>0$. From Equation (B.7), we have

$$\frac{a_{ef}^i P-a_{ep}^i F}{(a_{ef}^i+a_{ep}^i)(P+F-a_{ef}^i-a_{ep}^i)+PF}>\frac{PF-Fa_{ep}^f}{(F+a_{ep}^f)(P-a_{ep}^f)+PF}$$

Therefore, $s_i\in S_B^{AM}$ after (A.124). Thus, $S_B^{Op1}\subseteq S_B^{AM}$.

Secondly, we are going to prove $S_A^{AM}\subseteq S_A^{Op1}$. Suppose $s_i\in S_A^{AM}$. Then after (A.126), we have

$$\frac{a_{ef}^i P-a_{ep}^i F}{(a_{ef}^i+a_{ep}^i)(P+F-a_{ef}^i-a_{ep}^i)+PF}<\frac{PF-Fa_{ep}^f}{(F+a_{ep}^f)(P-a_{ep}^f)+PF}$$

- Suppose $(a_{ef}^i < F)$. Immediately after (2.3), $s_i \in S_A^{Op1}$.
- Suppose $(a_{ef}^i = F)$. It follows from

$$\frac{a_{ef}^i P - a_{ep}^i F}{(a_{ef}^i + a_{ep}^i)(P + F - a_{ef}^i - a_{ep}^i) + PF} < \frac{PF - Fa_{ep}^f}{(F + a_{ep}^f)(P - a_{ep}^f) + PF}$$

and Equation (B.7) that

$$\frac{F[(P - a_{ep}^i)(P - a_{ep}^f) + PF](a_{ep}^f - a_{ep}^i)}{[(F + a_{ep}^i)(P - a_{ep}^i) + PF][(F + a_{ep}^f)(P - a_{ep}^f) + PF]} < 0$$

which implies $(a_{ep}^f - a_{ep}^i) < 0$ because after Lemma 2.3.1, there are

$$F[(P - a_{ep}^i)(P - a_{ep}^f) + PF] > 0$$

$$(F + a_{ep}^i)(P - a_{ep}^i) + PF > 0$$

$$(F + a_{ep}^f)(P - a_{ep}^f) + PF > 0$$

Thus, $s_i \in S_A^{Op1}$ after (2.3).

In summary, we have proved that $S_A^{AM} \subseteq S_A^{Op1}$.

In conclusion, we have $S_B^{Op1} \subseteq S_B^{AM}$ and $S_A^{AM} \subseteq S_A^{Op1}$. Immediately after Theorem 2.2.2, Op1 → Arithmetic Mean. Since Op1 belongs to ER1, we have ER1 → Arithmetic Mean.   □

Proposition B.9 *ER1 → Cohen.*

Proof In order to prove ER1 → Cohen, it is sufficient to prove Op1 → Cohen. As proved in Appendix A, S_B^{Op1} and S_A^{Op1} are equal to the sets defined in (2.1) and (2.3), respectively, and S_B^C and S_A^C are equal to the sets defined in (A.127) and (A.129), respectively, as follows.

$$S_B^C = \{s_i \mid \frac{a_{ef}^i P - a_{ep}^i F}{P(a_{ef}^i + a_{ep}^i) + F(P + F - a_{ef}^i - a_{ep}^i)} > \frac{PF - Fa_{ep}^f}{P(F + a_{ep}^f) + F(P - a_{ep}^f)}, 1 \leq i \leq n\}$$

$$S_A^C = \{s_i \mid \frac{a_{ef}^i P - a_{ep}^i F}{P(a_{ef}^i + a_{ep}^i) + F(P + F - a_{ef}^i - a_{ep}^i)} < \frac{PF - Fa_{ep}^f}{P(F + a_{ep}^f) + F(P - a_{ep}^f)}, 1 \leq i \leq n\}$$

If $a_{ef}^i = F$, we have

$$\frac{a_{ef}^i P - a_{ep}^i F}{P(a_{ef}^i + a_{ep}^i) + F(P + F - a_{ef}^i - a_{ep}^i)} - \frac{PF - Fa_{ep}^f}{P(F + a_{ep}^f) + F(P - a_{ep}^f)}$$

$$= \frac{PF - Fa_{ep}^i}{P(F + a_{ep}^i) + F(P - a_{ep}^i)} - \frac{PF - Fa_{ep}^f}{P(F + a_{ep}^f) + F(P - a_{ep}^f)}$$

$$= \frac{F(PF + P^2)(a_{ep}^f - a_{ep}^i)}{[P(F + a_{ep}^i) + F(P - a_{ep}^i)][P(F + a_{ep}^f) + F(P - a_{ep}^f)]} \tag{B.8}$$

Now, we are going to prove $S_B^{Op1} \subseteq S_B^C$ and $S_A^C \subseteq S_A^{Op1}$.

Firstly, we will prove $S_B^{Op1} \subseteq S_B^C$. Assume $s_i \in S_B^{Op1}$. Then, $a_{ef}^i = F$ and $(a_{ep}^f - a_{ep}^i) > 0$ after (2.1). It follows from Lemma 2.3.1 that $F(PF + P^2) > 0$, $P(F + a_{ep}^i) + F(P - a_{ep}^i) > 0$, and $P(F + a_{ep}^f) + F(P - a_{ep}^f) > 0$; then because $(a_{ep}^f - a_{ep}^i) > 0$, we have

$$\frac{F(PF + P^2)(a_{ep}^f - a_{ep}^i)}{[P(F + a_{ep}^i) + F(P - a_{ep}^i)][P(F + a_{ep}^f) + F(P - a_{ep}^f)]} > 0$$

From Equation (B.8), we have

$$\frac{a_{ef}^i P - a_{ep}^i F}{P(a_{ef}^i + a_{ep}^i) + F(P + F - a_{ef}^i - a_{ep}^i)} > \frac{PF - Fa_{ep}^f}{P(F + a_{ep}^f) + F(P - a_{ep}^f)}$$

Therefore, $s_i \in S_B^C$ after (A.127). Thus, $S_B^{Op1} \subseteq S_B^C$.

Secondly, we are going to prove $S_A^C \subseteq S_A^{Op1}$. Suppose $s_i \in S_A^C$. Then we have $\frac{a_{ef}^i P - a_{ep}^i F}{P(a_{ef}^i + a_{ep}^i) + F(P + F - a_{ef}^i - a_{ep}^i)} < \frac{PF - Fa_{ep}^f}{P(F + a_{ep}^f) + F(P - a_{ep}^f)}$ after (A.129).

- Suppose $(a_{ef}^i < F)$. Immediately after (2.3), $s_i \in S_A^{Op1}$.
- Suppose $(a_{ef}^i = F)$. It follows from Equation (B.8) and

$$\frac{a_{ef}^i P - a_{ep}^i F}{P(a_{ef}^i + a_{ep}^i) + F(P + F - a_{ef}^i - a_{ep}^i)} < \frac{PF - Fa_{ep}^f}{P(F + a_{ep}^f) + F(P - a_{ep}^f)}$$

that

$$\frac{F(PF + P^2)(a_{ep}^f - a_{ep}^i)}{[P(F + a_{ep}^i) + F(P - a_{ep}^i)][P(F + a_{ep}^f) + F(P - a_{ep}^f)]} < 0$$

which implies $(a_{ep}^f - a_{ep}^i) < 0$ because $F(PF + P^2) > 0$, $P(F + a_{ep}^i) + F(P - a_{ep}^i) > 0$, and $P(F + a_{ep}^f) + F(P - a_{ep}^f) > 0$ after Lemma 2.3.1. Thus, $s_i \in S_A^{Op1}$ after (2.3).

In summary, we have proved that $S_A^C \subseteq S_A^{Op1}$.

In conclusion, we have $S_B^{Op1} \subseteq S_B^C$ and $S_A^C \subseteq S_A^{Op1}$. Immediately after Theorem 2.2.2, Op1 → Cohen. Since Op1 belongs to ER1, we have ER1 → Cohen.   □

Proposition B.10 *ER1 → Fleiss.*

Proof In order to prove ER1 → Fleiss, it is sufficient to prove Op1 → Fleiss. As proved in Appendix A, S_B^{Op1} and S_A^{Op1} are equal to the sets defined in (2.1) and (2.3), respectively, and S_B^F and S_A^F are equal to the sets defined in (A.130) and (A.132), respectively, as follows.

$$S_B^F = \{s_i | -F^2 + 4a_{ef}^i P + 2Fa_{ef}^i - 2Fa_{ep}^i - (a_{ep}^i + a_{ef}^i)^2$$

$$> 4PF - 4Fa_{ep}^f - (a_{ep}^f)^2, \ 1 \le i \le n\}$$

$$S_A^F = \{s_i | -F^2 + 4a_{ef}^i P + 2Fa_{ef}^i - 2Fa_{ep}^i - (a_{ep}^i + a_{ef}^i)^2$$

$$< 4PF - 4Fa_{ep}^f - (a_{ep}^f)^2, \ 1 \le i \le n\}$$

If $a_{ef}^i = F$, we have

$$[-F^2 + 4a_{ef}^i P + 2Fa_{ef}^i - 2Fa_{ep}^i - (a_{ep}^i + a_{ef}^i)^2] - [4PF - 4Fa_{ep}^f - (a_{ep}^f)^2]$$

$$= [4PF - 4Fa_{ep}^i - (a_{ep}^i)^2] - [4PF - 4Fa_{ep}^f - (a_{ep}^f)^2]$$

$$= (4F + a_{ep}^f + a_{ep}^i)(a_{ep}^f - a_{ep}^i) \tag{B.9}$$

Now, we are going to prove $S_B^{Op1} \subseteq S_B^F$ and $S_A^F \subseteq S_A^{Op1}$.

Firstly, we will prove $S_B^{Op1} \subseteq S_B^F$. Assume $s_i \in S_B^{Op1}$. Then, $a_{ef}^i = F$ and $(a_{ep}^f - a_{ep}^i) > 0$ after (2.1). It follows from Lemma 2.3.1 that $4F + a_{ep}^f + a_{ep}^i > 0$; then we have

$$(4F + a_{ep}^f + a_{ep}^i)(a_{ep}^f - a_{ep}^i) > 0$$

because $(a_{ep}^f - a_{ep}^i) > 0$. From Equation (B.9), we have

$$-F^2 + 4a_{ef}^i P + 2Fa_{ef}^i - 2Fa_{ep}^i - (a_{ep}^i + a_{ef}^i)^2 > 4PF - 4Fa_{ep}^f - (a_{ep}^f)^2$$

Therefore, $s_i \in S_B^F$ after (A.130). Thus, $S_B^{Op1} \subseteq S_B^F$.

Secondly, we are going to prove $S_A^F \subseteq S_A^{Op1}$. Suppose $s_i \in S_A^F$. Then after (A.132) we have

$$-F^2+4a_{ef}^i P+2Fa_{ef}^i-2Fa_{ep}^i-(a_{ep}^i+a_{ef}^i)^2 < 4PF-4Fa_{ep}^f-(a_{ep}^f)^2$$

- Suppose $(a_{ef}^i < F)$. Immediately after (2.3), $s_i \in S_A^{Op1}$.
- Suppose $(a_{ef}^i = F)$. It follows from Equation (B.9) and

$$-F^2+4a_{ef}^i P+2Fa_{ef}^i-2Fa_{ep}^i-(a_{ep}^i+a_{ef}^i)^2 < 4PF-4Fa_{ep}^f-(a_{ep}^f)^2$$

  that

$$(4F+a_{ep}^f+a_{ep}^i)(a_{ep}^f-a_{ep}^i) < 0$$

  which implies $(a_{ep}^f-a_{ep}^i) < 0$ after Lemma 2.3.1. Thus, $s_i \in S_A^{Op1}$ after (2.3).

In summary, we have proved that $S_A^F \subseteq S_A^{Op1}$.

In conclusion, we have $S_B^{Op1} \subseteq S_B^F$ and $S_A^F \subseteq S_A^{Op1}$. Immediately after Theorem 2.2.2, Op1 $\rightarrow$ Fleiss. Since Op1 belongs to ER1, we have ER1 $\rightarrow$ Fleiss. □

Printed in the United States
by Baker & Taylor Publisher Services